D0514289

The
Fighter
of
Auschwitz

The
Fighter
of
Auschwitz

The incredible story of
Leen Sanders who boxed
to help others survive

Erik Brouwer

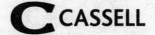

First published in Great Britain in 2023 by Cassell, an imprint of
Octopus Publishing Group Ltd
Carmelite House, 50 Victoria Embankment
London EC4Y 0DZ
www.octopusbooks.co.uk

An Hachette UK Company
www.hachette.co.uk

Distributed in the US by Hachette Book Group
1290 Avenue of the Americas, 4th and 5th Floors
New York, NY 10104

Distributed in Canada by Canadian Manda Group
664 Annette St., Toronto, Ontario, Canada M6S 2C8

ISBN 978 1 78840 430 3
A CIP catalogue record for this book is available from the British Library.

Printed and bound in UK
Typeset in 11/15pt Mrs Eaves OT by Jouve (UK), Milton Keynes

13 5 7 9 10 8 6 4 2

Publisher: Trevor Davies
Senior Managing Editor: Sybella Stephens
Translation from Dutch: Guy Shipton, in association with First Edition Translations
Copy Editors: John English and Laura Gladwin
Design Director: Mel Four
Cover Design: Two Associates
Assistant Production Managers: Nic Jones and Lucy Carter

Advisory note: This text explores the themes of racial prejudices in a historical context
and includes language which was once commonplace in society but is no longer acceptable,
and which some readers might find offensive.

This FSC® label means that materials used for the product have been responsibly sourced.

CONTENTS

PROLOGUE

The same dream came to him again last night. SS men continually attacking him, launching left- and right-hook punches, stamping on him with their boots. Normally, he would have defended himself with his famous double defence, but he was helpless. There were just too many.

He wakes from the nightmare, sweating, and thinking of Selli, Jopie and David.

It is the summer of 1975. Many times Dutch boxing champion Leendert Josua Sanders, hailing from Rotterdam's Zandstraat district, is now sixty-seven years old. His sparse dark hair is streaked with grey and he has a belly. His hands are large and rough; his nose, despite tens of thousands of blows, is relatively unscathed. He takes pills and is rheumatic; he forgets his keys, dates, stories and words. His left arm bears his concentration camp number: 86764. He has become an American citizen; he had to.

On the table in his living room there are letters, cards, sheets of A4 and forms, so very many forms. For years now he has been engaged in the application process for an Extraordinary Pension, a provision introduced in 1952 for 'persons invalided as a result of measures taken against them by the enemy in connection with resistance'. In his view and that of Dr Perloff, his American physician, Leen qualifies for this. He writes to an official that, following a trip to the Netherlands, he had gone to the pharmacy to buy 'hundreds of Mogadon sleeping pills'. He brought these back to his home in Los Angeles, where he takes them daily. How else is he to get to sleep after what has happened to him? He is also 'forever asking acquaintances travelling to Holland if they would bring me back some Mogadon'.

Had Leen Sanders been a resistance fighter both inside the concentration camp and outside it? Had he saved Dutch lives in Auschwitz because of boxing? Had he really been on the receiving end of violence from the SS? Is it true that he would howl and cry each night? The officials want names, dates and facts. They verify data and place question marks next to certain stories, and they talk about the difference between 'humanity' and 'resistance'.

Leen collects additional witnesses and writes letters to former camp inmates and ex-boxers; he phones, he pleads, he begs. He flies to the Netherlands in search of evidence to support his case. He goes to a doctor who saved his life in 1944. At boxing matches, he catches up with old-timers from the fight game who helped him during his pre-war resistance. He visits an Auschwitz survivor who has become a psychologist, and he thinks increasingly often about things he would rather forget: the bombing of Rotterdam; his time as a prisoner of war; his escape; his fight for the Dutch title with Nazis in the front row; the identity documents that he stole; the betrayal and the arrest; the SS men who assaulted him; the miracle that occurred thanks to his ear; the All-weights Auschwitz

Championship; the Death March and the Death Train. And always: Selli, Jopie and David.

What actually happened? How has Leen Sanders come to be the way he is? Although he has no desire to tell his story, he is compelled to do it all the same.

Part I

The boxers, the rabbi and the waffle baker

I.

It is dark and the wind has picked up as Leendert Josua Sanders walks out of his parental home in Rotterdam's Nieuwsteeg on 5 January 1925. He passes by the Notenboom storage depot, the De Groot roofing merchants and the warehouse for Droomer, the Jewish greengrocer. Houses lean askew, most of the roofs are missing tiles, rats crawl in and out of drains, and slum dwellings are declared by the council to be unfit for human habitation. A storm on New Year's Eve has left debris lying in the street.

He walks past sailors' taverns, *cafés chantants*, honkytonk piano joints and bordellos. Cripples and blind men stand outside lodgings. Men with barrel organs are asking for donations and pedlars carry suitcases containing yarn, soap, hairpins and razors. Jewish hawkers call out to the locals: 'Have you any rags?' Women are led by pimps to dosshouses.

After ten minutes he is standing outside the General Auction House on Goudschesingel, opposite the market. Some traders are dismantling their stalls, while others are carrying on for as long as they possibly can: 'Have a taste, young sir. See how good it is!'

Boxing fans are queueing up in front of the ticket counter. Boys are selling umbrellas, bars of Kwatta chocolate, raincoats and the newspapers *Voorwaarts*, *De Tribune* and *De Dageraad*. A man is shouting out the cost of the programmes – five cents – while uniformed doormen tell the waiting throng that they must have their tickets at the ready, and anarchists are handing out pamphlets against the harbour barons. In the minds of liberals, the Auction Room is the meeting place for the lower classes; dockhands and barrowmen frequently call for strike action there. Party members praise Lenin with rasping smokers' cries, and socialists from Rotterdam's working-class neighbourhoods agitate against capitalist bloodsuckers. Everyone can better themselves in this society if only we change the System.

Leen is sixteen years old, has thick brown hair and speaks in the broad Rotterdam dialect with a Yiddish accent. He is 1.65 metres tall, weighs 58 kilograms and has skinny legs and a narrow waist. He employs a closed defence technique when fighting and views boxing in the traditional British way as 'the noble art of self-defence'. He lives with his parents, five brothers, four sisters, his aunt Duifje and his uncle Joël at 10a Nieuwsteeg, where the walls are riddled with mould because of the leaking roof, the stairs are shot through with woodworm, and hardly any light filters through the small windows. His mother, Saartje, will often buy yesterday's bread; when seriously strapped for cash, she goes to the pawnbroker to sell a few bits and pieces. The box beds are creeping with lice, fleas and bugs. The youngest children have corns on their feet and suffer from hunger oedema as well as the infectious eye disease trachoma.

Leen's ambition is to become a pro boxer. A trainer has told him that this sport gives young Jews the chance 'to break out of always living in the shadows and instead bask in the sunlight'. Leen and his brother Bram would rather read boxing magazines than the Torah;

they scrutinize the matches fought by Georges Carpentier and Jack Dempsey – the best boxers in the world – when they're screened at Bram Tuschinski's cinema in Hoogstraat, Rotterdam's busiest thoroughfare. Their idol is the Jewish American boxer Benny Leonard, born Benjamin Leiner in the Jewish ghetto of New York's East Side. Benny began boxing as protection against Jew-haters, had a Star of David sewn onto his shorts and became world champion. A Jewish journalist wrote: 'Seeing him climb into the ring with the six-pointed Jewish star on his boxing shorts felt like revenge for all the bloodied noses, split lips and taunting laughter at pale, puny, skinny Jewish boys.'

The great hall at the Auction House has sold out. The smell is one of sweat, eau de cologne, smoke and massage oil. Chairs have been crammed together; spectators are reading either the programme or the local newspapers. Over the weekend Feyenoord has played against Haarlem on a rain-sodden pitch: 0–0. The evening edition of *De Maasbode* reports on the Maas having burst its banks, that stock-market prices have risen again, and there's plenty of work at the port; nightlife is flourishing. A few days earlier, the Italian leader Mussolini sang the praises of fascism. The weather forecast concludes with the message 'Be on your guard.'

Leen is making his amateur debut this evening. His eighteen-year-old cousin, Meijer, is boxing at the same event; both of them are members of the National Boxing Club, doing their training in a café cellar. Meijer lives a few doors along from Leen in Nieuwsteeg, where he and his eight brothers and sisters all sleep in the same cramped room.

The main lighting is switched off; the glimmer of a lightbulb flickers beneath low beams. Visibility is poor, thanks to cigars from overseas, pipe tobacco, Van Nelle shag and Chief Whip cigarettes. Ex-boxers boast about long-forgotten matches: 'Two left jabs to the chin, a fast one to the belly on top of that and, quick as you like, straight on the floor.' Policemen stand in place facing the public; boxing fans often carry knives and knuckledusters. Sailors sit alongside flower street-traders, pub landlords, socialists, pavement singers, counterfeiters, journeyman painters, hot-water salesmen, bargemen, dockhands, barrowmen, porters and eel sellers. Almost everyone is wearing a cap; jackets and waistcoats hang open, chest hair spilling out from open-necked shirts stained with patches of sweat; faces are grimy with the dust and soot of ten-plus hours of toil in factories or the docks. They are called 'men of the people', prone to utterances such as 'God-awful!' and 'Get stuffed!', their tall stories concluding with 'you can just imagine'. If there are any empty spots in the front row, they clamber their way down to sit as close to the ringside as possible, overturning chairs as they go, shoving aside crowd controllers and any like-minded spectators. A liberal journalist describes these flat-capped men as 'common people from the slums and alleyways, from basements and garrets, louts, loudmouths, numbskulls, scoundrels'. A fellow reporter comes up with the inventive expression 'bloody-nosed proletariat'; in Amsterdam and virtually all other Dutch towns and cities it is forbidden to organize boxing matches, so why then is the same not true in Rotterdam? For the flat caps in the Auction House the violence is what they love most about boxing, and any member of the anti-boxing brigade above their social class is simply called out as a 'ban-crazed maniac'.

*

Leen warms up next to the ring, where, as he would say later, 'a great many of the seats were taken by friends and acquaintances who didn't want to miss out on my first public performance.' Jazz and swing emanates from a loudspeaker while orders are placed at the bar for beer and whisky; a shot of Dutch gin costs five cents.

The promoter, Theo Huizenaar, climbs through the ropes wearing a white suit, boater, waistcoat, dress shirt, trousers and tie. He has applied a dollop of pomade to comb back his dark hair. During the Great War, Theo was given boxing lessons by a Flemish refugee and set up his own club. After the Treaty of Versailles, he organized his first tournament at the Auction House; fist fighting became popular in Rotterdam and – now, in 1925 – Theo Huizenaar is the most important boxing promoter in the Netherlands.

Leen appears in a bathrobe, a white towel draped around his shoulders. His opponent, Van Oers from Crooswijk, is much bigger than him. Van Lent, the announcer, is holding a megaphone and calls out to the crowd: 'Ladies and gentlemen, our referee for this evening is Schulp.' Leen's brother Bram is his 'second' – his ringside assistant – and he sets down a spittoon and a bucket of water in the corner. A small bag contains collodion, smelling salts, ammonia, iodine and plasters. The boxing-ring doctor checks the boxers' pupils; a previous bout had ended in a knockout and serious brain injury.

Sanders and Van Oers briefly tap gloves. Schulp calls: 'Seconds out! Round one! Box!' Leen fights more offensively than usual: feinting right, left hook, jab to the right, a hit straight to the chin. A dull thud sounds as Van Oers falls to the canvas. Blood seeps into the planking. An adjudicator strikes the gong: the end of round one.

Stools are placed in the ring and Leen sits down, breathing in and out. Bram waves a towel about and thrusts a wet sponge in Leen's face. Blobs of phlegm, blood and snot swirl in a bucket.

'Seconds out! Round two. Box!'

As the fight resumes, Van Oers manages to score a few hits to Leen's ear. In the next break, the ringside doctor lifts up the rope and pricks open the resulting bump with a needle. Some blood drips from it; Leen hopes there will be no swelling afterwards, otherwise he will end up with a cauliflower ear.

The tempo increases in the third round and the flat caps stand on their chairs, shadowboxing. Even the policemen have now turned around to face the ring and watch. Ex-pros commend Leen's agility, tactical skill, sportsmanship and discipline. Van Oers tires, and has to clinch on to Leen with both hands to catch his breath. Schulp calls out 'Break!', and after three minutes, 'Time!'

Leen wins by a sizeable number of points, and Meijer defeats his goy opponent in the next bout. In Leen's view this is 'a proper celebration for all of us'. The Jewish cousins set off for the dressing room. Their torsos glisten with sweat and massage oil, their faces are flushed and swollen, their lips crusted with scabs; they scrape off the blood and knit eyebrows back together with staples. A journalist observes how noses are 'reduced to raw pieces of flesh'.

II.

The railway cuts right through the city. It is always busy around Maas Station: traffic jams, hubbub, trams, lorries driving to the port of Rotterdam, anti-revolutionaries travelling to meeting rooms in the city centre, stockbrokers walking in haste to Beursplein. Every inhabitant of Rotterdam seems to own a bicycle, and every man thinks he is cycling champion Piet Moeskops. Traffic policemen stand at the busiest junctions, and in the evenings they sport white jackets to remain visible. A commentator describes this hustle and bustle as 'the nervous agitation of the times'.

It is half past seven on the Saturday morning of 12 June 1926. Leen passes through the great glass door to the station. He's holding a suitcase in his hand because, for the first time, he is travelling abroad – to Düsseldorf in the Weimar Republic. Two days earlier he was celebrating his eighteenth birthday at his parents' house in Nieuwsteeg, and he is the reigning champion in the featherweight and lightweight divisions. The train to Amsterdam is departing from Platform 1. According to the notice on the window, there is NO SMOKING for men and women in the first- and second-class waiting rooms. Hawkers are selling coffee for passengers to drink en route, and Saturday editions of the *Rotterdamsch Nieuwsblad* hang on view in a kiosk: the Wall Street Stock Exchange 'once again showed steady progress with lively trading', while shares in General Motors 'went up by a further 2%'.

It is 17°C and raining. A band is playing the *Wilhelmus*, the Dutch national anthem. The chairman of the Dutch Boxing Federation wishes the boxers and their coaches every success 'in beautiful Düsseldorf'. Mr Mulder is travelling with them as referee, while promoter and manager Theo Huizenaar is to supervise the boxers as a second. Fathers get handshakes, sweethearts a kiss, while friends and acquaintances call out advice from the platform: 'A clean left hook to those little German chins! Always works a treat!'

A porter hauls luggage into the luggage van, where the boxers' bags burst at the seams with bandages, nightwear, toiletries, mouthguards, ointment, camphor injections and chloroform. The stoker shovels coal into the firebox, steam billows from the boiler, and the train's wheels start to turn.

Leen is sitting in a carriage with three other boxers from Rotterdam. The teak seating is painted green; the ashtrays, only just emptied, are already nearly full again. Bep van Klaveren from Crooswijk is a year older than Leen.

Bep has straight, black hair and he boxes for Schilperoord School in Crooswijk. He usually calls men 'lads'; his opponents will be beaten 'to a pulp' or into a 'brain tumour'. Bep does not eat meat, which is seen as peculiar by the other boxers. His father is known to South Holland's underworld as Haagse Jan, and from what Bep says he is 'a very nasty piece of work': he once fought off seven policemen, smashing them all to smithereens. Leen and Bep represent the future of Dutch boxing, so it went without saying that they would be selected to visit Düsseldorf for this prestigious amateur boxing tournament, a dual challenge between western Germany and the Netherlands.

The train runs past Arnhem, Duiven and Zevenaar to North Rhine-Westphalia, where the Rhineland spreads out before them in a flat expanse of green. Belgian and French occupiers have left the region only recently and, seven years after the Treaty of Versailles, the Weimar Republic is at last to become a member of the League of Nations. During the Great War, Bep would sometimes go and stand on the Maas Bridge, from where he could hear the roar of cannon fire.

Customs officers board the train at the border town of Emmerich. They are amicable and polite – 'Do you have anything to declare? Coffee, tobacco, alcohol?' – and suitcases and travel bags are marked with chalk. 'Enjoy the rest of your journey, gentlemen. All the best in Düsseldorf.' Before the war it was much more difficult to cross the German border; since 1925, peace and feelings of fellowship have reigned in Western Europe.

The train passes through Oberhausen and Duisburg. Containers line the tracks, men are loading freight trains to the brim with coal and factory workers are lugging panels and pushing wheelbarrows. After more than four hours' travelling, the boxers and their coaches alight at the Hauptbahnhof in Düsseldorf. Herr Farber, chairman of the German Boxing Federation, bids them warm welcome. In Herr Farber's view, the peoples of Europe need to be brought closer together, and boxing can contribute towards that end.

Leen, Bep and the others are driven in the direction of the Rhine. Tents and buildings are spread out across a site encompassing

400,000 square metres. A month ago, it was here that the Weimar Republic opened its greatest exposition, GeSoLei (short for Healthcare, Social Welfare and Physical Exercise). Germany's birth rate has declined sharply; millions of men never returned from the war, and the nation's bodies and spirits have been weakened by malnutrition and mass unemployment. The exposition's motive was to signal the start of a German renaissance.

The boxers and their coaches explore the site aboard a miniature train. A white pavilion is housing an exhibition called 'Jewish Hygiene', an important subject in the Weimar Republic; misunderstandings about this have persisted for centuries, including in Düsseldorf. Jews are seen by German nationals as 'strangers with strange customs' that 'threaten Germans' public health'. Germany must create a 'body of people' composed of inhabitants sharing common descent; Jews and other 'foreigners' do not fit that mould, and at the exhibition, rabbis from Düsseldorf aim to dispel centuries of prejudice against them.

Leen, Bep and the others enter a different hall, its walls clad with drawings and information panels explaining the development of sport in Germany since the Middle Ages. Boxing features prominently, and is the most popular of German sports activities: the best boxers enjoy the same status as painters, generals, architects or novelists. One theatre critic calls boxing 'the perfect substitute for military service'; another wagers that German youth knows more about the American champion Jack Dempsey or the French boxing legend Georges Carpentier than it does about Hindenburg, Schiller or Goethe. In cafés, schools and workplaces, almost all the talk is about 'uppercuts, clinches and kidney punches'.

The Dutch delegation walks down a tree-lined avenue to reach the exposition's main entrance. Young Germans are arriving on

JAP motorcycles; petit bourgeois gentlemen are driving Opel cars. An orchestra is playing songs by Duke Ellington, Sam Wooding and Irving Berlin. 'Two-Step?' '*Gerne!*' (A pleasure!). Chorus girls with bobbed hair are dancing the Charleston or Black Bottom on the stage, and at the end of each number the crowd yells out 'Encore!' People are ordering German wheat beer and lighting up a quick Salem, Final, Nil, Eckstein, Camel or Lucky Strike. In Germany, you are not allowed to smoke during boxing matches.

The dual boxing tournament between western Germany and the Netherlands is being held in the largest building in the exposition grounds, the Planetarium. A local journalist describes the structure as 'a masterpiece of modern German architecture', and according to one Dutch visitor it is as 'grand and impressive as the Pantheon'. The guests enter the Planetarium by the main entrance, and their blood levels are then evaluated in a sports laboratory, while a doctor checks their blood pressure and heart rate. The main hall is roofed with a dome. When the curator presses a button, the roof elevates by four metres to reveal a gallery with room for eight hundred spectators. A light installation projects the constellations on to the ceiling.

Omnibuses and taxis halt in front of the Planetarium. Paper boys are selling the *Düsseldorfer Stadt-Anzeiger* and the *Düsseldorfer Nachrichten*, which contain previews of the tournament – Germany is favoured to win, and the German boxers are hailed as the *K.O.-Truppen aus Köln* (Cologne Knockout Squad).

The doorman tears tickets. Former frontline soldiers are allowed entry at a discount. Men in hats whisper '*Zigaretten*' to passers-by, but a few in the know twig that they are also selling cocaine. Black-market ticket vendors mutter: '*Wollense Karten? Zwei prima Ringsitze*' (Want tickets? Two terrific ringside seats). Inspectors tell spectators who have just arrived that queue jumping will not be tolerated: '*keine Vordrängelei!*' The *Schutzpolizei* (constabulary), known as 'Schupos' and carrying revolvers and truncheons, stand at the entrance to keep order. Since the fall of the German Empire, gangs of thugs, leaning to the left and right in politics, have been engaged in fighting each other on the streets, in cafés and at boxing matches.

The Planetarium is a sell-out and is hosting three thousand spectators. Former army chiefs are seated on a raised dais alongside leading industrialists and officials, as well as members of the nobility and judiciary. Laughing and flirting with their customers, waitresses in traditional dress traipse around with jugs of strong, dark lager and wheat beer. Men hawk and spit, the legacy of pneumonia caught in the trenches.

The chairman of the Boxing Federation lifts up the ropes at a quarter to eight. Herr Farber reaffirms the good relationship that has grown between Germany and the Netherlands since the war, and says that boxing brings about *Völkerversöhnung* (reconciliation between peoples) as well as being essential as a combat sport. Young Germans can cultivate their *Kampfgeist* (fighting spirit) in the ring and thus, through boxing, become strong patriots. There is no other sport as capable of reinvigorating the *totalen Mensch* (complete human being), and boxers are the very essence of the 'New Germans'.

A band plays both national anthems: the *Wilhelmus* and *Das Lied der Deutschen*. Germans hand bouquets to the Dutch and vice versa, while spectators clap and cheer as if Carpentier and Dempsey themselves were about to fight for the world title. A lady sings the first few lines from the exposition hymn:

O Germany, your body smarting still from its wounds.
War and hunger have consumed your strength.
And yet, my people, you must, you must recover.
Your fate can be overcome only by those who fight!

Leen, wearing a white shirt and orange shorts, is boxing in the third bout, and his opponent from Cologne is Franz Dübbers, ranked number two in Europe in his weight division. The victor will receive a plaque and a handshake from Herr Farber. Dübbers' blue eyes peer out from above his squashed boxer's nose; he combs back sparse blond hair over his scalp. He is fighting in a green-and-white boxing outfit and his shorts sport an eagle, the symbol of the Weimar Republic. Theo Huizenaar massages Leen's neck, hands him a water flask and whispers some final tactics in his ear. The referee calls out: '*Ring frei, kampf!*' A boxing warden sounds a gong and the spectators start to yell: '*Franz! Franz! Gib ihm Saures!*' (Give him the works!) '*Hoch Dübbers!*' 'Bravo Sanders!'

People are eating sauerkraut with bratwurst and are ordering still more wheat beer, schnapps and mulled wine; there's toasting, shouting and singing: '*Wir saufen wie die Schweine!*' (We swill it down like pigs!) Yes, it might all change in an instant, but right now wages are still going up every year, the Rhineland is no longer under occupation, the Kaiser is living in the Netherlands, and democracy seems to be winning out over conservatism.

III.

The double-decker tram is passing over Blackfriars Bridge to the other, less salubrious half of London. It is cold, dark and windy as the Sanders brothers pass industrial sheds, warehouses, flats, storage depots and a statue of Queen Victoria. Men drink tankards of Guinness outside a pub called The Blackfriar; war veterans walk on crutches to the Salvation Army shelter. The tram halts at the corner of Union Street next to an octagonal building known as 'the Fistic Temple by the Thames'. The sign on its domed roof reads: THE RING: BOXING ALL THE YEAR ROUND. A few months earlier, this is where British film director Alfred Hitchcock had shot his thrilling boxing-themed production *The Ring*.

The night before, Leen and Bram had departed Rotterdam from the quayside near the De Boompjes thoroughfare. Sailors of all nationalities walked up gangplanks to board their ships; anchor chains were freed; engine mechanisms ground and squealed back to life; captains advertised their imminent departures with steam whistles and ship's horns. The number of berths at the port had been further expanded; more boats needed to be built to handle all the work. The commissioners of the shipping companies wanted a capital increase, and stock-exchange prices for shipping companies were continuing to rise.

The Sanders brothers boarded the steamship *Batavier IV* and sailed past Schiehaven, Parkhaven, Sint Jobshaven, Parkkade, Vlaardingen and Maassluis. At Hook of Holland the waves were bigger and Leen spent some time slumped over the railings. The *Batavier* arrived in Gravesend at eight in the morning, where customs officers came aboard the vessel, asking questions and peering into suitcases. Several weeks had already passed since the profession in Leen's passport had been updated to 'Professional Boxer'.

It is Thursday 25 November 1926, and this evening Leen will be making his official professional debut. He weighs in at 60 kilograms; his brother, Abraham Joshua 'Bram' Sanders, is four years his senior, seven centimetres shorter and ten kilograms or so heavier. He has been boxing since 1924 under the name 'Battling Sanders'. A journalist writes that 'he cuts a somewhat unusual figure for a prize fighter, and it seems to us that a spot of running, wearing a couple of woollen pullovers on top of each other, might not only help reduce the excess weight, but also benefit this Battling Dutchman's boxing skills'. Leen would later confide that his brother was 'actually too fat and not as good as me'.

Bram and Leen cross the street to 196 Blackfriars Road, the address of the Fistic Temple. Titled gentlemen are being driven to the door in limousines and two doormen in gold-braided uniforms stand at the entrance. A Dutch correspondent declares that this lends The Ring 'a certain status' – a status that it does not merit. The programme booklet promises 'an evening you'll remember more than your wedding day'. Posters proclaim:

THE RING — BOXING'S PREMIER ARENA
UNDER THE DIRECTION OF MRS DICK BURGE
25 NOVEMBER 1926
IMPORTANT 6-ROUND CONTESTS
EDDIE PINN (MARYLEBONE) V BATTLING SANDERS
    (ROTTERDAM)
TOM WILSON (BLACKFRIARS) V LEN SANDERS (ROTTERDAM)

The Ring is nearly sold out and the stench of stale beer and dried blood is in the air. Five matches are scheduled for this evening's programme, but the main fight is to be between Great Britain's Len Johnson and his French challenger, Prunier. The programme describes Johnson as the 'Coalblack Lancashire Middleweight'; his father is African. According to the boxing reporter for the *Daily Telegraph*, 'darkie Johnson' versus Prunier is 'the big bout of the week'. Bram and Leen knock on an office door with a nameplate that reads: Mrs B. Burge.

At the time, Bella Burge is the sole female promoter in European professional boxing, nicknamed 'Madame Boxing' and 'Bella of Blackfriars'. Her late husband, Dick, had been the previous owner of The Ring. In 1918 he caught pneumonia while trying to rescue Londoners after a German air raid; on his deathbed he had asked Bella whether she wanted to carry on his work at The Ring – and she had promised to do so. Since then, Bella of Blackfriars has been in charge of negotiating fees with boxers and managers, as well as ensuring that unruly boxing fans are ejected from The Ring.

Spectators wearing drab jackets take the stairs to the gallery: traders or barrowmen from the fish market at Billingsgate and stevedores or dockworkers from Southwark or East Smithfield. They are drinking ale, gin and whisky, and smoking Wills' Gold Flakes, Churchman's Tenners, Herbert Tareyton's London or Craven A cigarettes. The men in the gallery are referred to as the 'betting boys' because of how much they gamble. If the match is lacklustre, they either choose a favourite and then over-enthusiastically encourage them, or turn their backs on the bout and sing hits by Al Jolson or Gene Austin at the top of their lungs. The French are always called 'froggies', while cautious boxers are labelled 'sissies' or 'Charley Howards' to rhyme with 'cowards' in Cockney rhyming slang. Jews are often serenaded with cries of 'Abie! Abie! Abie, my boy, what're you gonna do now?' An impoverished Broadway star has the sole task of shouting out 'Quiet please!' whenever the betting boys start to get too rowdy.

Ladies wearing rouge and lipstick pose with cigarette holders held aloft. Because of the cold they are wearing dresses that cover the legs, but in spring, summer and early autumn they swap these for shockingly short skirts. Almost all of them bob their hair, read novels by Scott Fitzgerald, dance until long into the evening at nightclubs in the West End, kiss fellows they barely know and, at regular intervals, go off to 'powder their noses' – quite literally so, in fact, with a little line of coke. These are the so-called 'bright young things' who are made to feel welcome by Bella of Blackfriars at The Ring.

Earls and lords sit only a few metres distant from the ringside, hence their designation as 'ringsiders'. They wear black top hats, cloaks, tailcoats and bow ties and beneath their seats are boxes of Corona cigars. They read the *Daily Mirror*, the *Daily News* or *The Times*: the coal miners' dispute seems to be in the past; production is already on the up again. According to the Foreign Secretary, Sir Austen Chamberlain, Britain's great enemy, Germany, is complying reasonably with the terms of disarmament imposed upon it after the Treaty of Versailles.

The in-house band plays 'God Save the King' and 'Rule, Britannia!'. Pickpockets collide against spectators while policemen chase after them, just like in the Mack Sennett films. Disabled veterans slide crutches under their seats; chaperones tell blind soldiers what's happening in the boxing hall. Vendors in white jackets carrying trays pass among the spectators crying 'Chocolate! Chocolate!' and 'Fine apples, fine apples!' In the United States, the sale of liquor has been prohibited for seven years, but at The Ring there are seven bars open for business and serving customers.

The Ring is also known as 'The Smoke'. Smog-like clouds of smoke billow beneath the domed ceiling, and one Dutch attendee is seated next to a man 'puffing away on his pipe as if fearful the tobacco merchants weren't already coining it in' – according to him, others hold 'a glowing brief for the fragrance of Virginia tobacco'. Neon signs proclaim that Player's Navy Cut makes millions of smokers happy throughout the world.

The betting boys descend the stairs and press coins into the hands of Birmingham gangsters who are running a sideline as bookies. During a previous visit to The Ring they'd set the press table on fire: notebooks were reduced to ash with weighty analyses of talented British boxers never to be read, and the firemen were only just able to prevent the domed ceiling from going up in flames.

The Master of Ceremonies climbs into the ring. He is wearing a black smoking jacket with a bow tie and dark, striped trousers. His trembling hands betray all the marks of old age, his head sports a lacklustre tuft of white hair and below his nose there is a walrus moustache with patchy nicotine stains in yellow ochre. His name is George Harris, a fact known to all; the spectators and boxers call him 'Old George'. His role is to announce the bouts in The Ring and, according to a Dutch journalist, 'he knows how to control or call to order the often boisterous crowd'.

A fierce, bright light shines on Old George as he raises the megaphone to his lips to announce that the galleries are brimming with 'petty thieves and men of more ambitious crimes', so valuables are best left in the cloakroom. It is just before eight o'clock when he declares the evening's boxing tournament open, loudly drawling: 'Lay-dees an' . . . ah . . . gentle-men . . . a six-round contest!' The wooden swing doors to the hall push open. Leen stands in the corridor dressed in his bathrobe, his ears assailed by the roaring, the pounding, the singing and the swearing. The reporter for the magazine *Boxing*, the world's leading boxing publication, describes the noise as 'that great swelling expectancy'. Leen climbs through the ropes into the ring and sits down on a stool, where there's a bowl filled with sawdust and a receptacle to hawk up in.

Old George informs the crowd that the referee will be Moss Deyong, and the betting boys jeer at him. At a previous match, Moss had let the wrong boxer win, whereupon they had stolen a cabby's cash box and pelted Mossy's bald pate with sharpened coins. Old George cries out: 'They are . . . ah . . . both ready!!! On my right . . . Len Sanderrrrs from Rotterdam! Featherweight champion of Holland! On my left . . . Tom Wilson from Blackfriars! May the best man win!' The MC lifts the ropes while Moss lights up a cigarette and climbs into his referee's high chair outside the ring. Nichols, the venerable timekeeper, takes his place behind a table and also lights up. Moss addresses Leen and Tom's seconds: 'Gentlemen, seconds out! Time!' and Nichols strikes the gong with a muffled hammer.

Leen and Tom cautiously approach each other; they jab, duck, clinch together and counterpunch. There are no doctors on hand – a sponge or injection is all that's needed to patch up a boxer, and in an emergency Moss has plasters to stick on to busted noses, eyebrows or lips. The spectators yell: 'Sock 'im in, Dutchie!', 'Move in, Tom!' and 'Ow, come on Len!'

In the second round, Leen launches attacks from his hermetic double defence, surprising Tom with uppercuts that the journalist writing for *Boxing* refers to as 'snappy'. Tom is having to back out and is saved by the bell. His eyebrow is torn, blood is streaming from his nose and he's seeing double. His speech is as slurred as if he'd just polished off a bottle of Dewar's whisky. A second gives him smelling salts and liniment and Moss applies plasters to the worst of the wounds.

Nichols sounds the gong for the third round. The betting boys bellow out: 'Finish 'im, Len!' and Leen sallies with a left and a right hook; Tom goes down again. 'Count 'im out! Count 'im out!' Moss counts down, but Tom does not get up in time. His seconds lug him to his stool and Leen punches the air with his fists. To show their appreciation for a good show, the betting boys shower the ring with pennies and shillings – loose change called 'nobbins' in the local slang.

Leen freshens up under a cold shower and sweeps away any talc and dirt from the floor; Bella insists on changing rooms being left clean. His eyebrows are cut and some blood drips from his nose. His right ear is red and swollen: a cauliflower ear.

IV.

Dawn is breaking and the waffle baker is trailing through De Dijk with his barrow. British sailors are calling out 'good morning', lorries full of vegetables are heading to the market next to Goudschesingel, and stockbrokers are walking to the stock exchange. The number 10 tram is already almost full, its passengers search their pockets for loose change for their tickets and conductors inspect the coins with a torch to check their authenticity. Policemen with truncheons are on patrol until early in the morning. According to them, women should be especially wary of 'seafarers' because, having been long at sea, they're not beyond groping under skirts and gowns or inside fur coats. The first cafés are opening their doors and filter coffee is percolating through machines; a cup will set you back ten cents. Trams come by De Dijk every ten minutes as cyclists mount the Maas Bridge to enter the city. At no. 21, literary works by local writers are being carried into Bolle's antiquarian bookshop. J.J. van der Vorst's shop window bears the legend ENGLISH BOOTMAKER. At nos 23–25, labourers smoke roll-ups in front of the Van Nelle factory building where they manufacture and package rolling tobacco, cigarettes, tea and roasted coffee.

Leen's father, Josua Jacob Sanders, opens the door to his waffle bakery at no. 54. A lightbulb hangs from the ceiling and an oil lamp illuminates a large copper mixing bowl. The counter has a cash register with a hand crank with an accounts book alongside. Indigent Rotterdammers can pay on tick; Josua takes a dip pen and writes down the sum owed in a notebook. It's going to be another busy day at the shop: tourists and day visitors from across the Netherlands always spend a while walking around De Dijk, and a butter waffle is as much a part of the Rotterdam experience as a visit to Museum Boijmans, a mariner's pub or one of those ladies, all lipstick and cleavage, in some red-lit backroom.

Josua brushes down the pavement. Indoors, his son Bram sweeps the floor clean of flour. He has lost ten of his last twelve bouts and has not actually won any. Battling Sanders has decided to throw in the professional boxing towel and work with his father instead. One of his colleagues is his brother Meijer, two years his senior, and Leen also tries to help out in between training sessions and tournaments.

Their father dons his long white apron, puts dough into a mould and sticks waffles together with dollops of caramel syrup. Signs in the shop window announce that galettes cost ten cents each and *stroopwafels* (caramel waffles) six cents, or fifteen cents for four mini-waffles. They are finely chequered, crisp, light, exquisitely flavoured and hygienically prepared. White lettering across the window proclaims the nature of the business:

J.J. SANDERS & SONS
FRESHLY BAKED EVERY DAY
BUTTER AND CARAMEL WAFFLES
BRUSSELS GALETTES
BISCUITS AND PASTRIES

A reviewer writes: 'The way Mr J. Sanders makes his butter waffles, caramel waffles and galettes has customers coming back time and again, and that's just the ticket!'

Leen's father is fifty-three years old. His brown hair is starting to lose its colour and his bristling moustache is flecked greyish-white. His military service card describes him as having a low forehead, grey eyes and a rounded chin. An official has judged his nose to be 'large', but his arms and legs are not, and thanks to his short stature he has not had to enlist.

The small kitchen used by J.J. Sanders & Sons is home to sieves, lemons, baker's moulds, whisks, egg beaters, waffle irons, greaseproof bowls, metal grills, weighing scales, a cutting machine and a piping bag. The smell is one of vanilla, cinnamon, burned butter and syrup. Ships are coming into Leuvehaven to dock and the air fills with cries in a multitude of languages. Migrant workers Randolfi and Sabatini are playing Italian songs on the organ or banjo, but their two beautiful daughters make a far more lasting impression as they pass the cap around. Cafés and honkytonk joints are playing 78s by Gene Austin, Duke Ellington and Paul Whiteman. Goys are buying chops and ribs from Bergers the pork butcher at no. 133. Against an illuminated sign, black lettering announces: ALCAZAR DANCE PALACE, and later that day, a 'jazz band' will be bringing 'ultramodern American dance music' to people's ears. Their great competitor, Mr Gelderblom, is advertising an alternative venue: DANCE AND HAVE FUN AT THE COSMOPOLIET.

Deothor Stein, the neighbour at no. 56, has straight, black hair and is short, squat and thickset. Over the years, his nose has taken on an increasingly bizarre appearance thanks to a series of uppercuts, jabs, hooks and counterpunches. Deothor became the Dutch welterweight boxing champion under the name Theo Kourimsky and opened a pub on De Dijk. Deothor's wife, Petronella, works behind the bar; she's nine years older than him and for a long time she worked as a prostitute. People call her Nel the Liar, and she is every bit as fond of gin as her clientele.

Devoutly Jewish customers of J.J. Sanders & Sons like to complain about assimilation, blaming it on sport and all the dancing events on De Dijk: Jews train and shower with goys, and at Cosmopoliet and Alcazar they flirt with Christian girls. Many mixed marriages are taking place, including in Rotterdam, and according to a pamphleteer from the *Nieuw Israëlietisch Weekblad*, fewer and fewer 'children of Israel' will be left as a result.

No blame can be laid at Josua Sanders' door: he has ten children and is raising his sons and daughters as devoutly as possible. His own youth was difficult, but through his belief in God he has continued to hope for a better future. Until he was ten, Josua lived in Schavensteeg, the poorest and most dangerous place in Rotterdam's Zandstraat neighbourhood. At first, his father, Jakob, made a poor living from rolling cigars, but he went on to become a waffle baker. His products were high quality but the returns were disappointing, and Jakob and his family had to move house many times. When the landlord raised the rent by a few guilders yet again, they'd lug their household goods on to a couple of barrows off to the next slum dwelling – usually at night, out of shame.

In 1900, at the age of twenty-eight, Josua had married a Jewish maidservant from Rotterdam called Saartje, seven years his junior. For the wedding Josua wore a tall black hat and black suit, Saartje a white dress with a veil, her long brown hair covered by a wig. Men sat below in the main auditorium while the women sat in the balcony, behind a curtain. The marriage had to be officially sanctioned at Rotterdam's City Hall in Hoogstraat, where the marriage certificate was read aloud by a goy official. Saartje's mother, Rozetta, and Josua's Amsterdammer mother, Sipora, a seamstress by profession, were obliged to confess that they had not learned to write, and signed their names with a cross.

The couple's first son, Jakob, was born in 1902. Josua and Saartje then lived in Zandstraat, the most notorious street in Rotterdam, where cafés stood alongside dance halls, cramped properties, lodging houses, bordellos and illegal distilleries. The comedian Louis Davids grew up in Zandstraat, where he sang his first ditties, and Abraham Tuschinski, a Polish refugee Jew, started up his first cinema there. On Saturdays and Sundays, tourists, as well as men seeking prostitutes, would loiter about in the Sanders' street, and Jews with barrows would ply their trade in a mixture of Yiddish and the Rotterdam dialect. Behind closed shutters, some places would be hosting illicit dog fights and cockfights. Policemen were called *dofgajes* (thug-thumpers), *kaasjagers* (named after the city's chief of bicycle-mounted police) or *blauwpijpers* (cocksuckers-in-blue). Pimps were *toffe jongens* (diamond geezers) or *gozers* (geezers), while a *knipje* (snare) or *rendezvous-huis* was a brothel, and prostitutes were *meissies* (girlies), *lichte vrouwen* (loose women), *gevallen vrouwen* (fallen women) or *vrouwen met zwakke hielen* (women with weak heels). Men of rank from respectable neighbourhoods would be set down from their coach and horses in front of the 'rendezvous houses', and seafarers' favourite ports of call were the Walhalla Dance Hall or the Nielsen Dance Hall. After imbibing far too much Dutch gin, they would be led off by a prostitute-thief to some dosshouse where they would be robbed by a 'diamond geezer'. Hardly any of the Zandstraat neighbourhood's residents trusted the police; a pickpocket or petty thief would sometimes run into the slums and alleyways surrounding Zandstraat with plain-clothes police in hot pursuit because a place to hide out was assured from any of the houses in the district.

Abraham 'Bram' Sanders was born in 1904, Meijer in 1906 and Leen on 11 June 1908. A midwife visited 17 Zandstraat at one o'clock that afternoon to assist Saartje. Afterwards, she went to the municipal registry to report 'a child of the male sex that is to be named: Leendert Josua'.

For the first two years of his life Leen lived in Zandstraat, but he grew up in Peperstraat. Local residents referred to the street ironically as the 'Rue du Poivre' and less ironically as 'a peppery area'. Belze Marie and Auntie Bet ran after-hours businesses there and stolen goods were sold under the counter at most of the shops; Mr Brisban's lodgings housed drunkards, counterfeiters, the unemployed, prostitutes, vagrants and bank robbers.

Saartje gave birth to four daughters in swift succession: Sipora, Rozette, Henriette and Sientje, and Joël and Mozes were born right after the Great War. Josua did not have enough money to maintain all these children, so his sons had to leave school at a young age in order to work. Leen was thirteen when his father started training him as a waffle baker. How much sugar does a gaufrette need? How do you make a galette, and what exactly is that? Syrup is runnier than caramel and makes waffles especially sticky as a result; egg whites have to be 'beaten into snowy peaks'; to make thirty butter waffles you need: 300g butter, 250g icing sugar, three eggs, two teaspoons of vanilla essence, 300g Hungarian flour, a tablespoon of milk and a pinch of ammonia. Good syrup drips down the chin when you take a bite from a waffle, which is precisely how it should be.

Leen preferred boxing to baking, and told his father so. Josua responded by saying that boxing was the goys' *naches* (Yiddish: their 'delight'): mindless pleasure held in esteem only by the goyim. The truly devout Yehudim devote *their* time and energy to study of the Torah and the Talmud . . . and to making butter waffles. Leen did not listen and, one year after his bar mitzvah, left his home in Nieuwsteeg for 79a De Dijk, a beer hall where the wall behind the bar was clad with mirrors and sailors ordered beers and nips of gin. The owner was Adrianus 'Janus' Riesmeijer, a divorced Catholic and chancer from a notorious Rotterdam family. Janus's older brother, Herman, pickpocketed sailors, bargemen and tourists, while his sister, Catharina, rented out rooms to 'geezers' and ladies of the night at exorbitant prices.

In the eyes of many Rotterdammers, Janus was just as untrustworthy as most of the other Riesmeijers. He had no knowledge of the 'noble art' at all, but began giving boxing lessons because it had become fashionable, and he never passed up a chance to earn some easy money. He read a few textbooks, learned the terminology by heart, bought dumbbells, mirrors, skipping ropes and a punchbag, then set up a business that he named the National Boxing Club because it sounded so much classier in English. As the brother of Battling Bram Sanders, Leen was the perfect acquisition. One afternoon in 1922, Janus led Leen down to the cellar at Café Riesmeijer. The planks creaked, and there, between casks of beer and assorted beverage bottles, were two boxing rings where Jews and goys would box beneath a lightbulb hanging from a thin wire. The heavyweight Arie Valk would shadowbox against one wall; Maupie Ploeg would jab at a punchbag; Piet van Dam would be using a skipping rope, and his younger brother, Jan, would be doing press-ups. Leen and his cousin Meijer would spar with Karel Veldt, a former cabin boy from Schiedam. After training, they would wash themselves from a bucket.

Josua Sanders closes his waffle bakery at six in the evening and within ten minutes has walked back with his barrow to his shabby dwelling in Nieuwsteeg. Saartje has a kosher dinner ready, and following the blessing for the meal, conversation at the dinner table centres almost as much on the 'noble art' as it does on butter waffles. Will Benny Leonard hold on to his title? Will Georges Carpentier make a comeback? Will Jack Dempsey take back his world title? By 1926, Josua Sanders has ceased to object to his sons' passion for boxing. One afternoon, he asks Leen to hand him a pair of boxing gloves. He takes them along to De Dijk, climbs onto a stool and nails them above the entrance to Waffle Bakery J.J. Sanders & Sons.

V.

A large building in London's East End district of Whitechapel bears the name PREMIERLAND. Barrow boys are calling out to the passers-by: 'Come and get yer ice cream! Peanuts, fresh today! Luvverly apples! Sharp's Kreem Toffees!' Beetroots, cabbages and black radishes gleam in the spring sunshine. Jewish and Irish workers are entering Charles Kinloch & Company Ltd, a wine, whisky and brandy factory. In 1888, Jack the Ripper murdered five women in this area. Street vendors cry out that they're selling the blood of Jack's victims and photos of the autopsies.

Whitechapel is referred to as 'the Jewish East End'. Houses here are even more askew than in Rotterdam's Nieuwsteeg. Scarcely any light permeates the alleys and slum dwellings. One Dutchman says that, beyond a shadow of a doubt, nobody apart from boxing fanatics would be seen dead here; he describes Whitechapel as 'a maze of narrow streets surrounded by outlandish houses and establishments'. Orthodox Jewish men sport tall hats and wear their beards long, while their spouses cover their hair with a *sheitel* (wig). Slum landlords rent out their premises at extortionate prices and shop windows advertise their business and wares in Hebrew and Yiddish. Broken panes of glass have been covered up with rags, paving is loose underfoot, rubbish is dumped in the middle of the street. A goy commentator for the *East London Observer* calls the Jewish East End 'a rubbish tip for foreign riffraff'.

It is the Sunday afternoon of 29 April 1928. Cars, taxis, horse-drawn carts and double-decker buses are passing along Commercial Road to Back Church Lane, a narrow road with equally narrow pavements on either side. Impecunious boxing fans have come on foot from the Aldgate East underground station, where a Jewish boy is waving the Saturday edition of *Reynold's Illustrated News*: Frederick Guy Browne has just been convicted for the murder of Police Constable Gutteridge on an Essex road; together with an accomplice, he has been found guilty at the Old Bailey and sentenced to death, a double hanging to take place on 31 May.

It is overcast and 17°C. Visitors from the affluent West End are parking in front of Premierland in their Chevrolets or Daimlers, and local kids are offering to wash their cars for a few pennies or to watch over them in case of thieves. Policemen on the beat are walking to and fro to discourage pickpockets; in the main, it is goys who are most likely to be robbed here. Posters proclaim:

PREMIERLAND
SUNDAY 29 APRIL, 1928
GREAT SPECIAL 15-ROUND CONTEST (3 MINUTES EACH)
BETWEEN
HARRY 'BUGLER' LAKE (PLYMOUTH, BRITISH CHAMPION,
    EUROPEAN CHAMPION)

V

LEN SANDERS (ROTTERDAM, DUTCH FEATHERWEIGHT CHAMPION)

Leen is nineteen and weighs 63 kilograms. He has enough talent to become a top-flight European boxer and is being compared to the new Jewish star from Whitechapel, Judah Bergman, born in the East End and a year older than Leen. He's nicknamed 'the Whitechapel Whirlwind' and 'the Carpentier of the East End', although most Whitechapel Jews call him 'Kid Berg'.

Kid Berg grew up a few hundred metres from Premierland in one of Whitechapel's many tenement buildings, accessed through a dark tunnel under the railway line at Conant Mews, a left turn off Cable Street. He was discovered as a boxer at the age of fourteen, when he knocked a couple of Jew-haters to the ground in front of the entrance to the boxing hall. Since then he's been fighting at Premierland every two weeks with a Star of David sewn on to his shorts.

According to British and Dutch experts, Leen is just as promising as Kid Berg. He's deceptively fast, has an above-average constitution and when lagging behind in points he's still able to bounce back in the final rounds. Cleverly, he always keeps his distance from the ropes, dishes out 'snappy jabs' and almost never takes a hit himself; his double defence is famous. British spectators will leap up, screaming their lungs out, whenever Leen takes the initiative from a closed defence stance. 'At those moments, [his fists] flash to chin or stomach, not with excessive force but with great precision, and when the astonished opponent seeks to retaliate, [Leen] has already retreated behind that hermetic defence of his.' British journalists sometimes refer to him as Frank Sanders, Lew Sanders or Len Saunders, and the Premierland programme describes him as 'Len Sanders: Forceful Pounding Machine'.

Leen is popular in England, where he can get a far higher fee than in his home country. This explains why he boards the *Batavier V* every few months to sail from De Boompjes to Gravesend. According to a journalist writing for *De Telegraaf*, 'the names of our Dutch boxers, such as Leen Sanders, [have] a golden ring to them, and if a "Dutchie" should feature in the programme, one can always be certain of sizeable public interest in them, because the Dutch have a reputation in the Boxing Union not only as courageous and sportsmanlike fighters, but, moreover, also as pugilists capable of handing the English a robust rejoinder and even of beating them at one of their most beloved sports.'

At times, Leen needs rest in order to recover from all the knocks and all the travelling, but his manager, Janus, wants to earn as much money as possible from his boxers, so his pupil is fighting in Portsmouth, Manchester, Newcastle, Edmonton (London), Birmingham and Ilford. A journalist for the magazine *Boxing* calls Leen a 'master in the art of avoiding punishment'; he is 'dour, strong and as clever and as cunning as a monkey'; the sole criticism is that Leen could have been a few pounds lighter. He is 'stocky', 'sturdy' and 'rugged', and during a match against a British opponent from Birmingham, he appeared 'to be something in the weights'.

Leen's status seems to increase in line with his weight gain. In 1928, he is the Netherlands' most successful Jewish professional boxer. One Rotterdammer claims that even Amsterdam aficionados are 'enthralled by the splendid way he champions the Dutch nation abroad'. Following his most recent win against Kid Berg at The Ring, the *Rotterdamsch Nieuwsblad* proclaims: 'Keep this up, Sanders, and you'll be . . . going far.'

Leen is proud to be able to represent the Netherlands abroad, but he will never conceal his Jewish identity. In 1926, Leen and his brother Bram pose together for the prominent sports magazine *Sportrevue/'t Stadion* dressed in white shorts embroidered with a Star of David in the same style as Benny Leonard and Kid Berg. Battling Sanders adopts a tough stance, his arms folded across his chest, while Leen has his hands on his hips as if throwing down a challenge: 'Just what are you anti-Semites going to do, eh? Just what have you got?'

Premierland opens its doors at half past two. The walls are overgrown with moss and the roof is leaking and rusted. Pillars obstruct the view. The urinals stink, chairs wobble, the benches have wood rot, lightbulbs are burned out and the oil lamps have almost run dry. Torn posters show pictures of Kid Berg, former world champion Ted 'Kid' Lewis, Samuel 'Dutch Sam' Elias and Daniel Mendoza: Great Britain's four best-ever Jewish boxers.

According to the expert writers for *Boxing*, Premierland is the primary training centre for Jewish boxers, and it commends 'that great people which has bestowed such top-class artists on the boxing world'. Clichés of every kind appear in the British media: Jews are such good boxers owing to their strict kosher diet; Jews are sober fellows and cautious by nature, which might seem a disadvantage in boxing, but it can reap its own reward: recklessness can be one's downfall. A few years earlier in the *London Evening Standard*: 'Do the Jews have fighting spirit? Answer: look at Daniel Mendoza, Dutch Sam Elias, Kid Lewis and Kid Berg. Some may take surprise at this, but if so they have a poor understanding of the Jews. For how could they have survived centuries of persecution without a fighting spirit?'

A few years before, a non-Jewish journalist from Rotterdam had gone to see Premierland for himself. He was taken aback by the combative eagerness, courage and passion with which a Jewish boxer would drive his goy opponent around the ring. Anti-Semites around the world persisted in calling Jews cowardly and inferior, but at the Premierland boxing ring 'the descendants of fierce Hebrew warriors' proved time and again that they 'are ideally suited to this profession in which the chicken-hearted, no matter how strong and well-built they might be otherwise, never get far'. According to a Jewish Dutchman, Jewish boxers have 'good responsiveness thanks to study of the Talmud, compelling them to be inventive and precise'. Jewish boxers are also, in his view, often tougher than their goy opponents 'owing to their struggle for survival'.

Leen is welcomed by Victor Berliner, a Jewish Pole with British nationality. He has straight black hair and a nose that points to the ground like a divining rod. Forty years ago, his parents fled their Polish village for London, and in his new country Victor came to own a haberdashery business, selling buttons, drapery and hats, but closed it in the early 1920s to coach Jewish boxers. As well as being Kid Berg's manager, he is also the manager of Premierland; one journalist wrote that he 'has the Hebrew instinct for earning money'.

Leen goes to the changing room and gets a cup of tea and a piece of toast. His English opponent, Harry, is sitting opposite. He comes from Plymouth and is much larger than Leen. According to a journalist writing for *Boxing*, his nose looks like 'a squashed prune', although in British boxing circles the usual term is simply 'flat nose'. Harry is wearing a white outfit bearing the Union Jack. He goes by the nickname 'Bugler' because that was his duty when he served in the army during the Great War.

Some Jewish lads from Whitechapel are sitting in silence on a bench opposite Leen and Harry. They fight under names such as Jewey Smith, Young Joseph and Cockney Cohen, and may enter the ring only if a scheduled match finishes too soon. Steve, a Jewish ex-boxer, now enters the changing room. He checks on how they are, asks questions, spars with them a bit, looks in their eyes and then selects two novice boxers who will be permitted to prove their worth. They have to seize that opportunity: the Whitechapel ghetto feels like a prison, and boxing can offer a way out. It provides money and status; you have only to look at Benny Leonard, Kid Lewis, Kid Berg and Len Sanders. Only in the ring can a Jew be the temporary equal of a Christian . . . or even his superior.

Premierland is a sell-out, with three thousand spectators. The poorest boxing fans have bought tickets at a penny or tuppence each and have to watch the matches from the balcony or stairs; some are even hanging from the roof's steel joists. As elsewhere, almost everyone is wearing some kind of hat at Premierland; as one Rotterdam journalist puts it: 'when tallied up, the flat cap will most definitely be declared the victor in *that* battle.'

Boxing fans from Whitechapel have brought food along with them: dried fish, gherkins and pickled herring. People are reading the *East London Observer* and the tabloids: Arsenal is playing a relegation game against West Ham this Saturday; continuing good news about the stock market, with a columnist trumpeting 'boom conditions!'; Marmaduke the escaped monkey has been spotted in the West End, where police made a failed attempt to capture her at the corner of Oxford Street and Tottenham Court Road.

Ted 'Kid' Lewis enters the hall, a Stetson on his head and clad in a fur coat, waving with his walking stick to friends and acquaintances. The crowd gives him an ovation. Kid Lewis was born in the East End as Gershon Mendeloff, and in 1914 won the European featherweight title at a sold-out Premierland. He is friends with Charlie Chaplin, has affairs with goy music-hall stars, goes out in the West End with 'bright young things' until three or four in the morning and every so often has his chauffeur drive him to Premierland in a limousine.

A bald Jewish gentleman steps into the ring: Lewis Cohen, the Master of Ceremonies at Premierland. Spectators chant 'Lew! Lew! Lew!' Just like Victor Berliner, MC Lew grew up in Poland, fleeing his homeland because of the increasing frequency of arson attacks on Jewish Poles' homes. As MC Lew announces the first match of the evening, the crowd hurls fruit peel and bits of pastry towards the ring. Afterwards, Leen describes the atmosphere in Premierland as 'unfriendly', while a Rotterdam journalist writes: 'If people think that Rotterdam has the monopoly over unruly nights out, they are sorely mistaken.'

The door to the changing room opens and Steve walks in to pick up Leen and Harry 'Bugler' Lake. They walk through a central aisle towards the ring. Jewish and goy spectators touch Leen and Harry, shouting out: 'Bash 'im, Dutchie!', '*Mazel tov!*' and '*Zje klug!*' (Be smart!) Steve lifts up the ropes a fraction and Leen climbs into the ring, sitting himself down on a stool. His second is a Jewish former boxer who has adopted the name 'Fred' in England; Leen has to pay him fivepence from out of his own wages. In return, Leen gets his neck massaged, has water squirted into his mouth, liniment rubbed into his eyebrows and a towel wrapped around his head in the breaks between rounds.

Premierland employees throw sawdust into the ring. MC Lew screams out: 'Ladies and . . . ah . . . gentlemen . . . they are . . . ah . . . both ready! On my left . . . the one and only . . . Haaaarry "Buglerrrr" Lake! On my right, from Rrrrotterdam, the Netherlands, featherweight and hard-hitting Dutchman Len Sanderrrrs! A great international fifteen-round contest!' The victor is to receive prize money of fifty pounds. MC Lew mentions that the on-site 'medical man' is Dr Cohen, responsible for intervening in the event of a life-threatening situation for either of the two young fighters. A twenty-one-year-old boxer had already died at Premierland in 1925: a bone splinter pierced his brain. As the reporter for *Boxing* put it, he'd been 'knocked out for ever'.

Leen shadowboxes in the ring for a few seconds as Hyman, the Jewish timekeeper, checks his timepiece. Dr Cohen shines a torch into 'Bugler' Lake's eyes. Lew explains that the contest will be refereed by Jack Hart, born in the East End under the name Moses Solomon. Leen removes his bathrobe and Premierland's spectators erupt into 'a cacophony that defies sight and sound' when they realize what Leen is sporting on his blue shorts: picked out in white is a Star of David. The Jewish boy from the Zandstraat ghetto punches the air with his boxing gloves. He's as much a Rotterdammer as Bok de Korver and Bep van Klaveren, but also as Jewish as Victor Berliner, MC Lew, Dr Cohen, Kid Berg and, of course, Benny Leonard.

VI.

The boxing manager leans over the beer tap. Ashtrays are overflowing, curtains reek of nicotine and the carpet is beer-stained. Seated on stools at the bar there are Norwegians, Frenchmen, Czechs, Englishmen, Germans and Dutchmen wearing slouch hats, baggy trousers and red baize shirts, their hands tattooed with anchors. Blackboards give the prices for coffee and sandwich rolls, but customers at Café Riesmeijer can also order a hot meal of meatballs and fresh liver.

Kees the Bootblack comes in, a battered carrying case and greasy polish under his arm. He is cheap and not a dawdler; the seafarers soon have the best-shined boots in all the world. The wife of Kees the Bootblack is called Antje the Rag on account of the black rag she wears in her crocheted cap in an attempt to disguise her baldness. Miss 'Dollface' looks sweet and can sing well, but her knife will skewer any sailor unwise enough to let his hands wander. Drunken Riekie is best not provoked, as she might stab you to death with her hairpin. Flip the Eelman sells hot sausages with sauerkraut and eel; he enters the pub calling in his clear, sing-song voice, and after ten minutes or so will say: 'Nobody else? Had the lot of you? Then, byeeee!'

It's March 1929. Stocks continue to rise in value on Wall Street. The front page of the *Rotterdamsch Nieuwsblad* informs readers that 'Prof. Dr Albert Einstein, scientist, musician and man of integrity' is fifty years old. The sports pages report that 'the celebrated Rotterdam boxer Leen Sanders is departing for Berlin, where, on Friday evening, he will be pitted against Gustav Eder.' German boxing experts believe that, within a few years, Leen's opponent could become European champion, and perhaps even world champion.

Leen is twenty. He is living with his parents in Leeuwenlaan, an alley in the Zandstraat neighbourhood. One journalist has written that, following recent victories at Premierland and other British boxing venues, Leen 'has restored the reputation of the Dutch as a sporting nation'. On the other hand, things could be better for Leen's manager and café landlord, Janus: his youngest brother was arrested a few weeks earlier. According to the public prosecutor, Marinus Riesmeijer was running 'a vampire-like business' for the exploitation of women, and he's been given a seven-month prison sentence.

Janus wants to keep on the straight and narrow, believing that Leen is going to be his ticket to riches. From the cellar of his café he negotiates new fights and calls reporters at *De Maasbode* and the *Rotterdamsch Nieuwsblad* to get his best pupil into the paper. In October 1928 he sent a letter to the International Boxing Union to register Leen for the title match in the lightweight division of the European championships against the Spaniard, Rayo: 'That lad has no clue what is coming his way.' Janus drew up a list showing the results of Len's matches, showing a succession of wins and draws against celebrated British boxers at The Ring, Premierland, the Ilford Skating Rink and other well-known arenas. Janus then sent off the registration fee of 1,000 francs to the International Boxing Union. Everything was pointing towards the Union granting Leen a European title fight, and any doubt was removed when, on 15 October 1928, he received the news that the challenge had been accepted.

Janus and Leen made plans. The Auction Rooms? Too small, too dingy. It had to be not just big, but bigger still . . . the biggest: the Sparta football stadium, for example, with more than ten thousand Rotterdammers cheering Leen on just as they did on Sundays for Sparta's star player, Bok de Korver.

On 19 November 1928, a new letter from the IBU arrived. Janus tore open the envelope quickly only to read that Leen's registration had not been accepted after all. Janus demanded an inquiry: how it was possible that a favourable decision made on 15 October could be simply withdrawn over a month later? He received no reply, which meant that there was only one thing for it: Leen and Janus had to get to Berlin. Winning against Gustav Eder would be a sensation, and then a European title match was sure to be arranged within a few months.

The train runs via Osnabrück and Hanover to Berlin-Hauptbahnhof. Clinker bricks are being tapped into place; steam hammers drive piles into the ground; excavations are underway behind fencing, as there is still more of the underground railway network to come. Leen and Janus are walking over planks. No other European city is witnessing the construction of so many new dance palaces, department stores, brothels, theatres, restaurants and beer halls. A Rotterdam journalist writes that Berlin is 'the modern Babel-on-the-Spree'.

Boxer and manager take the metro to Kurfürstendamm. They alight after five stops and pass by beer gardens on three floors, the

Berlin Zoo on Budapester Straße, the American restaurant Röberts and the Zoo Palast, Europe's largest cinema. Men use long poles to light streetlamps; cars honk their horns; buses and taxis jam the streets, and horses pull carriages of tourists to Alexanderplatz. Shop-window mannequins display the latest Berlin fashions and ladies with *Bubiköpfe* (bobbed hair) board trams, metro trains or taxis to get to the department stores Tietz or Kaufhaus des Westen. National Socialists with swastika armbands are selling newspapers and pamphlets in front of the fashion store Wertheim; writing on the wall exhorts passers-by to BUY GERMAN, NOT JEWISH! In 1928, their leader, Adolf Hitler, had given an address at the Berlin Sportpalast, where the auditorium was as full as for a Carpentier or Dempsey boxing match with an audience of sixteen thousand.

Leen and Janus walk past bookshops and newspaper kiosks, where journals and magazines give previews of Leen's match against Gustav Eder. One journalist calls Leen 'a somewhat thickset but plucky boxer' who issues left hooks in a 'propeller-like tempo'. The sports page of *Vossische Zeitung* describes him as 'the much-acclaimed little Dutchman', the 'outstanding Dutch welterweight' and the 'technically marvellous Dutchman Len Sanders'. This praise owes itself to a previous match in Berlin against Fritz Kracht from Hamburg in which Leen had won, with spectators chanting out his name at the end: 'Len! Len! Len!' An editor from the newspaper *Nachtausgabe* came up with the headline 'Dutch Boxing Lesson'.

The article reads: 'Yesterday, the little Dutchman Leen Sanders . . . managed to leave us somewhat astonished. The boxing technique that he displayed at the sold-out Spichernsälen [boxing hall] was simply staggering, and he belongs undoubtedly among Europe's top flight boxers.' The journalist writing for the *Vossische Zeitung* felt he was one of the best boxers ever to have stood in a German boxing ring and added: 'From the first round, Sanders demonstrated what being able to box actually means. It was a pleasure to be able to see him at work.' The esteemed magazine *Box-Sport* printed his photograph, which showed Leen standing in the ring alongside Fritz Kracht, his bathrobe half open, looking confidently into the lens. The headline: 'Great future'.

It is dark when Leen and Janus cross Nürnberger Platz to Spichernstraße in the notorious Berlin district of Wilmersdorf. Street hawkers are crying out: 'Juno cigarettes! Twenty pfennigs! Sportsmen's cigarettes of choice!' Men on benches whisper: 'Psst! Coke, hash, morphine?' Berlin Jews wearing skullcaps or tall black hats are walking hurriedly back home: it's Friday evening, and the chicken soup is nearly ready, the candles will soon be lit, the pear kugel has been left to cool in the kitchen. Having reached no. 3, Leen and Janus find themselves in front of a lofty building. The poster outside reads:

SPICHERNSÄLEN BERLIN
FRIDAY 15 MARCH, 20.00 HOURS
GRAND INTERNATIONAL BOXING MATCH EVENING
MAIN FIGHT:
LEN SANDERS (DUTCH WELTERWEIGHT, DEFEATED FRITZ
    KRAFT)
VERSUS
GUSTAV EDER (BIELEFELD/DORTMUND, DEFEATED ONLY
    ONCE)

Boys are selling roast chestnuts and salted pretzels and newspaper vendors are calling out *'Illustrierte! Berliner Abendzeitung! Nachtausgabe! Welt! Grüne Post! BZ am Mittag! Vorwärts! Vossische!'* Bratwurst sausages and onions are being charred on griddles and the odour permeates pullovers and jackets that were not so freshly scented to start with. Men queue up at the ticket counter; most of them no longer have jobs, and have moved back in with their parents because of the housing shortage. Tickets for the theatre, cinema or a boxing event at the Berliner Sportpalast have become too expensive – only tickets for the Spichernsälen are just about affordable. They sit in the cheapest sections and view the bouts through binoculars; otherwise, they can only hear the slap of boxing gloves and the boxers' grunts.

Inspectors from Berlin's homicide division show their police ID-cards to the doorman and are allowed in without paying. Anyone who wants to solve a crime goes to the Spichernsälen, where gangland leaders gather together in conspiratorially whispered conversation. Outside the boxing hall they emerge from Mercedes limousines, Austin 7s and BMW Dixis wearing fedoras and carrying wraps of cocaine in their pockets, accompanied by women in petite colourful hats, open-necked blouses, suspender belts and high heels.

Bank directors, film stars and criminals order Escorial beer at the Prominenten Bar, and bottles of champagne at thirty marks each are placed on the table in a cooler. Seats at the bar are given to journalists, as bar seats give the best view of the ring. The beer garden benches at the sides are all packed. Signs on the Spichernsälen walls declare: RAUCHEN VERBOTEN! (Smoking Prohibited!) According to the programme booklet, 'the matadors [can] provide the top-class sport expected of them by the public only in a smoke-free atmosphere.'

Leen and Janus enter through an arched gateway. The hall is lofty but cramped, its windows barred. Workmen are rolling casks of strong lager through the goods entrance. The two Dutchmen have a meeting in Pepi Burda's office, where two table lamps and a pot of mustard grace the desk. The curtains are closed and a gaslit crystal chandelier radiates warm light. Pepi grew up in Bohemia but fled to the Weimar Republic because of its better treatment of Jews. He's managed to build a secure life for himself in Berlin, but recently even Pepi has faced threats: supporters of Adolf Hitler are provoking Jewish, socialist or communist boxing fans, and Pepi strongly advises against Leen boxing with a Star of David on his shorts.

Steep stairs lead them to a dark tunnel with recesses and side-passages. The ringside doctor, Dr Von der Esche, has the largest room in this maze of corridors. Leen has to undress in a room so small that Janus can hardly fit next to him. There's a pocket mirror on top of a small cabinet, a flickering lightbulb hangs from a wire, and the wastebasket is an old gherkin barrel. Janus fills a jug with murky tap water and tells Leen what his fight plan needs to be: of his own free will, Eder often allows himself to be coerced into the ropes and tries to strike only when his opponent is no longer expecting it. Janus's advice is never think that Eder has been beaten, and watch out for his right hook, which is among Europe's finest. Piet van Dam, Leen's teammate at the National Boxing Club, lost to Eder and found him 'a tremendously tricky man to box'.

Dr Von der Esche weighs over a hundred kilograms and climbs with difficulty into his high chair, puts on his spectacles and flips open his notebook, as he has to write a medical bulletin later on. Janus gives final instructions to Leen as they leave the changing room and walk through the subterranean corridors. The announcer picks up a megaphone and bellows out: '*Damen und Herrrren,* Ladies aaaand gentlemen, *Freunde des Spichernrings!*' Referee Max Pippow, from Hamburg, is wearing a white shirt with rolled-up sleeves, white trousers and white shoes. There are no adjudicators; it is Pippow who determines who has won at the end of each bout. The announcer introduces Leen as 'Len from Tulip-land, the victor against Fritz Kracht', and the spectators cry '*Hoch Sanders!*' and 'Bravo Len!' His opponent, Gustav Eder, receives almost as much applause. Referee Pippow calls: '*Ring frei! Kampf! Box!*'

Len 'from Tulip-land' and 'Ironside' Gustav approach each other. Each one circles around the other guardedly, but never cautiously: one of the most quoted boxing maxims in Germany is *Vorsicht ist die Mutter der Knock-out* ('knockouts are born of caution'). Pippow is monitoring the boxers from only a few centimetres away; he shouts out orders such as '*Nicht halten! Wiederkämpfen!*' (No clinching! Fight on!) In the third round, Leen lands a heavy blow to 'Ironside' Gustav's nose and mouth. Part of his face tears open and Pippow pauses the match to have the blood swept away. Dr Von der Esche staples up Eder's face and signals to Pippow that the match can continue. Leen keeps on dodging Eder's strikes, countering them with short, fast attacks that catch him on the chin, ear, lip and temple. 'Ironside' Gustav is continually pushed back; when will his second throw a towel into the ring? Not just yet, but Leen keeps coming at him, his left fist going to work just as it did against Fritz Kracht, like a propeller, resulting in hits to the chin and punches to the stomach; Eder can hardly breathe. After the eighth round, the gong sounds for the final time. Referee Pippow declares Leen the winner. According to the journalist for *Box-Sport*, Leen had won the fight hands down.

The spectators file out. Behind a table in the press office, a German journalist is typing up words of praise for Len Sanders, the conqueror of Fritz Kracht and Gustav Eder. That same journalist will be meeting Leen again in 1943 . . . in Auschwitz.

Part II

An exceptional boxer, especially for a Jew

I.

———

Astride his Gazelle bicycle, the champion fighter is cycling through the city; first he emerges from Leeuwenlaan, watching out for loose bricks in the road, then turns the corner at Achterom. Pedlars with barrows offer their wares at 'depression prices', and posters and advertising columns announce a forthcoming event:

TUESDAY EVENING, 18 FEBRUARY 1930
ARTS & SCIENCES BUILDING, SCHIEDAMSCHESINGEL 27
LEEN SANDERS, NATIONAL BOXING CLUB (TITLE HOLDER)
VERSUS
BEP VAN KLAVEREN, THE PUGILIST (CHALLENGER)

Leen has to get to the weigh-in and, needless to say, he cannot turn up late, so he keeps on pedalling. The city remains busy, even in the Great Depression. He picks up the pace and passes City Hall on Coolsingel; the venue Dancing Pschorr has a jazz orchestra playing at eight o'clock this evening with wind and strings sections and a double bass; neon signs at the Cinema Royal are advertising the comedy duo Watt and Halfwatt (also known as Long and Short). He comes to a halt at 103

Coolsingel, leans the bicycle against a tree and remembers to lock it . . . after all, the neighbourhood is getting worse; since the Crash of '29, criminality in Rotterdam seems to be turning American in character.

The Wall Street Crash, the fall in stock values, the panic in New York, Black Thursday. It happened on Yom Kippur, the holiest of all Jewish festivals, and Leen was with his father, brothers and cousins at the Great Synagogue near De Boompjes. His mother, sisters and aunts were watching from the gallery, heads were covered and appropriate clothing worn; stomachs empty from early in the morning until into the evening, they were listening to Rabbi Cohen recite from passages about suffering, human shortcomings and atonement.

News of the Crash became known the day afterwards. According to the correspondent writing for *De Maasbode*, 'a real state of panic was being felt' in New York; share prices kept on tumbling. A 'shouting and raging crowd' gathered outside the Wall Street Stock Exchange and fresh reports followed in succession about 'staggering losses in some fund or other' and then 'the hubbub would rise still more'. Stockbrokers, speculators and commission agents fell ill and were taken to hospital; men clutching their briefcases leapt from rooftops; millions were made bankrupt. Traders on the Amsterdam Stock Exchange had as little faith in a recovery as their American counterparts; quite legitimately, harbour barons in Rotterdam issued warnings about mass redundancies. At the Leuvehaven docks, ships were being put under embargo with increasing frequency, sailors were left without work, dozens of cafés on De Dijk ceased trading. As a Rotterdam newspaper put it, the expression 'lower living standards' has become the slogan of the times.

One month after the Crash, Leen is boxing for the Dutch title against Florijn, the lightweight boxer from The Hague. In the twelfth round he floors his opponent with his less good right hand; the flat-capped crowd laughs and cheers: 'One! Two! Three! Four! Five!' Florijn gets to his feet again just in time, but Leen is not about to surrender his points advantage and is awarded the championship belt in the ring.

Westbroek, the boxing-union chairman from Kralingen, is just about to make a speech when a small, suntanned man climbs into the ring: Bep van Klaveren, Olympic boxing champion in 1928 and, in the view of the press, 'the coming young man', 'our all-the-rage Bep', 'the most talked about boxer in our country' and 'a cheeky chappie'. Bep bumps his not-so-broad chest against the champion and says in his trademark high-pitched voice: 'Leen, I'm challenging you!'

The contract is signed on 10 February 1930. Despite the Crash, the harbour barons have been prepared to offer quite sizeable prize money. Nobody wants to miss out on seeing the Dutch champion Leendert Josua Sanders from Leeuwenlaan fighting against the challenger Bep van Klaveren from Van Rijnstraat. It promises to be the match of the century, on the scale of Dempsey versus Carpentier in Rotterdam: Leen Sanders, the best defensive boxer in the Netherlands, against Bep van Klaveren, the best offensive boxer with the warning motto 'Get busy with your fists or you're gonna get whacked'.

Leen walks to the intersection of Van Oldenbarneveltstraat and Aert van Nesstraat. He enters café-restaurant La Paix, where the customers are grumbling about the economy and complaining about the mild winter. The General Commission for Trade in Rotterdam 'has ceased payments; the creditors have been convened to ascertain whether there is still any possibility of avoiding insolvency.'

Inside the café, the kitchen staff are rinsing cups, plates and cooking pans; leftovers can be taken home in sandwich bags. Van Meel, the proprietor, welcomes Leen, and together they walk up a curved marble staircase to a room on the third floor. Inside, there are boxing managers, promoters, journalists, 'diamond geezers', photographers, out-of-work men who shortly before had been queueing at the unemployment office, and men whose bosses have given them an hour off to see Rotterdam's best boxers at close quarters. Other participants at the event are seated at tables, waiting for their turn to be weighed. They have brought with them little tubes of castor oil, senna powder and cascara to rub into the skin; they need to lose just that little bit more weight to reach their target, and these remedies help them shed water more quickly. Emetics help too, of course, and in an emergency they resort to old-fashioned techniques: walking up and down stairs, wearing several pullovers at once and, lastly, body wraps.

The promoter of 'Leen v Bep I' enters the room: Adrianus 'Janus' Riesmeijer, the former beer-hall patron on De Dijk and chairman, as ever, of the National Boxing Club. His café had been receiving ever-fewer customers with only a very few seafarers at the bar, and the serving girl spending the greater part of the day sweeping the floor. Janus sold his café, became a boxing promoter and offered his former pupil a tidy sum to defend his Dutch title against Bep. Leen is in desperate need of the money and a chance like this might never come again. He has agreed to the fight, conscious of the risk he is taking. He is good, but Bep is probably better. Earlier that year, Bep had won five times in a row against strong British opponents. *Boxing*, the sport's most important professional journal, had Bep's photograph on the front page with the caption: 'Bep van Klaveren from Rotterdam, Holland. A possible future world champion.'

Applause and cheering as Bep comes in with his thick, dark hair and tanned face, looking like the best-dressed dandy in the city – boxing's Douglas Fairbanks, the Rotterdam Valentino. His coach and manager, Theo Huizenaar, walks alongside him. Huizenaar shakes hands, takes a box from his long-panelled winter coat, removes a Corona cigar, lights it and blows a cloud of smoke to the ceiling. Bep changes clothes, returning five minutes later in a silk bathrobe with finely stitched borders. He embraces Leen; they know each other from boxing events and their trip together to Düsseldorf in 1926. Huizenaar was then Leen's second in the ring, and regarded Leen as 'a nice, sociable chap', an 'outstanding boxer' and 'a great defensive champion'. Bep steps into the boxing ring (set against one wall) and hands his bathrobe to a team member. A journalist notes: 'If a sculptor in these lands should ever take on a project requiring the depiction of strength and energy, he should ask Bep whether he'll pose as the model with his coffee-brown body.' The challenger is wearing only underpants when he steps on to the weighing-scale platform; women suppress the temptation to squeal and the needle twitches upwards. Westbroek, the union chairman, leans forward and says: 'Van Klaveren, 61 kilograms.' Leen walks to the scales straight after Bep, bathrobe removed, woollen underpants, the trace of a belly. Westbroek studies the figures: 'Sanders, 61.2 kilograms.' Just like Bep, Leen has reached his target weight; boxers in the lightweight class may weigh no more than 62 kilograms.

Next, Leen and Bep go to the gym for a massage. The hours tick by and the tension rises. The whole of Rotterdam seems to be talking about the match: Leen or Bep, Bep or Leen – who is the more likely to win the national lightweight title, and who could be the first Dutchman to become European champion? A preview article in the *Rotterdamsch Nieuwsblad* reports: 'Only a superior boxer can take on Sanders, and for that reason everyone in the boxing-mad Netherlands will be eager to see what the sterling Van Klaveren will do against a man like Sanders.'

The doorman is standing in front of a large wooden door at the entrance to the Arts & Sciences Building at 27 Schiedamschesingel. It is half past seven in the evening, and boxing fans fumble nervously for their tickets as upper-crust ladies walk to the practices of Dr Van der Sluis at no. 58 or Dr Levie a little further on. Servants are walking their employers' pedigree dogs. The people returning home from work – notaries, headmasters, solicitors, barristers, politicians and bailiffs – visit the Arts & Sciences Building only when a piano recital is being held. To them, the 'noble art' is the perverse pastime of villains and rogues.

The queue continues to lengthen and photographers are turning their lenses on Rotterdam celebrities. Here comes Theo Huizenaar, the most important man in Dutch boxing: 'the Boss'; Bep calls him 'the Big Man'. Bram Sanders is there as well, of course. He is now working as a tailor and is trying to secure a loan to start up his own boxing school. The J.J. Sanders Waffle Bakery on De Dijk has gone into insolvency, and Bram's father now rents out barrows on Nieuwsteeg. He still occasionally sells his famed butter waffles at fairs in Limburg, Gelderland, Brabant and South Holland. Customers call him 'Uncle Jan'.

The spectators gather in a hall with arched windows and a domed ceiling. Folding chairs fill the ground floor, lamps hang from cables above the ring, and an electric clock shows the time: 19:57. The evening is a sell-out, with an audience of four thousand. Leen's Jewish fans are described as 'the Salomons with their kiss-curls' and 'a dark-tinted crowd'; their chatter is 'different' and they look like 'foreigners'.

Van Lent, the announcer, climbs into the ring at eight o'clock, megaphone under his arm. He is wearing a dark jacket, white trousers and white suede shoes, as if his plan immediately after the fight was to head off to the Cosmopoliet or Alcazar dance halls on De Dijk to dance the Charleston. The first match begins with murmurs, catcalls: 'Punch his nut; that bloke's knocked silly,' 'Blow me if he ain't croaked in a day or two; know what I mean?'

The sound of the gong: match number two. Newcomers try to make the best of it; the flat caps hang over the balustrade, bored; nobody seems bothered to watch. The third match: only family members show any interest. Ten o'clock in the evening: cheering and stamping – the main event is about to begin at last. Calmly, Van Lent takes up his megaphone and announces: 'Ladies and gentlemen, I now welcome you to today's chief fight: a contest for the Dutch lightweight championship. A maximum of fifteen three-minute rounds between the title holder, Leen Sanders from the Riesmeijer School, and the challenger, Bep van Klaveren from the Huizenaar School. Ringside judges: Hutteman, Van Vliet and Schulp. This evening's referee will be Westbroek.'

Lights go off and then on; Leen and Bep walk forwards, shadowboxing. They climb into the ring and Dr Frenkel checks their pulse. Both boxers receive bouquets because of the huge impression they made the last time they were in Great Britain; in Van Lent's view, they've 'held aloft the reputation of Holland'. Bep's mascot, a woollen mouse, dangles from a string in his corner.

Leen takes off his red bathrobe. He's combed back his brown hair with brilliantine and the sides have been shorn with clippers to bare millimetres: he's a street lad from the ghetto, the Benny Leonard of the Zandstraat. The referee, Bertus Westbroek, has a quick word with Leen and Bep: they may not get into clinches, no head-butting and never any punches below the belt. He will issue only one warning; anything more means disqualification. Blows to the kidneys or the back of the head will result, without notice, in a defeat. Leen and Bep shake hands.

Leen goes to his corner and puts in his gumshield. Bram is Leen's second and coach. He rubs dry talcum powder into his brother's hands, whispers tactics in his ear and wraps Leen's fists in protective tape. The referee is looking on from above, stooping; are those tapes not too long? The next stage: boxing gloves on. Once again, Westbroek observes: no weights or reinforcements placed inside? Are the laces too tight? Everything is in order, likewise for Bep.

'Seconds out! Box!'

The gong: first round. Leen and Bep step forwards, circling each other, watching, waiting, getting each other's measure. Stepping back, minding the footwork, keeping a high defence, turning, reversing, ducking, hovering. Westbroek yells: 'Break!' and Leen and Bep take a step back. 'Box!' Leen blocks Bep's thrusts and counters with low jabs to the stomach region. The tempo quickens in the second round; Bep goes repeatedly on the offensive and, as expected, Leen pulls back into his defence, gloves in front of his face, sneaking glances at Bep, the peek-a-boo tactic. Keeping calm, peeking, into defence, peeking. Is Bep weaker or in fact stronger than he lets it seem?

From the third to the sixth round, Leen seeks out lines of attack more often than predicted; Westbroek hardly ever needs to call out 'Break!' It is only in the seventh round that Leen has to go into retreat; he is evasive and withdraws into 'the shell', as Bep has previously nicknamed Leen's hermetic defence. In the ninth round, one of Leen's lefts gets Bep's eye, causing the tear ducts to spring into action; Bep bleeds and can no longer see. Leen's fans stand on their chairs, mimicking the uppercut as an attendant cries out: 'Sit down people, please just sit down!' Westbroek calls the match to a temporary halt while Bep's second wipes his eye clean; he has a minor cut to the eyebrow, and Dr Frenkel enters the ring to stitch it up. A hush falls with murmured conversations: can Bep carry on? The spectators feel that he must, and they're in no hurry to return home; what would they do there anyway? The roof is leaking; the baby is crying; the wife just nags and the stove is cold because the price of coal has gone up again. Fortunately, Dr Frenkel signals that Bep can keep going.

Leen's challenger continues to be troubled by his right eye. It is swelling up, the bruising turning from red to purple – a hindrance to Bep, although he tries not to let it show. Boxing is also the art of pretence.

After fifteen rounds, the final gong is sounded and the Netherlands' best boxers shake each other's hand. Bep's vision is a blur; the swelling has grown considerably. 'A win on points for Bep van Klaveren,' announces Van Lent, 'the new Dutch lightweight champion.'

According to a journalist from the *Rotterdamsch Nieuwsblad*, both boxers receive a prolonged ovation. The fight had been at an international standard: the best Dutch boxing match ever. Decades later, Bep recalls Leen as 'a tricky bloke, a difficult bloke to box against'.

Referee Westbroek hands over the championship belt to Bep. Spectators climb into the ring and the boxers are lifted onto shoulders. A photographer asks whether they would pose together, and Bep's manager, Huizenaar, laughs; Leen looks a lot less pleased. With the title lost, he must start all over again from scratch – he's never going to become Rotterdam's Benny Leonard like this, and for now he can kiss goodbye to that European title fight as well. Leen showers, walks outside and, now long after midnight, cycles with his brother Bram across an empty Coolsingel back to Leeuwenlaan.

II.

On the afternoon of Wednesday 29 June 1932, Leen is twenty-four and riding in a horse-drawn carriage through Rotterdam. He wears a tall black hat with a wide brim, a black tie and a tailored black suit with a breast-pocket handkerchief; passers-by cheer him on, calling out advice and warnings. It's 20°C with a light breeze, and overcast. The front-page headlines in *Het Volk* read: 'The Nazi terror carries on', 'Serious clashes throughout Germany', 'Nazi bloodhounds murder workers'.

Leen alights at De Boompjes by the Maas and walks past the Swedish Lutheran church and the former headquarters of the Dutch East India Company towards a slightly dilapidated building surrounded by high fences: the Great Synagogue. Bridesmaids are holding posies, and Leen's sisters wear beribboned hats, full silk skirts and white gloves. From the harbour front, seafarers from across the globe can tell the time just by glancing at the synagogue's clock tower, and ships bound for distant lands are setting sail.

Leen's fiancée is Sellina: she comes from Kampen, is twenty-two and has curly chestnut hair; friends and relatives just call her Selli. She has sixteen aunts and uncles, and her grandfather, Jankef Goudsmit,

used to work in Kampen as a rag-and-bone man and scrap merchant –
virtually every business in Overijssel knows him. Her uncle Sam has
written several rustic Jewish novels about him. In one of his stories,
Selli's mother, Geertruida, is described as having 'the kindly, robust
face of a Jewish peasant woman with voluptuous eyebrows'; according
to Sam, she grew up in 'the Ghetto, the provincial ghetto, but ghetto
all the same'.

Women enter the Great Synagogue by a side door and take the stairs
to the gallery, while men are allowed in by the main entrance. Heads
are covered with hats, skullcaps, bandeaux or wigs. Chandeliers hang
from the ceiling, and candlesticks and candelabra have been placed on
the railings. It is crowded; allowing any more people in is impossible,
so latecomers must sit on the steps. Announcements on sheets of paper
state that extraordinary services are to be held at the synagogue over
the next few weeks in view of 'the seriousness of the times'.

Leen's sister Rozette has come with her husband, Simon. He
is a tailor, fights as a bantamweight at boxing events and, just like
Leen, is a member of the National Boxing Club. Leen's younger
sister Henriette has just turned eighteen. She has thick black
hair but thin lips to which she will sometimes apply lipstick – to her
father's displeasure. At sixteen, Sientje is Leen's youngest sister,
who dreams of one day becoming a salesgirl at De Bijenkorf on
Schiedamschesingel, a newly opened fashion department store with
escalators and carpeting with electrically heated underlay. Seated
next to Sientje is Leen's mother, Saartje: dark hair and a small wart
above one eye. Her children usually address her as 'Ma', but Josua
Jakob is always 'Father'.

Leen's friends and sparring partners at the National Boxing

Club are identifiable on account of their flat noses and cauliflower ears, and the chairman, Janus Riesmeijer, is also in attendance. Nowadays he is working as a 'purifier', as his profession euphemistically terms it: kitted out in a mask and protective clothing, he sets off for ships, tenements, lodgings, hostels, mental asylums or dosshouses, where he exterminates rats, mice, fleas, bedbugs and cockroaches. His business card states: 'Confidentiality guaranteed'.

Leen's uncle Joël has strolled to the Great Synagogue from his house in Josephstraat. He was trained to be a waffle baker, as were all male members of the Sanders family, but resolved to become a musician after passing a little café on De Dijk and hearing 78rpm records by Duke Ellington and George Gershwin being played. He has had little work since the Crash, and in the *Rotterdamsch Nieuwsblad* he advertises himself as an 'Accordionist, pianist and also jazz drummer. Modern repertoire; rates: reasonable.'

Selli's uncle Sam has come down from Amsterdam. He writes about Jewish matters in a socialist magazine and for months has been issuing warnings about the seemingly unstoppable rise of fascism. The popularity in Germany of former frontline soldier Adolf Hitler will result in 'blood and destruction', and the Jews are already getting 'the full Shylock pound of flesh' from 'their fair-haired friends'. The inevitable consequences: 'sinister torments, castration, the crushing of people's spirits, expulsion'. Sam has also written a poem, '*Der Jude ist an allem schuld (Hitler)*', which includes the lines:

> Dissolute are the noses, of the noses beware;
> They smell the burnt odour of their screaming flesh for a century.
> [. . .] Moses and Rebecca, dancing around in the flames.

Rabbi Cohen enters the Great Synagogue, prayer shawl about his shoulders topped off with his tall black hat, and Leen follows behind in his black *chuppah* suit. He's accompanied by his father, Josua, and his future father-in-law, David. Leen and Selli climb the wooden steps to the *bimah*, the dais from which the Torah is read aloud during services. Leen takes his place next to Selli under a canopy (the *chuppah*), symbolic of the little house in Kipstraat where bride and bridegroom are soon to be living together. Most of Selli's curls are hidden beneath a white hat.

A photographer from the *Rotterdamsch Nieuwsblad* takes photos of the couple: Leen has become a Rotterdam celebrity thanks to a rematch in 1931 against Bep van Klaveren, once again at the Arts & Sciences Building, where he boxed even better than the first time. Even so, he still could not quite regain his title; it was left at a draw. Boxing experts praised his style; Leen had looked, waited, parried, come up with countermoves, and thought three rounds ahead. They described him as an 'exceptionally difficult opponent thanks to his double defence', a 'master of self-defence', 'the ring regular who has mastered boxing as a defensive sport to perfection' and the 'Max Euwe of the ring'. Bep may still have been the champion, yet he felt forced to admit to Leen at the end: 'I couldn't break through your defence.'

Selli's father is sitting next to his twenty-year-old son Jozef, apprenticed to be a baker in Rotterdam. Dozens of relatives – butchers, kosher butchers, scrap merchants – have driven from the provincial ghetto of Kampen to Rotterdam. Selli's fourteen-year-old sister Elisabeth is seated next to her mother in the gallery.

Leen's first witness is Samuel Hijman, his father's best friend, and his second is his eldest brother, Jakob, twenty-nine and a furrier by profession. His hair is already beginning to thin; early-onset baldness runs in the family, unfortunately. Jakob swapped Rotterdam for Brussels when Leen was sixteen, but returned at the start of 1930. Business fared badly after the Crash, and Jakob felt he might just as well plod along in Rotterdam – at least he would be with family. He's now living in Leeuwenlaan again with his parents, brothers and sisters. Leen's father is seated on a wooden bench alongside his sons Bram, Meijer, Joël and Mozes.

Rabbi Cohen gives the blessings and expressly counsels Leen and Selli to bear many children, who must be brought up according to Jewish teachings. Assimilation is a pestilence that must be strictly opposed; recently, the Synagogue has seen troublingly low attendance and mixed marriages are much in the ascendant; birth rates are declining among Jews; fewer than twenty Jewish weddings have taken place at the synagogue that year. Nowadays, it's only on high holy days that the Great Synagogue is as full as at Leen and Selli's wedding.

Leen slips a ring on to Selli's right index finger and says: 'Behold, you are consecrated to me with this ring according to the laws of Moses and Israel.' They drink wine from the same cup and their union is established. Leen breaks a glass underfoot: even in good times, devout Jews must reflect for a moment on the destruction of the Temple in Jerusalem more than two thousand years ago.

The couple walk out of the synagogue to cries from friends, family and acquaintances of 'Mazel tov!' and 'For many years to come!' There is chatter and laughter: 'Leen a *chatan* (bridegroom)! Who'd have thought it? What with eyebrows always cut up and that cauliflower ear of his!' Selli is 'the Flower of Israel', a 'nice decent girl', 'madly pretty'. A columnist from the magazine *Groot-Rotterdam* wonders 'whether Leen Sanders, our famous boxer, will indeed win the match, because as strong as he may well be, if your weaker other half is in a bad mood, it is only your fancy footwork that can save you!'

A photographer from the *Rotterdamsch Nieuwsblad* is standing on the steps of the synagogue, where Leen poses with a white pocket handkerchief in his hand, and Selli's left hand clutches a bridal bouquet. Bride and groom laugh together. They're in love; no man will put them asunder until death do them part.

Leen and Selli begin married life at 32 Kipstraat, right next to Hoogstraat, Goudschesingel and Gedempte Binnenrotte. De Vries, the pharmacist at no. 43, sells remedies for urinary complaints and 'women's problems'; Jewish tourists lug their suitcases to the kosher Hotel Sprechter at no. 93c. Piet Heniger's window at the junction with Korte Pannekoekstraat is emblazoned: A HENIGER HAT OR CAP IS ALWAYS STURDY, RELIABLE, COLOURFAST AND INEXPENSIVE. For reasons that are unclear, the head of a cow hangs above the door of lamb butcher Isedore Lezer at no. 63; a sign in his shop window reads: 'EAT MORE LAMB — HALF A KILO COSTS 1 GUILDER'. The unemployed are waiting outside the modest building at no. 72 that's selling semi-mouldy butter. Fights often break out over this because the price is low and the stock is soon exhausted; mounted policemen then appear, with officers brandishing drawn swords and striking and making arrests.

Selli is pregnant when Leen signs a contract for two matches at the Spichernsälen in Berlin. He buys a return ticket at Maas Station; expenses will be reimbursed later. Selli wants him to watch his step in Berlin; something is brewing there. Early in 1932, her uncle Sam had written in his poem '*Der Jude ist an allem schuld (Hitler)*':

Assembly, comrades, chairman, editors,
To speak! We request to speak!
Once more it's us, we thought as much!
Once more we are the n****** of Western Europe.
The grapes of Germany
are bursting with the blood of Jews.

III.

A Nazi party member stands on the steps to Berlin's Spichernsälen boxing hall; Erwin Thoma shows his press card to the doorman, but it's not actually required. Everyone in the German boxing world knows who he is; they worship him, they are in fear of him, and he gets the best seat at every boxing arena. Thoma writes under the pseudonym 'Punch' for the authoritative journal *Box-Sport*.

It's 14 October 1932. A poster announces:

> BIG FIGHT EVENING
> LEN SANDERS (ROTTERDAM, VICTOR AGAINST FRITZ
>   KRACHT AND GUSTAVE EDER)
> VERSUS
> KONRAD STEIN (NO. 2 IN GERMANY, MUNICH)

In 1929, Punch had seen Leen box against Fritz Kracht and Gustav Eder. At the time he had praised the Jewish boxer with the Star of David shorts, but three years have passed since then and it's not something he will be doing any more. In his view, NSDAP-leader Adolf Hitler embodies 'a respectable male image': Germans need him. Things have gone badly for their country since the treacherous defeat of 1918. Jews, liberals and Marxists are dominating the Weimar Republic and destroying Berlin as well. The homeless are drifting aimlessly throughout the city, their women and children in tow; fathers lug heavy bags or have loaded their household goods on to wheelbarrows. War veterans hold up signs that plead WE SEEK WORK, pensioners are selling matches and shoelaces, ninety per cent of young people are without a job, the number of suicides is rising. Women offer themselves at Alexanderplatz, on Kurfürstendamm, in Joachimstaler Straße and at Berlin-Hauptbahnhof railway station: 'Might I give you some "pleasure" for a small fee?'

According to Punch, only the Führer is capable of ensuring peace and order in their country. Men will be prepared to fight again, whether on the battlefield or in the ring. Just as in the past, women will devote themselves to the three Ks: *Kinder, Küche, Kirche* (Children, Kitchen, Church). Thanks to Hitler and his storm troopers, the 'lying/Jewish press' and the 'Communist pigs' will have to call a halt to their subversive work.

Punch also views the sport of boxing from a fascist perspective, and he knows exactly what the German people want. Elitist liberals have no right to pen articles about German boxing – they commend Jews, the handicapped, blacks and Roma, and they use the English word 'boxing' instead of the term *Deutsche Faustkampf* (traditional German pugilism). In Punch's opinion, the new owner of the Spichernsälen should be ranked among the greatest enemies of German pugilism. Ernst Zirzow may not be Jewish, but Punch loathes him just as much as his predecessor, Pepi Burda. The Spichernsälen boss is fair-haired, short and corpulent, and he snorts when having to walk any distance; Punch refers to him in *Box-Sport* as a '*großmäulige Jahrmarktfigur*' (a loud-mouthed fairground barker). On a number of occasions Zirzow has overturned chairs or adjudicators' tables because of the referee's decision, and he expels Nazis from the hall if they yell '*Saujude!*' (Jew pig!) or '*Drecksjude!*' (Jew filth!) at Jewish boxers.

On 9 January 1932, Zirzow had had Johann 'the Gypsy' Trollmann fight against 'Beasley the Negro' – according to Punch, only the latest 'black import' of many; the fight might have succeeded as a circus act, but it had had nothing to do with professional sport. In Punch's view, Beasley had fought as had come to be expected of 'black imports': with a lot of show and strength, little sophistication and a lack of foresight owing to an inferior intellect. Punch writes disapproving articles about Trollmann nearly every week.

Ernst Zirzow had become Trollmann's manager in 1931, and in the following year, the Roma boxer became a sensation by beating one blond-haired-blue-eyed opponent after another. Punch also says that Trollmann fights in an 'un-German style', employing silly footwork, grimacing at spectators and, at the end of almost every round, blowing kisses to female boxing fans. Punch rejects this as 'eccentricity' and argues in *Box-Sport* for the permanent expulsion from German boxing of 'the highly problematic Gypsy'.

In many ways, Punch sees Jews as an even greater threat to the sport. 'Talentless' boxers are suddenly beating favourites-to-win at the Spichernsälen; of course, this has been staged by Ernst Zirzow and his moneygrubbing Jewish business partners. They gamble heavily on matches that have been bought and, through such deception, become even richer – their foremost goal in life, alongside world domination. The problem is that Jews are also winning titles more often; this sits uneasily with far-right preconceptions that Jews are physically inferior. On 22 April 1932, for example, at a sold-out Spichernsälen, the Berliner Jew Harry Stein had won against the 'racially pure' Paul Noack, and for the first time Germany had a Jewish boxing champion. Punch's article has it that Harry Stein must have won his title through foul play; 'Aryan' boxing managers needed to conduct a root-and-branch investigation into the matter.

Fortunately, thinks Punch, the interlopers will not be able to exert their destructive influence for much longer. In the summer of 1932, Adolf Hitler's National Socialist German Workers' Party (NSDAP) had received 37.3 per cent of the vote, making it the largest single party in the nation's government . . . and the Führer was a supporter of German pugilism. Punch's idol had written in his bestseller, *Mein Kampf*: 'Boxing and jujitsu have always seemed to me more important than any inferior, because incomplete, training in marksmanship. Give the German nation six million bodies with flawless athletic training, all glowing with fanatical love of their country and inculcated with the highest offensive spirit, and a national state will, in less than two years if necessary, have created an army [. . .]'

Punch knows from a reliable source that Hitler, following his inevitable appointment as chancellor, has plans for German pugilism that will be more revolutionary still. *Untermenschen* (subhumans), such as Trollmann, the Roma, and the Jews Burda and Stein, will be expelled from clubs and federations. Only then will racially pure *Deutsche Faustkämpfer* (German boxers) once more 'be able to breathe free'.

Leen is twenty-four and, according to national and international expert opinion, ranks among the best European boxers in the welterweight division, a fact acknowledged even by Punch. The Flemish magazine *Sportwereld* names him an 'international-level boxer', 'the ever-dangerous and tough Dutch fist-flourisher Leen Sanders' and the 'sole boxer to defeat the German champion Gustav Eder in Berlin'. Leen had made his own case for the right to a European title match, having sent a telegram to the European Boxing Union in order to challenge the Italian title holder, Cleto Locatelli. After a few weeks he received a return telegram: BELGIAN FRANÇOIS SYBILLE TO FIGHT LOCATELLI — STOP — TRY AGAIN LATER — STOP.

Helmeted and armed with swords and revolvers, *Schutzpolizei* officers are walking back and forth in front of the Spichernsälen entrance. Are they seeking Nazis from the *Sturmabteilung* (SA: the party's paramilitary wing known as 'brownshirts') who are harassing Jews, Roma people or communists, or are they seeking communists or socialists intent on harassing Nazis? Recently, ninety-nine people have been killed and more than fifteen hundred injured in street fighting. In 1931, the Jewish New Year had fallen on 12 September, and two thousand Nazis went to Kurfürstendamm, fifteen minutes' walk from the Spichernsälen. Jewish men were shoved, spat upon and punched, while the Hitlerites shouted out: *'Juda verrecke! Deutschland erwache!'* (Perish Juda! Germany awake!)

Leen's return to Berlin is not a cause of celebration to Punch; why should Germans go to watch a foreigner Jew and, above all, one who often fights with a Star of David on his shorts? It is a matter of 'racial shame' that Ernst Zirzow should be giving Sanders the opportunity, twice in a row, to prove himself in the ring against Aryans. But liberal fellow-journalists at the *Vossische Zeitung* are more enthusiastic – preview articles praise Leen's 'murderous left hooks' and say he is 'on top form'. According to the Berlin correspondent for *Het Vaderland*, he is 'always a welcome guest in German circles'.

Leen had arrived a few days earlier at Berlin-Hauptbahnhof where he was met by Ernst Zirzow, with whom he was offered lodgings for two weeks, plus training sessions with his boxers. He had attended a match at the Spichernsälen between Johan Trollmann and Rinus de Boer from Rotterdam, at which the 'artful Gypsy boxer', as Trollmann was called in the *Rotterdamsch Nieuwsblad*, appeared in a camel-hair coat, blew kisses as usual to all the Aryan women in the front row, and waved to the hundreds of Roma fans in the gallery who had come to Berlin from all over Germany especially to see him. Prior to the match, Hitler supporters had been at beer halls in the vicinity looking for reds, Jews and Trollmann fans. In *Box-Sport*, Punch had written: 'Is that any wonder with three million unemployed?' Vendors of the left-wing newspaper *Vorwärts* were assaulted by members of the SA, who broke windows at the Spichernsälen and chalked on the walls JEWS AND GYPSIES OUT! Ernst Zirzow had had to hire additional security.

Bottles of sherry cluster beneath the desk in Ernst Zirzow's office. The Spichernsälen boss takes a large round glass and fills it to the brim; he sniffs it, holds the sherry to the light and makes continual observations to showcase his knowledge on the subject. Every few minutes he fumbles in his cigarette case, lighting up one Muratti after another.

Zirzow has good news: the Spichernsälen has sold out, thanks to Leen, and he hands over an envelope full of marks, which Leen takes with him to the changing room. The poorest and most fanatical spectators mount the stairs to the gallery. Zirzow has given them a discount, as they were among the first Germans to have lost their jobs after the Crash.

The announcer opens the evening: '*Damen und Herrrren, Freunde des Spichernrrrrings!*' He tells the crowd that the hall has sold out 'to the very last seat'. Leen is introduced as 'the victor against Gustav Eder and Fritz Kracht', and he climbs into the ring. His opponent, Konrad Stein from Munich, is a much bigger man. Punch sits on a stool next to far-right reporters from the *Völkische Beobachter*, *Der Angriff* and *Der Stürmer*. The ventilation fans are broken again; the place reeks of sweat, bratwurst, refuse and wheat beer; mouse and rat dropping litter the corners. Punch comments on the 'pitiful state' of the place, calling the Spichernsälen a 'tumbledown shed' and a 'squalid palace'.

NSDAP members take their seats alongside members of the *Stahlhelm* (paramilitary wing of the monarchist German National People's Party), the SA and the SS. Hitlerites are kitted out in their brown uniforms, the side of which is adorned with a large swastika, long banned in the Weimar Republic. At times they break out into the Horst-Wessel song (the party anthem) or the national hymn dating from the German Empire, '*Die Wacht am Rhein*' (The Watch on the Rhine):

> *The cry resounds like thunder's peal,*
> *Like clashing waves and clang of steel:*
> *The Rhine, the Rhine, the German Rhine,*
> *We all shall stand to hold the line!*

Leen removes his bathrobe. As usual, he is wearing his shorts with the Star of David. The female ringside assistant, Martha, holds up a signboard: ROUND I. Policemen with truncheons and light rifles stand with their backs to 'Len from Tulip-land' and focus only on the public. The lights above the ring glare down into Leen's eyes. He must win in order to remain in contention for a European title fight. Jew and Aryan tap each other's gloves; referee Koch has a quick word and then says: '*Ring frei, box!*'

IV.

—

'Quicker, and follow on.'

'Man-to-man.'

'Hit hard!'

'Closed defence.'

'Keep your hands higher, lad. Those hands are too low down.'

Leen is in his coaching sweats and is working in small premises on a narrow street called Meent, not far from the Auction House, where BRAM SANDERS GYMNASIUM FOR LADIES AND GENTLEMEN is emblazoned on the door. The walls are hung with photographs of Benny Leonard, Leen Sanders, Jack Dempsey and Georges Carpentier. The wooden floor is strewn with dumb-bells, barbells, medicine balls, groin guards and boxing gloves, with a punchbag dangling from a rope. Cupboards contain notepads listing the telephone numbers of boxing managers throughout Europe, and there are also the latest editions of *Box-Sport* and the British publication *Boxing*. Binders contain newspaper cuttings of Leen and Bram's fights in London, Birmingham, Newcastle, Ilford, Cardiff and Edmonton. Posters and sheets of paper alert the reader:

EMERGENCY FOR GERMAN JEWS!
AN APPEAL FOR SUPPORT!

Refugees from Germany are arriving every day, abruptly robbed of their own livelihoods, their morale utterly broken. After the misery they have suffered, we can and must provide them with sustenance and, above all, rest! Donate to the 1934 Emergency Fund to alleviate the dire need of the German refugees!

It is December 1934; Leen is twenty-six. He is living with his wife and two little sons in Sint Laurensstraat, just four minutes' walk from the boxing school opened by Bram in 1931. Jopie is two and David was born on 27 June this year. Rotterdam remains the premier city for boxing, despite the Depression . . . or even because of it. The 'noble art' provides hope, solace and relief at a time of rising fascism, collapsed stock-market prices and mass unemployment.

Six months earlier, Leen had become Dutch middleweight champion, but he is much more popular abroad in Germany and Great Britain than he is in his own country. He gets few offers to box at major matches, even in Rotterdam, owing to a style people perceive as monotonous. The bloody-nosed proletariat call him 'the Mobile Wall', preferring brawlers like Bep van Klaveren with his up-and-at-'em left-and-right-punches approach; they get bored at Leen's matches, become boisterous, whistle, jeer and turn their backs on him. Theo Huizenaar, his promoter, knows that Leen is technically and tactically among the best of Europe's boxers, but he is attracting ever fewer spectators, which is why Leen has had to take on a secondary job as an instructor at Bram's boxing school.

The first pupils come in at around five o'clock in the afternoon and warm up with skipping-rope exercises. Every three minutes Bram calls 'Time!' Next exercise: sparring. Leon Greenman from Helmersstraat is not much taller than Leen, and a deal thinner. He was born in London, and most of the boxers at Bram's boxing school refer to him as 'the Englishman'. Heavyweight Arie Valk was originally a member of the National Boxing Club and, like Leen, fights with a Star of David on his shorts. Leo Zurel is the same weight as Leen; he's an apprentice plasterer, but still helps his father, Isaac, in his flower kiosk on Hofplein on Sundays and public holidays.

A lot of Jewish boxers train at Bram's school – three of them have become Rotterdam champions, and one Jewish boxer from Rotterdam has won the Dutch title. Leen teaches them the 'shell' technique: double defence. A reporter from the *Weekblad voor Israëlitische Huisgezinnen* advises all young Jews to learn the 'noble art' at the Bram Sanders Gymnasium: 'Jewish A.J. Sanders is an able instructor, a very well-known former international boxer and a qualified referee'; Leen is cited as 'the featherweight, lightweight and currently middleweight champion of the Netherlands' and 'one of the best boxers in the world'. He is the 'only person to defeat the German and European champion Gustaf Eder' and in Nazi Germany is considered 'an exceptional boxer, especially for a Jew'.

Leen feints with fast left-hook jabs, retreats behind the 'shell' and then goes on the offensive again, launching a careful blow to a chin. The best boxer at the school is called Arnold 'Nol' Lagrand – he's seventeen and also known as 'Little Lagrand'. Bram aims to coach him towards becoming European featherweight champion. One journalist writes that Nol has lived 'the hard life of the socially underprivileged' – never a bad thing for a boxer – the Sanders brothers had grown up just the same. Bram provides Nol with food, advice and career management; Leen will say later that his brother did this with a 'fatherly loyalty'.

After training sessions the talk is increasingly about the 'seriousness of the times'. Joseph Goebbels, the German Minister for Public Information and Propaganda, has said in a speech that 'our government will be carrying its racial policy forward; the German people are as one in standing behind the Führer', and anti-Semites looking for trouble are increasingly walking the streets of Rotterdam. The newspaper *Voorwaarts* dubs them 'Holland's Hitlerites'. They are as much in thrall to 'Mussolini the Great' as to the Führer.

The ordinary Dutch citizen is almost as agitated by the German refugees as these extremists. Jews are crossing the border en masse; should they be given shelter out of decency, or is that asking for trouble? As yet, there are relatively few German Jews in Rotterdam, but in the view of most of the city's residents that still does not mean they should come. Stop them at the border, send them back; in the long run Hitler is sure to be fine – after all, he spent time in the trenches himself. The new chancellor with his toothbrush moustache and loud mouth is not going to want a war, and those refugees are not going to go away after two or three years, are they? And who can say for sure they will *ever* want to go back again?

Leen has strong views on the subject: Hitler is not fine, not now and not in the future. He is in touch with German boxers such as Harry Stein and Erich Seelig, who are also Jewish . . . and Jews are in grave danger.

*

It happened a few weeks after Adolf Hitler's election victory of 1933. The head of the German Boxing Federation predicted a renaissance for German pugilism and cried out three times '*Sieg Heil!*' (Hail victory!). According to the Führer: 'Germany's young men of the future [must be] agile and lean, as fast as greyhounds, as tough as leather and as hard as Krupp steel.' Boxing can bring this about, and German politicians should have invested in German pugilism years before the Great War; if only that had been done, Hitler writes in *Mein Kampf*, 'a German revolution [in 1919] by pimps, deserters and similar rabble would never have been possible'.

A few days after Hitler's victory, directors of the Verband Deutscher Faustkämpfer (German Boxers' Association) had convened to cast their votes concerning their Jewish members. Most officials wanted their organization 'purged of foreign elements' as soon as possible, and hundreds of people were dismissed. Pride in the association had to be reinstated, and that was possible only without 'corrupt Jewish leeches' and 'communist enemies of the state'. In the view of Punch, writing in *Box-Sport*, 'parasites' such as Pepi Burda, the former manager of the Spichernsälen, had rightly been 'frozen out' and such a 'rigorous purge' should have been done much sooner. In recent years, boxing had been a sport managed by a 'clique of unscrupulous, corrupt Bolshevik businessmen'.

Leen has heard from the German boxer Erich Seelig that, since 4 April 1933, Jewish boxers and managers may no longer so much as *enter* a boxing arena. Seelig was the reigning German middleweight champion and was to defend his title in April 1933: he feels both Jewish *and* German, but that was insufficient. He was threatened by Hitlerites: 'the Jew must die.' The fight did not go ahead, and almost all German boxing managers felt that was for the best. On 11 April 1933 it was announced that Erich Seelig 'the Jew' was no longer a champion.

Adolf Hitler celebrated his forty-fourth birthday on 20 April 1933. German boxing managers sent the Führer a telegram which began: 'To the German Chancellor Adolf Hitler! The German Boxers' Association extends to our Führer, revered by us all, the very best of wishes!' Above all else, their leader was enjoined to carry on as he was doing; the association's membership would, 'with clenched fists, defend [his nation] against all enemies'; they had already taken measures against 'vermin'. The national boxing championships took place one week later. Before matches, the shrill cry was uttered:

> *Es lebe Volk und Vaterland und Führer!* (Long live the people and fatherland and leader!)
> *Heil Hitler!* (Hail Hitler!)

Victors received a framed photograph bearing Hitler's signature; a Nazi official gave a speech that emphasized the Führer's passion for German pugilism. A singer sang the Horst-Wessel song, an ode to the SA leader murdered by communists in 1930. Spectators would place a hand on their heart and sing:

> *Raise the flag! The ranks tightly closed!*
> *The SA marches with calm, steady step.*
> *Comrades shot by the Red Front and reactionaries*
> *March in spirit within our ranks!*

Erich Rüdiger, the new boss of the German Boxers' Association, is known as the Führer of German boxers. One of his speeches begins with the words:

> My comrades in sport must give thanks to Adolf Hitler from the bottom of their hearts. His robust action has ensured the advancement of our movement in ways hitherto unknown to us; thanks to our Führer, our sport at last has its place in the sun so long desired by us. Boxers can take pride in being supported by the Führer in this way, and we are now doubly obliged always to come to the defence of Führer, people and fatherland!

A year before Hitler's appointment as chancellor, Leen had won against the German welterweight Erwin Volkmar, a staunch communist and anti-Nazi. On the night of 20 April 1933, Volkmar went to a café on Hohenzollernplatz in Berlin-Neukölln. He was meant to be boxing at the Spichernsälen on the following day, so he was the only one to stay sober. At half past midnight members of the SA came in, celebrating Hitler's birthday and intent on provoking customers who were communists or looked Jewish. One SA man approached Volkmar, pushing and pulling at him, hounding him. The man was assisted in this by other Nazis and blows were exchanged. Volkmar defended himself with hook jabs, swing punches and hits to the kidneys; noses bled; eyebrows needed stapling; SA men could no longer breathe. The fight continued on the street. One SA member drew a pistol, pointing it at Volkmar. The boxer defended his face with closed fists, but they were no barrier to the bullets; he fell to the ground bleeding. An ambulance drove in haste to the Britz Hospital in Neuköln, where Erwin Volkmar died early in the afternoon of 21 April. He was the first sportsman to be murdered by a Nazi.

A few days after Volkmar's death, Harry Stein, German champion and Leen's former sparring partner in Berlin, fled to Prague. Johann Trollmann, another former sparring partner, resolved to stay and on 9 June boxed in front of fifteen hundred spectators against twenty-year-old Adolf Witt from Schleswig-Holstein. This posed a major problem for the Nazis: Trollmann, the 'racially inferior Gypsy', defeated Witt, the 'Aryan', and became champion. Some solution had to be contrived, and soon: after three days, Trollmann's victory was declared invalid owing to 'un-German boxing'.

Nevertheless, in July 1933 Trollmann was permitted to appear again against Gustav Eder, the most popular boxer in Nazi Germany. The Roma former champion was ordered to fight in 'the German style'; he was decidedly not allowed 'to dance like a Gypsy'. Trollmann dyed his black hair blond and whitened his skin using flour; according to one liberal journalist it was 'a caricature of an Aryan and a protest against discrimination'. In the first rounds Trollmann fought in the allegedly German style: technically a good job, but from a clinical perspective without any frills or risk. After a few rounds he fell back into his old routine; he danced frivolously around Eder, provoking him, laughing, waving to acquaintances and pretty women. Halfway through the final round Trollmann became fatigued and Eder landed two blows to his head and two to his body. Trollmann was knocked out, and then counted out by the referee. Most of the spectators suspected they were being cheated, crying out '*Schiebung!*' (Swindle!)

Not a single fight offer came Trollmann's way after that. His manager, Ernst Zirzow, distanced himself from the boxer and

Trollmann was never to enjoy top-level boxing again. By then, most of Germany's Jewish boxers had already fled the country.

By 1934, thousands of exiles were living in the Netherlands. Some went to Rotterdam, where they were housed in the Montefiore building, founded in 1883 'to support transient Jewish foreigners in need'. A few times every week, Leen's mother, Saartje, and his sisters Sini, Roosje, Jetty and Sipora walked from their home in Rotterdam's city centre to Van Speykstraat 105 armed with pans of soup and freshly made matzo balls.

Leen has a subscription to *Box-Sport*. Gustav Eder is often shown laughing on the cover, his fists in the air. The journalist Punch says he is the perfect German idol for the 'new age', 'the best representative of Nazi Germany' and the 'pillar of *Deutsche Faustkampf*'. Before title fights, Eder raises his right boxing glove into the air and shouts '*Heil Hitler!*'

On 10 June 1934, Eder becomes European champion by beating the Belgian boxer Chalier in Berlin. According to Punch, it was the first great international victory for the 'New Germany' and an 'auspicious omen for the advancement of our movement'. In the Nazi view, nobody but Eder fights in a style more German; he is even more important to the Führer than Max Schmeling – the most popular German boxer and future world champion – because nine times out of ten Eder boxes in Berlin or other German cities. The same cannot be said about Schmeling, and what's more, his manager is Jewish.

Who is to be the next international opponent for Eder the 'Master'? Punch writes in *Box-Sport*: 'At present, there is no welterweight in Europe even close to Gustav Eder. Each victory that the pride of our nation secures makes it more difficult to find a worthy adversary.'

A journalist from the *Rotterdamsch Nieuwsblad* passes on this news snippet. Leen calls him, saying he would like nothing better than to fight Eder; for some time, in fact, he has been in negotiations with Eder's manager, Walter Englert. It had seemed on a number of occasions that it might go ahead, but Englert was asking for a fee 'that was ten times as high' as could be offered and the prize money pledged for Leen was, by contrast, 'ridiculously low'. What is underlying all of this? What are Eder and Englert frightened of? As the newspaper puts it a day later, could it simply be that 'Leen Sanders was the only welterweight to have beaten [Eder] both gloriously and with ease?' Or is it, perhaps, because Leen is Jewish?

V.

The steamship *Sidi Brahim* departs early in the morning from the port of Marseille. Leen's destination is the Algerian coastal city of Oran. His opponent there is Evelio Celestino Mustelier from Victoria de Las Tunas in Cuba, who fights under the pseudonym 'Kid Tunero'. A few days previously, Leen's French manager Maurice Operti had written in a telegram to the promoter: TELL TUNERO WE SHALL WIN — STOP — LEN LEAVING ROTTERDAM TOMORROW VIA PARIS — STOP — ORAN PUBLIC WILL BE PLEASED — STOP.

It is Tuesday morning on 27 October 1936. Leen is twenty-eight and still the Dutch middleweight champion. He is getting even fewer invitations to fight in his home country than in previous years and has engaged a French intermediary so that he can box in Paris and Oran. He had taken the train to Gare du Nord and then walked to Operti's modest office on Rue Véron, where they discussed Leen's dream of one day boxing in a rematch against his Nazi nemesis Gustav Eder. Firstly, Operti arranges two serious matches in Paris. In the event of a double win, Leen will stand a good chance of becoming Eder's challenger.

His first adversary is Victor Deckmyn, who was born into a peasant family; Parisians can barely understand him. His nickname is *le Dur Nordiste* (the Tough Northerner), and Leen calls Deckmyn 'one of the best French welterweights'; journalists describe him as 'the great expert at fierce fighting', a noble savage who 'regularly lets [his opponent] enjoy the sensation of artificially induced sleep with his terrible right hook'. Deckmyn had won the French title in 1933. Painters, writers and singers invite him to drink absinthe with them in little Montmartre cafés, and he has become the favourite French boxer among Parisian *sportifs* – men who hop between boxing and cycling halls, eager to be seen in the company of famous sportsmen.

At around six in the evening, Operti drives Leen to the Central Sporting Club at 57 Rue du Faubourg. Boxing fans and tourists are getting baguettes and croissants from the boulangerie at no. 55, while *sportifs* are drinking beer, calvados, absinthe or wine at the Bar aux Sportifs at no. 51. Wafting from the doorways and windows of cafés, brasseries and dance halls there are hits by Carlito Gardel, Josephine Baker, Django Reinhardt, Maurice Chevalier and Charles 'The Singing Madman' Trenet. Posters announce:

AT THE CENTRAL
MAKING HIS DÉBUT IN FRANCE
AN INTERNATIONAL STAR
LEN SANDERS, DUTCH CHAMPION
VERSUS
THE TOUGH NORTHERNER, VICTOR DECKMYN
RUE DU FAUBOURG ST DENIS

The Central Sporting Club is small with a low ceiling, and nowhere else in Paris are spectators seated so close to the ring. It has been a sell-out, the opposite side of the room blocked out by smoke. Bohemians with narrow Clark Gable moustaches sit beside nightclub dancers on wooden folding chairs next to the ring. Less moneyed Parisians watch the matches from the balconies, leaning over the railings with caps askew and shabby shoes dangling over the edge. Four lamps are suspended a few metres above the ring. Journalists from *L'Auto, Paris-Soir, Le Figaro, Le Journal* and *Paris-Midi* bash away at their Remingtons as if they were Hemingway. The announcer climbs into the ring: bushy moustache, bow tie, eyes bloodshot from the smoke and announces the main match as '*le grand combat international*' and '*le match vedette*'. As in London, Leen is known as 'Len' in Paris. The announcer introduces him as 'the victor against Gustav Eder' and 'a champion in a class of his own'. Most of the spectators are still unfamiliar with Leen, despite the sports newspaper *L'Auto* having described him as one of the stars of international boxing. Whatever the case, French observers know for a near certainty that Deckmyn's 'terrible right hook' will soon be breaking straight through that little Dutchman's defence.

Leen starts off in surprisingly offensive style, using uppercuts and left hooks, and he goes on to impress the *sportifs* with a technically faultless demonstration of the 'noble art'. It's in the third round that Deckmyn pulls out his 'terrible right hook'; his fist meets with Leen's right eyebrow, causing blood to stream over his eye and cheek, preventing him from seeing. The referee brings the fight to a temporary halt as Leen gropes his way back to his corner and dabs at the wound with a hand towel; once the bleeding has tailed off somewhat, he is able to carry on.

In the rounds that follow, most of the *sportifs* are yelling incessantly: 'The right hook! Go for the right hook!' Deckmyn pursues his bleeding opponent, but Leen has already retreated behind his double defence, every bit as famed as Deckmyn's 'terrible right hook'. *Le Dur Nordiste* is not quite able to catch his much smaller adversary and, according to a journalist from *Le Miroir des Sports*, 'Deckmyn's devastating punches' are 'blocked with great mastery by the Dutch champion'. By then the *sportifs* have become as fanatical in their encouragement of Leen as they are for Deckmyn, which one Parisian regular maintains never normally happens at the Central Sporting Club. Towards the end, Leen decides unexpectedly on a renewed offensive tactic, catching the 'Tough Northerner' on the nose, ear, chin and liver. Blood is still dripping down Leen's face when the referee declares him the winner. The Dutch correspondent for *Het Volk* writes how the spectators had given him a 'prolonged ovation and, on account of his performance, he had managed to conquer a Parisian public which, in fairness, is not easily surprised by much'. One *sportif* is reported by the boxing expert for *L'Auto* as having said: 'What might Sanders have done to his opponent if only he'd had two eyes?'

Leen receives telegrams from Bram and from his pupils. *Het Volk* writes: 'Rotterdam's Leen now occupies a more than satisfactory position in the international boxing world'; the sports reporter for the *Weekblad voor Israëlietische Huisgezinnen* writes: 'The press is hailing this scion of our city as one of the best boxers in Europe and one who will certainly be eligible for the European championship.'

Leen returns to Rotterdam with all the French newspapers under his arm. The man who beat Deckmyn is described as 'the elusive Dutchman', 'a great champion' and 'a tough pugilist, quite brilliant in the art of defence and evasion'; a journalist from *Paris-Midi* writes: 'Sanders had been announced as a top-class champion and he turned those expectations into reality.' One headline reads: 'Sanders defeats Deckmyn with one eye' and this is displayed on the wall at Bram's gym.

Leen sends a telegram to the International Boxing Union to

challenge Gustav Eder for the European title, and the reply is good news: Eder must defend his title against 'Deckmyn's conqueror'. Leen wants to fight in Rotterdam, but the French sports magazine *L'Auto* writes that 'such a great event' cannot be held in the Netherlands – the boxing halls in Leen's native city are just not big enough. In Operti's view, Germany is 'not an option for Len Sanders either, because he is Jewish, as many of you are perhaps unaware'. Operti's proposal is that this titanic battle should be held in Paris. A Jew against an Aryan at the Vélodrome d'Hiver stadium or the Palais des Sports: the grandstands would be packed; tickets would be selling on the black market for thousands of francs, Reichsmarks or guilders; journalists from around the world would be writing about it. And that is good for Paris, for boxing and, perhaps, even for world peace.

But Eder does not want to box in pernicious Paris. His manager tells Leen that the April 1936 fight will be held in Berlin after all, and that the challenger should submit his terms as soon as possible. Leen telegraphs back that he has no need at all to submit terms, because he refuses to fight in Nazi Germany. At the time, most Dutch sportsmen are indeed travelling to German championships and contests, returning with glad tidings: perfect organization, metro trains running on time, the inhabitants adoring the Führer, not a single sign to be seen declaring JUDEN RAUS! (Jews Out!) The Olympic Games are scheduled to start in Germany at the end of July 1936, and Jewish and black athletes are welcome as normal; it is to be a celebration of fraternity.

Leen stands his ground. If Jews are being treated better, it is only temporarily so, and just 'an Olympic interval'; 'Jewish blood would be flowing again' after the Games. Leen receives praise from socialists, communists, Jews and anarchists alike. *Het Volk* writes:

Whereas several boxing clubs and unions have recently decided to participate in the Nazi Olympiad, or to allow their members freedom of choice to participate, it is especially pleasing to us that the celebrated Rotterdam professional boxer Leen Sanders should be the one to set the example to his sporting brethren. May Dutch amateur boxers draw lessons from this and with utmost haste rescind their decision to take part in the Nazi Games. Bravo, Sanders!!

To avoid the fight, Eder boards a ship for the United States. The title is taken from him and, at a stroke, Leen finds himself allowed to fight the Fleming Felix Wouters for the European championship. Punch is incandescent about this; without Gustav it is 'a surrogate championship'. As he goes on to write in *Box-Sport*: 'Weak title holders are a disgrace to the whole movement'; 'Master Eder' has been robbed of his title, which has clearly come about through the Jewish lobby. In Punch's view, German boxing managers must break all ties with the International Boxing Union: faithful followers of Adolf Hitler never let the British, French, Dutch or Spanish dictate to them what has to happen.

On 23 July 1936, Leen's Jewish fans from Rotterdam board a hired bus bound for Brussels and arrive in a boxing hall that is three-quarters empty. Scarcely any Dutch reporters have come: too far; story not interesting enough; a devalued charade. Even Leen's home paper, the *Rotterdamsche Nieuwsblad*, barely gives the title fight any mention. Almost all articles are about Hitler's Games, which are due to commence in four days.

Leen and his opponent climb into the ring. One Flemish

newspaper reports that the match began in an 'atmosphere of apathy and coolness'. It is only Leen's fans who raise spirits at all with choruses of voices and Jewish wisecracks. In 1937, Leen says that, despite everything, this title match was the 'most important fight that I delivered'; in a previous encounter he had beaten the 15 centimetres-taller Wouters in a knockout win, but 'in the fight for the title I wasn't able to stay the pace and so I lost on points.'

The *Sidi Brahim* sails past Mount Murdjadjo and the Fort of Santa Cruz, and after twenty-eight hours finally arrives at the port of Oran. For lack of funds, Leen is now his own trainer and coach; for the same reason, he does not have a doctor or second with him. The foreign press is particularly endeared to him as a result: a man alone, small in stature, stocky, muscled and not afraid to wear a Star of David in a hostile world.

The sun is shining and it is well over twenty degrees. An Algerian journalist observes: 'Our visitor is short, burly and strong. Given his physique and the information obtained from Parisian colleagues and other foreigners, he would seem to be the perfect boxing specimen.' In a telegram to local newspapers, Leen's manager, Operti, describes Leen as A SMALL BOXER WITH A VICIOUS LEFT HOOK – STOP.

Leen is met by the French boxing promoter Avernin, and they drive past colonial bungalows, palms and carob trees, passing bearded men in djellabas referred to by Western journalists as 'Mohammedans', 'Orientals' or 'Mussulmen'. Most of the churches and cathedrals were once mosques and French tricolours fly high atop flagpoles. Avernin warns Leen that he should also be on his guard in Oran: the West has been using Algeria as a cash-cow colony and there are fears of rioting;

Oran's Jewish population surmise that they will be the first victims. In the most recent elections, local politicians employed the lies and slogans heard everywhere in Nazi Germany; people waved swastikas, screaming out 'Death to the Jews!' The North African correspondent for the Dutch newspaper *Centraal Blad voor Israëlieten* writes that 'the issue of race, that eternal and brutal struggle, is on the brink of erupting here.'

Leen is dropped off in Oran's main thoroughfare, Rue Larbi Ben M'hidi. White-turbaned hawkers are selling dates, figs, mint, cumin, chocolate and almonds and the stone-built buildings bear advertisements: L'ATELIER DE BIJOUTERIE; PHARMACIE HENRY GIRAUD; LIBRAIRIE ANDREO and CORDONNERIE LUC BORGEAUD. A tobacconist is selling newspapers and tickets for the boat to Marseille. The front-page headline for *Oran-Matin* is: LA GUERRE CIVILE D'ESPAGNE: General Franco's army has advanced to within eleven kilometres of Madrid.

Leen walks along a narrow pavement past white stucco townhouses four storeys high with balconies. On outdoor terraces, men play chess, cards or draughts; in Oran, you can drink absinthe and other liquor without falling foul of the law. Market shoppers cast their gaze over tomatoes, aubergines, fennel and bananas; boxes are swaddled in canvas to protect the contents from the worst of the heat. Posters hang from the windows of Chez Serra kiosks:

SATURDAY, 31 OCTOBER AT 21:15 HOURS
AT THE CASINO BASTRANA, RUE TURIN
THE LONG-AWAITED INTERNATIONAL FIGHT
KID TUNERO (THE ONLY MAN TO DEFEAT MARCEL THIL)
VERSUS

LEN SANDERS (VICTOR AGAINST GUSTAV EDER)
+ 5 OTHER MATCHES
PURCHASE YOUR TICKETS FROM CHEZ SERRA KIOSKS.

On Fridays, the Tenoudji brothers' Colisée cinema shows the latest films, although the venue also plays host to jazz bands and press conferences for major sports events. The owner, Felix Tenoudji, shakes Leen's hand while Avernin fills jugs of water. Leen walks to the stage in the main auditorium, where the red curtain is open and the walls are hung with posters of Cary Grant, Bette Davis, Hans Albers and Katharine Hepburn. He takes his seat at a long table, where he finds himself in the company of journalists from all the chief newspapers in Morocco and France.

Avernin speaks: 'Len Sanders is less well known to us than Kid Tunero, but he is the official champion of the Netherlands and deserves to be pitted against the great stars. His fighting spirit brought him great acclaim in England, where he often fought in London and Liverpool. In the Netherlands he shares the status of Bep van Klaveren, and away from home he has had very flattering results: wins against Eder, Deckmyn, many British boxers and the European champion Felix Wouters in a knockout. It would be small wonder to us if he were able to bring about a surprise against Tunero.' There is applause, combined with cries from French and Algerian *sportifs* of '*Allez Len!*'

Through an interpreter, Leen says: 'Thank you to the people of Oran for your warm welcome; your city is beautiful and its people friendly. I'm in good shape and I know the reputation of Kid Tunero, the only man to win against Marcel Thil. I'll be fighting with everything I've got to please my countrymen, whom I thank for all the telegrams I've received. This match is very important to me; a good performance will give me the chance to box in even more contests of importance.'

Gustav Eder's conqueror stands, and is taken by Avernin to the gym for training. The next morning he awakes at seven o'clock to jog through Oran. Page 2 of *Oran–Matin Sportif* shows a photograph of Leen in boxing pose with the heading: LEN SANDERS, DUTCH CHAMPION, ARRIVED YESTERDAY.

A preview article comments:

Oran is on tenterhooks. On every street corner, all one hears is:

'Do you know the name of Kid Tunero's next opponent?'

'*Non.*'

'If you don't know it, my friend, it's the Dutchman Len Sanders, the man who beat the former European champion Gustav Eder and the man who beat the reigning champion Wouters in the fifth round in a knockout.'

'*Ce n'est pas possible!*'

'It's completely true, my friend, completely true.'

'*Oran-Matin! Echo d'Algers! Chronique à Oran! Radio Ciné Sports!*' The street vendors are hawking their newspapers in front of the Casino Bastrana on Rue Turin, next to the port of Oran. The last tickets are being sold from a pyramid-roofed tobacconist and Algerian boys are waiting outside the entrance to catch a glimpse of Kid Tunero. Casino Bastrana itself is a stately building defined by arches, arched windows and pillars. Two thousand spectators are pushing and shoving to get inside; Avernin calls the return on sales *formidable*. Algerians of

Spanish, North African, Italian and Jewish descent sit alongside French generals, lieutenants and politicians. According to a local journalist, the assembled public is both 'knowledgeable' and 'difficult'.

The ring has been placed in the orchestra pit to allow even those in the cheapest seats to see Kid Tunero. The communist flamenco singer Angelillo – a friend of Kid Tunero – sings his hit 'Soy un pobre presidiario'. He had frequently performed in Madrid for the Republican army, but fled to Oran in 1936 when General Franco's soldiers put him on their death list.

It's nearly midnight when the announcer finally speaks: 'Ladies and gentlemen, the long-awaited middleweight fight with two stars from the European boxing rings: Kid Tunero, 74 kilograms and the only man to have won against Marcel Thil, versus the representative from Tulip-land, Len Sanders, 71 kilograms and the victor against Gustav Eder and Felix Wouters.'

Tunero is the first to enter the hall with, in his wake, a doctor, his manager, sparring partners, two coaches, a trainer, a PR man, two seconds and a masseur. Leen is followed only by a boxer from Oran who, for a few francs, has agreed to be his second. The referee calls out: 'Box!'

Just as with Deckmyn, Leen causes surprise by going on the offensive sooner than expected, and radio announcers praise his superb left hook. At the end he is dubbed the 'Yiddish Crack'; a French-Algerian reporter writes that '[this] little man, without groomers, without a coach and without a trainer, presented a lesson on how to box.' A Dutch journalist describes Leen as 'the most astonishing character in the world of Dutch boxing'; a short, plucky man who has no need at all of any manager 'as he is that himself, just as he is his own instructor and, if needs be, his own promoter. It was on his own that he left for Africa, where he gave the famous Tunero a merciless bashing such as only those best acquainted with him will know.'

Leen takes the boat back to Rotterdam and is once more at home with Selli, Jopie and David early in November 1936. He fights on his home turf for the first time in ages, successfully defending his title against Arie de Jong. A journalist writes: 'Sanders may be older and heavier set than before, but he is still our best middleweight.'

The coffers of the Jewish Refugees Committee are depleted, so fundraising events have to be held to raise money. Leen often helps with this and has become the full-time boxing and gym instructor at the Jewish sports club Zerizoeth. According to its newsletter, the club was founded to fortify young Jews 'in body and spirit within their own Jewish milieu for the battle for existence awaiting them'. Zerizoeth has more than fifty members between the ages of fifteen and twenty-two, who learn Hebrew and listen to tales about 'musclemen Jews' from the glorious past, such as Judas Maccabeus and Simon bar Kokhba, heroic warriors fighting against goy overlords. Leen reinforces his pupils' agility through Swedish gymnastics and makes them more resilient by instructing them in the 'noble art'. The Zerizoeth newsletter notes that, 'especially in times such as these, a healthy mind in a healthy body is a necessity of life for young Jewish men and women.'

All the while, Leen is waiting for new match offers in the Netherlands. He calls up promoters and relates how well he boxed in Oran against Kid Tunero, the only man to vanquish Marcel Thil. Nobody's interested. He tries challenging Van Klaveren; even Leen's detractors will want to see a Leen v Bep III match. However, either Bep is not in the mood or does not have the nerve.

VI.

Leen the reservist is wearing a grey-green uniform and an army cap that smells of mothballs. He has leg bindings that pinch, boots with worn-through soles, a rusty rifle and a gas mask that may well not actually work. His jacket is a little tight across the chest, there are holes in his socks and his trousers look like they've shrunk in the wash.

It's 29 August 1939 and the announcement for mobilization was posted up throughout the city a day ago. Hundreds of people assembled on Coolsingel along with sighs, chatter and bellyaching: 'What does Hitler want?' 'Why doesn't Chamberlain let him have more territory?' and another commonly heard refrain in Rotterdam: 'It's not like they'll ever come here.'

Leen is thirty-one. He weighs 70 kilograms, which is 12 kilograms more than at his debut in 1925. At home he's not so keen to talk about boxing, but he has given Jopie and David a pair of boxing gloves each and is teaching them the principles of the 'noble art' at his own gymnasium, which he has opened in a small street known as Oppert, very close to his house in Sint Laurensstraat. He had taken out a loan and bought dumbbells and medicine balls, strung up punchbags and punchballs, and had two boxing rings, a balance beam and a pommel horse installed. At the opening, a boxing manager commented: 'Teach your pupils the "noble art" as if you were master of it yourself!' Leen doesn't earn much; it is the Depression and times are hard.

He has been Dutch middleweight champion since 1934, but it has been quite some time since he defended that title. He fought again in March 1938 – an international contest in Rotterdam against Oscar Descheemaecker, the champion in Flanders. According to a journalist from *De Telegraaf*, his comeback in the Netherlands was 'not an unqualified success'. The amount of hand-to-hand combat 'marred the fight' and 'it seemed to us that Sanders did not appear fully fit in the ring and that boxing so little lately has done him no favours'. After this, Leen had had to wait another six months before once more being able to box in the Netherlands for a decent fee: at the Krasnapolsky Hotel on Dam Square in Amsterdam, against the Belgian Jean De Schrijver.

Before this, he paid visits to Jewish colleagues at Jewish boxing clubs in Amsterdam, such as Olympia and Maccabi, asking what the situation was like in their city; were they getting trouble from members of the Netherlands' National Socialist Movement (NSB); were they ready to defend themselves against Hitlerites? The answer to the last question was quite probably a 'yes'. In 1938, Amsterdam's Jewish writer Maurits Dekker initiated the Foundation for the Defence of Jewish Cultural and Social Rights, whose members met twice weekly with the objective of 'arming' themselves because 'Throughout history, we as Jews have repeatedly taken it all lying down. Now, the time has come for us to take action ourselves.'

In the 1920s Leen had boxed as an amateur against the famous Jewish boxing coach from Amsterdam, Joël 'Joop' Cosman. After Kristallnacht in October 1938, Joop decided to set up a Jewish commando group to patrol through the city in order to attack NSB members and other German sympathizers in Amsterdam with fists, knees or iron weapons. Jewish pacifism had to be consigned to the past; anyone wanting war would get just that. On one occasion, Joop Cosman's boxers were walking past Muiderpoort Station when NSB members started shouting out: 'The Jews are our downfall!' and 'Netherlands awake!' After a volley of left and right hooks, anti-Semites were strewn over the ground, gasping for breath and with eyebrows split. Not long after, the Jewish boxing champion Bennie Bluhm from Joop Cosman's Olympia Club was strolling along Utrechtsestraat in the company of fellow boxer Japie Casserus and wrestler Teddie Goldsmit. A member of the *Weerbaarheidsafdeling* (WA: the paramilitary wing of the NSB), kitted out in his black uniform, thought he could push them off the narrow pavement. Bennie, Japie and Teddie tossed him through the air and through a shop window.

In Rotterdam, Leen's brother Bram is giving training sessions to Jews to make them more resilient. What should they do if pushed by an NSB member or a Nazi in civilian clothing? Bram supplies answers in small premises at 45 Gedempte Botersloot. There's also an advertisement in the *Weekblad voor Israëlietische Huisgezinnen*:

BRAM SANDERS' GYMNASIUM FOR LADIES AND
   GENTLEMEN
PHYSICAL CULTURE AND DEVELOPMENT
INDOOR TRAINING AND BOXING FOR SELF-DEFENCE

Leen is walking to Delftsche Poort Station. A small band is playing marching tunes, men are beating drums, majorettes throwing

batons into the air. From open windows you can hear songs by Snip &
Snap, the Ramblers and the Rhythm Five headed by Levie 'the Dutch
Louis Armstrong' Bannet. Women throw flowers down to the street;
everyone seems in the mood for quick, snappy mobilization. It won't
come to war anyway. Leen has just paid a visit to his parents and has
promised his sons he'll be back very soon. Bram is taking over his
training classes and Selli is getting government money to keep them
from going hungry.

Leen had interrupted his boxing career in 1928 to do military
service. At that time, Janus had called an editor at the *Rotterdamsch
Dagblad* to inform him that his pupil 'was going to be paying his dues to
his homeland'. It was sometimes claimed that Jews held dual loyalties
and had no wish to fight in the Dutch army, but Leen was a good patriot
who felt both Jewish and Dutch, and he would always be prepared to
fight for his country.

Twenty-five thousand Rotterdammers are being called
up. Men and teenage lads are travelling to their stations from
Blijdorp, Crooswijk, Feijenoord, Overschie, Delfshaven,
Spangen, Kleinpolder, Charlois, IJsselmonde and the Zandstraat
neighbourhood. Rotterdam's electric tram company has laid
on additional cars to cope with the extra demand; notices on the
doors and windows state: FOR SERVICEMEN ONLY. Farmers are
leading horses by halters through the city, either singly or several
at a time; the army needs thirty thousand of them. Vendors of the
Rotterdamsch Nieuwsblad are crying out: 'Mobilization! Call-up for all
Dutch soldiers and reservists!' and talk on the radio is about nothing
else. Experts predict a hopeless defeat if Germany were to invade the
Netherlands within the next few months. The soldiers' motivation
seems low; nobody sees the gravity of the situation. Mention is made

of the 'pitiful physical condition of our people'; it is an impossible task 'to spruce up sickly Dutchmen for some kind of defensive war'. You only have to look at the shabby appearance of most of the soldiers – reservists have sold off their boots during the Depression and hundreds of men called up for service in Rotterdam turn up in civilian footwear.

The military have erected additional fencing at the main entrance to the station; civilians have to keep behind it. Mothers, wives and sweethearts in their Sunday dresses tearfully hug their men. Mounted police have cordoned off requisition areas where requisitioned horses and vehicles are vetted, registered and forfeited; officers hand a document to the owners, who sign it and return home on foot or by tram. NSB members distribute pamphlets among the soldiers: 'Politicians sowing hate against Nazi Germany', 'Hitler really wants peace; the Jews have brought misfortune upon themselves', and policemen intervene. In the next day's *Rotterdamsch Nieuwsblad*: 'Opposition mounted against such elements fomenting unrest cannot be strong enough!'

More than one thousand reservists are already waiting on the platforms and comprise fifteen batches of men drafted into military service, all packed up and ready to go. The first batch served in 1924 and the last one in 1938. Bram hasn't had to report as he is overweight and flat-footed.

The platform is becoming increasingly crowded, with soldiers nipping off to the kiosk for a carton of cigarettes and waving farewells to relatives. Newspaper boys are hawking extra editions of *De Maasbode* and the *Rotterdamsch Nieuwsblad*, all dealing with mobilization. An advertisement assures its readers: SOLDIERS AND CIVILIANS: YOUR SKIN IS SAFE WITH SWING RAZOR BLADES.

Most reservists have to go to Utrecht, Arnhem, Amsterdam or Maastricht, but Leen is going to the 'Dune and Bulbs Region' of the western Netherlands. On arrival, a doctor shines a light into his eyes, after which he has to mount weighing scales and have his pulse taken. His belly fat is deemed to have no impact on his speed and condition. His right ear looks peculiar, but that is immaterial on the battlefield; his eyes are fine, and he is neither lame nor deaf nor colour blind; they cannot detect any underlying diseases in him. He is just tall enough to pass the inspection, and thanks to his famed double defence his mental faculties are well enough intact.

He marches from the station to the barracks, where his bed is even filthier than in the hostels arranged by Janus when Bram and Leen travelled through England. Tunics, helmets and weapons are in short supply; forks are rusty, knives are blunt; the lavatory seats in the latrines are as befouled as at the Spichernsälen in Berlin. Following the foundation of the League of Nations, military confrontation with the Weimar Republic or any another European country had seemed out of the question and the army has undergone considerable cutbacks.

Leen does target practice in the dunes using Schwarzlose M.08 machine guns and puts up roadblocks using barbed wire. Armed with his bayonet, he sprints towards the imaginary Hun, levelling a jab straight to the heart; the marching is good for his endurance.

Each morning he is awakened by the bugle blare of the reveille. Soldiers fetch tea, coffee, and bread and butter; they make their beds, the sheets having to be folded into a square. It's still dark when the sergeant enters and shouts: 'Stand by your beds!' At his rear there is an officer who performs the inspections: are the lockers tidied, have weapons been oiled, are the gun barrels free of rust? Any breach of the rules receives a warning; strict officers make an immediate entry on a soldier's reprimand report.

Leen is given permission to do boxing training: perhaps one day he'll get the chance to prove himself again in a major match, and he feels he's too good to stop now. He spars with amateur and professional boxers and gives boxing classes. The resilience of Dutch soldiers has to be improved; the Nazis will soon attempt to conquer the country, despite all expectations to the contrary. They use ropes to rig up an improvised boxing ring in the middle of the barracks; the roof is a little too low and Leen has to duck down to avoid bumping his head. He always spars for four two-minute rounds; the room sentry keeps time, with the chef rattling a tin can at the end of each round.

He loses weight through a combination of training and poor diet. All the same, he does manage to do a few hours' exercise almost every day, training his balance on sawn tree trunks, his muscles by using a pull-up bar, and the spring in his feet by jumping over crouching companions. Late in the evening he plays draughts or chess and beats sergeants and lieutenants at the board game halma. In a later interview, Leen commends military service: 'As a result, I have a distraction and don't need to keep thinking about my profession, boxing. And a distraction is a splendid thing. In the past I was already in the habit of never talking about boxing at home, purely and simply so I could be living in a different environment for once.'

Soldier Sanders is promoted to the rank of corporal. At weekends he rides in an army truck along with other drafted boxers to visit barracks in South Holland, where he instructs brothers-in-arms in the 'noble art'. One officer says of boxing that it is *essential* for a serviceman; it promotes all-round physical development and instils in them courage, self-confidence and endurance'. For some time, politicians abroad have recognized the importance of boxing – you only have to look at Germany. The *Wehrmacht* (unified armed forces) has made boxing mandatory there; it's even mentioned in Hitler's election manifesto. This is logical to a Corporal Wassen because 'Boxing fosters stalwart men.' Another army officer comments: 'Let a soldier play tennis and he'll become a tennis player. Teach him to play football and you might get a football player out of him. But teach him boxing and he'll become a warrior.'

Leen is still living in a barracks when, for the first time in years, he is once again given the opportunity to prove himself in a major fight: he is to defend his middleweight title against sergeant and boxing talent Hens Dekker. Posters sporting the Dutch flag announce:

DUTCH MIDDLEWEIGHT CHAMPIONSHIP
8 JANUARY 1940
DE DOELEN, COOLSINGEL
LEEN SANDERS (ROTTERDAM, TITLE HOLDER)
VERSUS
HENS DEKKERS (THE HAGUE, CHALLENGER)
12 3-MINUTE ROUNDS
MILITARY PERSONNEL BELOW THE RANK OF NCO AT HALF
    PRICE FOR AS LONG AS TICKETS LAST

Leen has combed his hair into a side parting, his ears seeming to stick out more than ever. Journalists refer to him as 'the old-timer of the boxing ring', 'the little Rotterdammer with the iron fists', 'the boxer you'd break your hands against' and 'the old champion'. His most memorable victory is that against 'the famous Gustav Eder'; unfortunately, that was more than ten years ago now.

Leen has been booked because Bep was not available. Bep's mother, Marie, has no faith in things working out with the Nazis and so, immediately after Hitler's plundering of Poland, her son boards a ship for the United States. Which boxer could attract just as big a crowd as Bep? Leen hadn't come up for consideration at first; none of the promoters thought him still capable of standing his ground. Even so, in the absence of any appealing alternative since Bep's departure, the promoter Huizenaar had come up with the idea of unleashing 'an up-and-coming' and brave 'knockout fighter' on Leen. The boring old-timer of boxing may have been champion since 1934, but that might now be brought to an end.

Hens Dekkers, the challenger, is the firm favourite among most spectators. He is 15 centimetres taller than Leen, a deal slimmer and seven years younger.

Leen starts off calmly, but in the third round he is so much improved that, in the words of a journalist, he 'seems to have ten arms and hands'. In round four Leen shows that he can also box in offensive mode; the flat-capped brigade stand up from their seats, laughing out loud, astonished. Just what has happened to 'the Mobile Wall' at those barracks? Leen wins by a wide margin. With the match over, a lad climbs through the ropes: Luc van Dam from Crooswijk, nineteen years old and, according to his manager, Huizenaar, a greater talent than Bep. Luc challenges the old-timer and the match is set for a month later. Will Leen be able to win yet again, pitted against a boxer who, as well as being 'an up-and-coming man', is also being hailed as 'the best knockout fighter' since Bep?

Leen enters the De Doelen events hall in his grey-green tunic, green cap, green trousers and clodhoppers. Almost all of the lads from his company are sitting in the gallery. A journalist comments: 'So enthusiastic are Soldier Sanders' brothers-in-arms that they lend him the strength to emerge all at once as an attacker.' Leen wins easily again: 'Sanders the serviceman appears to be quite a different boxer from Sanders the civilian,' writes another journalist. 'Urged on by his barracks mates, the champion more or less broke with his former exclusively defensive style and, to everyone's amazement, and not least that of his challengers themselves, let fly without, however, neglecting his well-nigh legendary double defence.'

Another match follows, two weeks later, once more against an up-and-coming boxer and knockout fighter; De Doelen is sold out yet again. Leen wins overwhelmingly against Bob Rieger from Rotterdam. *De Telegraaf* writes: 'His long absence from the ring no longer weighs upon him. Sanders is the reborn champion, and he seeks to re-establish his name internationally as well.'

It's Monday evening, 4 March 1940: the date of Leen's fourth fight in eight weeks. In all honesty it's not really a bona fide proposition – in Selli's view, and that of Leen's doctor and his parents, it should not be allowed to proceed, but the reborn champion is fit and popular, the hall is always a sell-out when his name is on the posters, and he has never taken home such good money before. This time his opponent comes from abroad: a fascist and a good friend of Mussolini's, Cleo Locatelli defeated Bep van Klaveren in 1932 in a European title fight and is nicknamed 'Satan'. Preview articles describe him as 'the world-renowned Mussolini supporter' and 'the fiery southerner who never gives his opponent a moment's peace'. Almost all the officers and soldiers from Leen's company are back at De Doelen again. During an interval, Van Lent, the announcer, calls for Leen to enter the ring; he climbs through the ropes and his army comrades start howling. A Dutch army officer is holding two large boxes, and after a 'spirited short speech' he hands them over to Corporal Sanders, who opens one. His brothers-in-arms erupt in fresh howls of laughter as the contents are revealed: shiny military boots with steel toecaps, perfect for endless marching in dunes country. The second box contains a grey military jacket, which one newspaper describes as 'a singular item'. The collar bears emblems in gold thread usually worn only by the army's highest-ranking officers.

The gong rings out: the end of the tenth and final round. Van Lent proclaims: 'Sanders, the winner of this bout.' Leen receives an ovation. A journalist from the *Rotterdamsch Nieuwsblad* is of the view that this is 'a well-deserved, albeit late, reward for his difficult and often thankless career', adding that 'precisely because [Sanders chooses] cunning technique and self-defence above the brute violence of the knockout, the boxing public demonstrates in this match that they set greater store by sportsmanship than they do by sensation.' The heading in another paper: 'Oats sown late may yet grow!'

Owing to the 'unpleasant international situation', Leen is unable to box abroad and is challenged by the next up-and-coming man and knockout fighter, Tin Dekkers. Corporal Sanders returns to his barracks, continues sparring and shadowboxing and develops a plan to defeat Tin. What are his strengths? He ponders on this during sentry duty and while marching, jotting down notes when lying on his bed. Should he start off the first round cautiously or do the opposite and once again show that he is more than 'a mobile wall with ten arms and hands'?

It is late March when Huizenaar informs him of the date; the reborn champion is to defend his title on 15 May 1940, and is sure to be cheered on again by his army comrades, his family, the flat-capped brigade and even Bep fans. Except that . . . as it turns out, the match never takes place.

Part III

Vryheid vergaat niet

(Freedom does not fade)

I.

It's 14 May 1940. At twenty-seven minutes past one on that Tuesday afternoon the air-raid sirens start up: Stukas and Heinkel bombers are in the skies above Rotterdam. Armed, helmeted Germans glide earthwards on parachutes, shells explode in shopping streets. An eyewitness writes: 'De Blaak [street] is on fire, Hoogstraat is on fire, what street isn't on fire?'

Bombs fall on the Mennonite church built in 1775 at 59 Sint Laurensstraat. The St Lawrence Church ceiling caves in; its restoration had only just begun. The wooden scaffolding catches alight; a builder flees; a plasterer lies dead beneath the rubble. Men, women and children race to their cars, some household items hastily thrown into the boot. It is near impossible to get through, with tyres punctured by shards of glass among the debris littering the streets. One of Leen's second cousins recalls later how 'everywhere people were in panic, seeking shelter, dreadful clouds of smoke hanging over the city. But the firehoses weren't working; nobody had been prepared for this.'

Leen's house is a little further along the street. Its windows have been blasted out of their frames; the walls shudder as if in a force-12 hurricane. Selli, Jopie and David are at home, and feel as if their skulls are being crushed. Wall clocks, crockery and mirrors are shattered and broken; Jopie and David's boxing gloves melt; scrapbooks of newspaper cuttings, books, photographs, editions of *Boxing* and *Box-Sport* go up in flames; furniture, trophies and medals are all lost. There's a whistling noise, followed by a momentary silence. Then new bombs, fresh panic. Piet Steijl's ironmongers at no. 71a, Maltha's painting firm, the 't Hoen shoe shop, Cor Kindt's French fries business, Boot's haberdashery and the Van Staal café have all taken a hit. The boxing old-timer Herman van 't Hof had had a boxing school in Sint Laurensstraat; now it lies in smoking ruins.

The Bram Sanders Gymnasium for Ladies and Gentlemen on Gedempte Botersloot no longer has a roof; dumbbells and posters of past fights are blackened; the boxing ring, the punchbag, the medicine balls . . . everything is destroyed. Address books with the names and numbers of boxing managers are turned to ash. After the war, Bram's eldest son, Jakob, confirms that his parents' house on Gedempte Karnemelkshaven was 'bombed flat'. Josua, Saartje, their son Mozes and their daughters Jetty, Sipora and Sientje flee from their home and wander through the city like street pedlars without any wares to sell. The window panes at J.J. Sanders Handcarts and Carrier Rentals on Kalverstraat now lie shattered on the pavement. Theo Huizenaar, the Netherlands' most important boxing promoter, cycles from his home in Hugo de Grootstraat to 74 Lange Torenstraat, near St Lawrence Church and Leen and Selli's house. The smoke can be seen from far away. Theo tries to run inside to save his most precious boxing belongings, but firemen restrain him; he would have died from smoke inhalation. Theo weeps as he cycles back home, while bombs continue to fall around him.

The bridges crossing the Waal have been blown up. The prison on Noordsingel is now without a roof; convicts with broken skulls are lying dead in their cells. The Coolsingel Hospital has been hit, its patients injured or killed; the De Bijenkorf department store has collapsed; beer halls, lodgings and bars on De Dijk no longer have doors and windows. At the Gerzon department store the window-display mannequins have melted; paintings at Museum Boijmans have been brought to safety in the nick of time. Ships and boats at the Leuvehaven dockside have been sunk. A Red Cross flag flies at a hospital; it suffers a hit by an incendiary device all the same. The Great Synagogue on De Boompjes suffers irreparable damage and Torah scrolls burn just as during Kristallnacht.

Peace appears to return at twenty to two in the afternoon. People venture cautiously on to the streets – is it safe or is it a trick? Selli, Jopie and David leave their house and head for Overschie, an outlying village where they know someone, and where bombs are unlikely to be dropped. Selli's mother, father, brother and sister are thinking about going to The Hague, but everyone else has the same idea and, anyway, how are they to get there?

Rotterdammers sweep debris from the pavements. Dogs bark, babies cry. One girl thinks her little brother has been crushed, crying out: 'His head's missing! His head's missing!' It feels as hot as a sauna. It is hard to breathe or see far because of all the dust and smoke. People are screaming out the names of relatives. Rotterdammers of German descent are being arrested by the city's servicemen and detained at the De Doelen hall on Coolsingel. Everywhere beneath the rubble there are bodies. A boy is searching for his father. People are pushing wheelbarrows. Canaries perch on shoulders; cats are being carried or are trying to keep up with their owners. Trams are at a standstill.

Cars are full of bleeding passengers. A man lumbers by holding a goldfish bowl, a radio and a vacuum cleaner. Greengrocers are being looted.

At four o'clock in the afternoon Sergeant Major Van Ommering waves a piece of cloth nailed to a broomstick, spotted with blood; earlier in the day he had used it to bandage a wounded marine. At a quarter past six, German tanks and army trucks drive through Proveniersstraat and into the city via Stationssingel. Soldiers smirk as they survey the damage; the Führer will be pleased.

On 15 May 1940, Queen Wilhelmina gives a wireless broadcast to announce the capitulation. By then, Leen has already been in Wassenaar for five days as a prisoner of war in German hands. On 10 May he had been sleeping in a requisitioned holiday cabin in the dunes where, at half past three in the morning, he was woken by the sound of machine-gun fire and hand grenades. The doors to the cabin were shot off their hinges; Germans shot through the windows and knocked the glass out with their rifles. Leen's comrades lost arms, legs or faces, and medics were needed at the double. The battalion commander went for cover behind a dune, sergeants dived for the ground, horses fell backwards. A major took to his feet to finish off a German, but was shot in the attempt. Twenty soldiers were killed.

The Nazis kept on shooting at cabins, tents and dwellings. Orders were barked: 'Raus! Alle raus!' (Everyone out!) Soldiers and officers escaped over a fence towards a wood, while grenades skimmed their helmets and the wounded lay bleeding to death in the sand. Dutch officers shouted: 'Ditch your equipment. We've got no chance!' White handkerchiefs were tied to bayonets and hands raised up in the air: '*Nicht schiessen!*' (Don't shoot!) Leen also surrendered and was arrested. He was allowed to keep his helmet and uniform, but his rucksack, army knife and firearms had to be handed over. At a cabin in the dunes, the prisoners of war had to take turns sleeping as there was hardly any room to lie down. They were given no food; buckets of water were all that the guards brought. The dead were buried in the garden.

Rumours abounded that they were to be taken to Germany, where they would end up in the prisoner camp at either Dachau or Sachsenhausen. Leen had no desire to await *that* eventuality and managed to escape, returning to Rotterdam. There, disaster tourists from across the Netherlands were walking and cycling through the city centre, where the city council had set the unemployed to work, issuing them with brooms to clear up the rubble. Carts went through the city laden with corpses, labels tied to the toes stating the place where they were found. The mayor laid wreaths all day long. Dozens of Rotterdam's Jews hanged themselves after the capitulation.

In the street where, until 14 May, his house had stood, Leen now sees only lampposts lying in the road like matchsticks. All that remains of his house is a heap of bricks and debris, and the nearby Leen Sanders Gymnasium has fared no better. After the war, Leen said that he had 'lost both home and livelihood as a result of the German bombing'.

Where are Selli, Jopie and David? He has no idea where to look for them. Two days pass, then a third and a fourth. It takes a week before he finally finds them – in his own words – in a farmer's barn in Overschie. Jopie and David have been sleeping badly, afraid that the bombers will be coming back again.

*

Rotterdam is still smouldering as Leen, together with boxing friends Nol Lagrand, Van Creveld and Louis van Sinderen, goes running through the Kralingse Bos (parkland at the edge of the city). All the boxing halls lie in ruins, and a journalist from the *Rotterdamsch Nieuwsblad* observes that boxing 'is probably the sport most affected by the situation'. Leen and his friends carry on training regardless – their city will have to be rebuilt from its foundations, but boxing can at least give victims of the bombing some pleasure and a temporary diversion.

Three days after the air raid, boxing promoter Theo Huizenaar is once more cycling behind his boxers and shouting out words of encouragement. After four days he decides to build a new gymnasium, drawing up plans for its reconstruction and fixing a date for the first sports event after the bombing. Since winning against Locatelli the Mussolini supporter, and against future hopefuls Hens Dekkers, Luc van Dam and Bob Rieger, Leen is now Rotterdam's biggest crowd-puller. Huizenaar offers the 'Mobile Wall' (along with his ten arms and hands) one of the best contracts of his life: but will the occupiers allow a Jew to be a champion?

II.

It has rained nearly all summer long. Soon Leen will be defending his middleweight title for the fourth time, and just as in February 1940, his opponent is to be Luc van Dam: nineteen years old and, according to Huizenaar, the greatest Dutch boxing talent since Bep van Klaveren. Luc's right hook might be even harder hitting than Bep's, and one journalist describes him as 'the Dutch Carpentier'. Sanders versus Van Dam II is the first major sporting event since 'the Fateful Day', as people in Rotterdam now refer to 14 May 1940. A preview article in *Het Volk* notes: 'Faster than was thought possible, boxing here in this city has recovered from the damage inflicted upon it.'

Leen had started preparations in late June. Like thousands of Rotterdam's other Jews after the bombing, he has moved with his wife and children to The Hague, where he has found a job as a sports instructor at the J. Nicolaas Gymnasium on Prinsesselaan in Rijswijk, a ten-minute drive from the city. As its proprietor, Johannes Gerardus 'Jan' Nicolaas, keenly advertises, YOU'LL ONLY LEARN TO BOX WELL WITH J. NICOLAAS, 6 YEARS NETHERLANDS CHAMPION. Leen spars and trains with him and his whole musculature hardens; his arms scarcely fit into his undershirt any longer; his legs become quite lean and toned. Jan lives in one of the smart villas on the outskirts of Rijswijk; his boxing school is part of his house, and Leen is able to have a hot shower there after training sessions. Chickens and cockerels peck about in the garden, and sometimes Jan's wife gives him a slice of bread and a fresh egg.

Every day, Leen and Jan run for hours along the beach at Scheveningen while German soldiers stroll along the boulevard at the pier. Children pose with them for photos, touching their helmets, and the occupiers chuckle and pat their heads. 'You see, Germans aren't so bad after all.'

Leen also does his training at the Kreek cycling track on Rotterdam's Stadionweg, which is where the title fight is to be held because German bombs have laid waste to De Doelen, the Arts & Sciences Building, the Auction House and the Odeon auditorium. Out of necessity, the first major sports event since the Fateful Day is going to be held in the open air. Leen wants to get used to this change of setting; boxing outdoors is a whole different type of sport; it's heavier going, and who knows whether it will be windy or raining. He spars with his brother Bram's best pupils (Lagrand, Van Creveld and Van Sinderen), who will also be boxing for titles of their own.

On the morning of the match, Leen travels from The Hague to Rotterdam. Walls and advertising pillars are plastered with posters:

NETHERLANDS MIDDLEWEIGHT CHAMPIONSHIP
LUC VAN DAM V LEEN SANDERS
KREEK RACETRACK
SUNDAY, 11 AUGUST 1940 — 15.00 hours

OTHER MATCHES:
LAGRAND V DISCH
VAN CREVELD V SERNO
AND MORE BESIDES

A chill wind is blowing and it looks like being yet another miserable summer's day. Fifteen hundred spectators are braving the rain to get to the Kreek racetrack, where promoter Theo Huizenaar has had a canopy-covered boxing ring put up on the track. Nazis in civilian clothing have been allotted the best front-row seats. At the bar, ration-card traffickers are floating about waving bank notes: they've hired a whole section, yelling away as if Feyenoord were playing Sparta and placing bets on the winner, and delaying placing their bets until the last moment. According to the *Rotterdamsch Nieuwsblad* reporter, 'the outcome is as precarious as a youngster's first crush.' Another writes: 'It's difficult to make a prediction right now. Both boxers have suffered on account of the war. It may be that this has affected one of them more greatly than it has the other.'

Tables are shunted against the ring, ready for the press in attendance. A journalist from the *Nederlandsch Dagblad: Orgaan voor het Nationaal Front* sits alongside the boxing expert from the *Deutsche Zeitung in den Niederlanden*. The first edition of that German newspaper had appeared three weeks after the occupation, and the editors would have it that the Dutch welcomed the Nazis with flowers and that everyone is happy to belong to the Thousand-Year Reich. A preview article calls the 'victor against Gustav Eder' a *Faustkämpfer* with a 'phenomenal routine', 'strapping arms' and 'fast moves'.

Leen watches the event's first matches from a sixth-row seat. Occasionally, Rotterdammers will approach to hand him cuttings of matches he fought against Bep or of his trips through England and Germany – he'd lost his own cuttings forever on the Fateful Day. The writer of an article in the programme feels that what 'the veteran Leen Sanders has shown of himself in the past two years [has been] admirable, highly admirable: a man living constantly in the shadow of Van Klaveren's popularity and one who, owing to his boxing style, could never conquer the sympathies of the boxing enthusiast masses'.

Huizenaar is wearing a long beige raincoat, a warm white scarf and a grey homburg. He talks to journalists about his new boxing ring; the former ring had been in the basement of De Doelen on Coolsingel. On 14 May he had gone to see whether it was still in one piece, but its metalwork was burned through and the ropes charred. He'd decided to order a canopy as well; it had been such a poor summer already and it might easily rain, even on 11 August, and just look . . . spectators with umbrellas and winter coats, men in flat caps sheltering under bushes.

In the first bout Lagrand, Leen's training partner and Bram's pupil, fights to an undecided finish against the Rotterdam lightweight champion, Robert Disch. Leen's Jewish training partner Van Creveld beats Amsterdam's Jaap Serno in a knockout; Serno is carried out on a stretcher while a second administers chloroform to relieve him. Bram oversees his pupils in the ring as a second and coach, handing them flasks of water, rubbing liniment into eyebrows and, between rounds, talking essential tactics to them. Leen's little boys, Jopie and David, are also here to watch the main match alongside their Uncle Bram. This is the first time they've attended a gala event – allowed only because this an afternoon bill. The boys have inherited not only their father's thick eyebrows, but also a desire to become professional boxers when they are older. After the first fight against Luc van Dam,

Jopie goes up to Leen and says: 'Father, keep the title for just a bit; then I can take it off you.'

There are hearty cheers of support as Leen climbs into Huizenaar's new ring in his colourful kimono. He waves to friends, acquaintances, his sons; he laughs, beaming his smile. He keeps his kimono on for some time, springing up and down to keep warm. At around five o'clock, the announcer, Van Lent, starts the proceedings: 'The championship match for the middleweight title; the title holder Sanders: 70.6 kilograms; the challenger Van Dam: 70.3 kilograms. The referee is Schulp.'

Beneath his kimono the title holder has donned dark shorts without a Star of David. The first major sports event since the bombings is about to begin. The wind has not slackened and it's still pelting down; Leen's thin hair is plastered to his scalp. Men in flat caps surge forwards to be able to see the fight from underneath the canopy; policemen make futile attempts to impede them. An adjudicator sounds the gong.

Leen wins the first eight rounds; thereafter, Luc improves somewhat. Just as before the war, the old-timer retreats behind his 'shell'; the 'mobile wall' tactic still works, and in the view of a journalist writing for *Volksdagblad*, Leen shows 'splendid examples of his legendary defence'.

The gong for the final round. Leen goes on the offensive again as if he were Bep; he hits Luc time and again with his left hook, and the wonder is that the 'Dutch Carpentier' has not been knocked out. Spectators are cheering Leen on even more raucously than at his previous matches against young challengers.

It is still raining when the adjudicator, Westbroek, beats the gong for the final time. Bram embraces Leen, Luc congratulates the champion for his well-deserved victory, fans from the now utterly devastated Zandstraat neighbourhood climb into the ring, and a victorious father lifts his sons into the air. Huizenaar asks the announcer to declare the result. A woman is in the ring holding a bouquet of flowers. Huizenaar has the champion's belt in his hands. Van Lent picks up his megaphone: 'Van Dam is the winner of the match.'

At first there is silence; *what* was that he just said?

The words slowly sink in; Leen's fans start to mutter, then whistle and boo; a chair is thrown towards the ring and policemen arrest the perpetrator. The *Rotterdamsch Nieuwsblad* reporter writes: 'The adjudicators' verdict came as a complete surprise to virtually everyone, because the champion, Sanders, had not exhibited a single moment's weakness; he had maintained the upper hand for the full fifteen rounds and had given his challenger very little chance indeed to corner him.'

Initially, Leen is too taken aback to protest. He speaks to Bram, Lagrand, Van Creveld and Van Sinderen, and it's then that he gets angry. The next day the *Rotterdamsch Nieuwsblad* reports: 'Sanders has lost his title, but he cannot be reconciled to that in this manner. The sport of boxing has been ill-served by this decision, as will be surely borne out.' Every other Dutch reporter is of like mind concerning the scandalous nature of the result. Headlines include: 'Questionable defeat of Sanders', 'Van Dam wins undeservedly against Sanders', 'Dubious victory', 'Unfathomable adjudication error'.

Why has Leen been judged the loser? Has his Jewish background had something to do with it? Huizenaar will say nothing; boxing managers will say nothing; and the new title holder dares say nothing. It is only decades later that Leen discovers the truth: a high-ranking Nazi official had ordered the adjudicators to ensure that the title holder lost.

The swindled champion jogs for three days every week through the Kralingse Bos with Bram's pupils Lagrand, Van Creveld and Van Sinderen: he's training to take back his title. In the afternoon he drives to The Hague to give boxing classes at the Strang Gymnasium on Brouwersgracht. It's on one of his days there that he receives a visit from a *Telegraaf* journalist. Leen tells him that he is trying to rebuild his 'gymnasium destroyed in Rotterdam' in his new city of residence and that his ultimate goal is to take revenge on Luc. The journalist writes that the 'boxing old-timer with the granite defence' has only 'out of necessity bidden farewell to the title wrested so unjustly from him'.

While training in Kralingse Bos, the boxers go in search of material dropped from British aircraft and find leaflets bearing the title VRYHEID VERGAAT NIET (Freedom does not fade), commissioned by Britain's Royal Air Force. The front page of the first edition, dated October 1940, contains headlines such as:

GERMAN U-BOAT DROWNS 77 CHILDREN

MORE THAN 2,400 GERMAN AIRCRAFT BROUGHT DOWN
ALREADY IN ASSAULT ON ENGLAND

NETHERLANDS MINISTER FOR FOREIGN AFFAIRS TO
DISCLOSE GERMAN OUTRAGES TO USA

The compilers of VRYHEID VERGAAT NIET 'are pleased to be the bearers of glad tidings about the world war against Hitler' and write: 'neither you, nor we, shall ever forget the bombing of Rotterdam', and that the 'royal couple has arrived in England after a miraculous escape from bombing raids and machine-gun fire'. Queen Wilhelmina has said in a speech: 'I urge my countrymen and women in our motherland, and wherever else they may be, however dark and difficult the times, to keep faith in the final victory.'

Leen gathers up the leaflets and stuffs them into his sweats. The occupiers are barbarians; nobody in the Netherlands should be left in any doubt. Together with Nol, Leo and Louis, he has the leaflets copied and disseminated throughout Rotterdam and The Hague as a rebuttal of German propaganda. They're well aware that an arrest could result in a one-way trip to Dachau or Mauthausen, more popularly known as *Moordhausen* ('murderhouses').

III.

Leen's identity card has had a 'J' stamped on it in black ink. Early in 1941, a civil servant in The Hague had noted down his name, date of birth and last address in the Greater Germanic Reich. The most important question: how many Jewish grandparents do you have? Leen had given the honest answer: 'four'. He had to be fingerprinted, and a photograph was stuck on to his identity card.

Leen meets up from time to time with a man by the name of Zandbergen. They know each other from before; in his early days, Zandbergen was a frequent presence on De Dijk when working as a police detective in uniform, official cap and truncheon in hand. His nickname had been the 'Sherlock Holmes of Rotterdam', and Leen described him later as 'the famous detective'. Zandbergen had solved quite a number of crimes, including the murders of Blonde Mien and Black Betty, 'working girls' on De Dijk. One newspaper observed how pimps, pickpockets, counterfeiters and bank robbers lived in fear of his 'punches, respected even among Rotterdam's professional boxers'.

Zandbergen has been in the resistance since May 1940 – a little reluctantly at first. After the German invasion, arrested members of the NSB had been singing Nazi songs to celebrate the victory, and Zandbergen had given the traitors blows to the neck with his truncheon. He'd been required to explain his actions before a judge, resulting in the surrender of his pistol and a fine. Zandbergen had resigned from the police, gone underground and regained his pride through undermining the occupiers. In 1941 he is collecting identity cards, and Leen is assisting him.

Leen, Lagrand, Van Creveld and Van Sinderen visit the Nenijto racetrack in Rotterdam and other sports facilities, where they change clothes and scout around. It makes perfect sense for them to be there – they are professional athletes, after all. They slip hands into jackets and bags and steal passports – as one of them says after the war, 'to help Jewish people wanting to pass as Christians'. Zandbergen takes the documents to master forgers where the stamped 'J' is removed and Salomon suddenly becomes Henk, Sarah is now Saskia. Zandbergen never tells Leen about the recipients of these identity cards; that sort of thing could put him in danger. If Leen were picked up and tortured by the barbarians to extract information about Zandbergen and his people, it could lead to dozens of arrests, executions or, for a few, deportations to Mauthausen.

The boxers arouse suspicion. A German policeman-cum-boxing fan called Röschmann tells Van Sinderen that Leen's name has been placed on the list kept by the *Sicherheitspolizei* (SiPo: the German Security Police), and since then Leen has been watching his step even more than normal.

In 1941 Leen is living at 11a Paviljoensgracht in The Hague. His new district is reminiscent of the Zandstraat area and is known as 'the Neighbourhood'. Its slum dwellings and alleyways are dark and narrow. Café Engels is the local pub at 109 Gedempte Gracht; it traffics ration cards for the purchase of extra bread, meat or flour, for which prices range upwards to 300 guilders. Leen and his wife and children are sharing the first floor of a house with the similarly Jewish De Winter family; most of the people living in the Neighbourhood are Jewish. The Lely brothers at no. 29 repair bath chairs, tricycles and wheelchairs. Izak 'Sakkie' van Leeuwen is the local drunkard; he is often heard screaming at his wife because of yet again failing to manage the narrow winding stairway. The poorest of the Neighbourhood's Jews sit for much of the day in Sloume Blok's café in Kranestraat. The Jewish Centre at no. 27 is one of The Hague's last bastions in resisting assimilation, where young Jews learn Hebrew and Jewish history and girls are given needlework courses; Leen sometimes demonstrates boxing skills there.

Leen often goes to the bookshop run by his downstairs neighbour, Mr Jacobson. In the summer of 1941, most of the Neighbourhood's locals make a point of buying a copy of the *Joodsche Weekblad* (Jewish Weekly), which nearly every week cites the latest anti-Jewish regulations. Since July 1941, Leen has no longer been able to train on the beach at Scheveningen because Nazi soldiers check the identity cards of suspect beach-goers. Jopie and David are no longer permitted to feed the ducks at the Palace, and Selli may now shop only at specifically kosher butchers or Jewish greengrocers. Her father, David, is a baker, selling bread and biscuits, and since the summer of 1941 he's been allowed to sell his wares solely to other Jews. Signs have been put up in the windows of cafés on Grote Markt, the Buitenhof and the Binnenhof, stating JEWS PROHIBITED. Leen and Selli are no longer welcome at the Mauritshuis art museum or at the National Theatre. Jopie and David used to love going with their parents to the

Flora cinema in Wagenstraat but, following a new regulation, that is now forbidden as well. Jews can no longer book rooms at Mr Deijers' Hotel Corona on the Buitenhof and in September 1941, Jopie and David have to leave their mixed school. A Hague politician comments that this is inevitable after 'incessant complaints resulting from the coexistence of Dutch and Jewish children at the same school'. According to NSB members, teachers were showing favouritism to Jewish pupils and action had to be taken against 'Jewish influences'. From now on, Jopie and David are going to a Jewish school in Bezemstraat, a side street off Gedempte Gracht in the heart of the Neighbourhood.

Anti-Semites often pass through the district; passers-by receive blows and barrows are pushed over. Pious Jews dare not hang mezuzahs (cases holding verses from the Torah) up above their doors; men prefer not to wear skullcaps on the street; orthodox Jewish women ask the Almighty, Everlasting and Merciful God for forgiveness for temporarily not covering their heads. Graffiti slurs appear on walls: THE JEWS ARE THE PLAGUE/MAKE A CLEAN SWEEP! The windows of Jewish shops in the Neighbourhood are graced with the slogan BUY FROM YOUR OWN PEOPLE! Christian neighbours wear NSB badges and no longer greet Leen in the street. He's also on his guard against the police in The Hague: the inspectors Spaans and Dusschoten force entry into homes and search rooms to loot diamonds or other valuables. Officer Tinus Osendarp is more feared than any other in the Dutch police. At the 1936 Olympic Games in Berlin he had won bronze medals for the 100m and 200m sprint events; journalists wrote that he was 'the fastest white man'. Both before and after the games he sang the Führer's praises and in 1941, as a mounted police officer, his adoration of Adolf Hitler has become greater than ever.

Leen's family is also banned from attending the Grand Synagogue in Wagenstraat, only three minutes' walk from their house. On 20 April 1941, Hitler's birthday, members of the NSB and WA had gone there and broken down the door, poured petrol over the pews and the Torah ark and set them alight. The windows were smashed in and they daubed the walls with JEWS OUT! and JEWISH BLOOD IS THE DEVIL'S BLOOD. The embroidered Torah curtain, the silverware and the Torah scrolls all had to be thrown away; restoration would take months.

Leen may no longer box against 'Aryans' such as Luc van Dam, nor can he continue as an instructor at the Strang Gymnasium in The Hague or at the J. Nicolaas School in Rijswijk. He now gives training classes from his own home in Paviljoensgracht, and Jopie and David spar with each other in their father's makeshift gymnasium. Jewish locals come by two or three times a week for training sessions advertised in *Het Joodsche Weekblad*:

MASSAGE
PHYSICAL CULTURE
AND SWEDISH GYMNASTICS CLASSES
LEEN SANDERS
FORMER NETHERLANDS CHAMPION
PAVILIOENSGRACHT 11A, THE HAGUE

A sombre mood prevails at Leen's home whenever there is a boxing match at which, under normal circumstances, he would have been

present. It is 2 December 1941 and the Arts & Sciences Building on
Zwarteweg in The Hague has sold out to 2,200 spectators. The 'Dutch
Carpentier', Luc van Dam, is boxing at eight o'clock this evening
against the pride of Nazi Germany: Gustav Eder. The latter, the most
famous welterweight in Europe, had arrived at Staatspoort Station
the day before. Members of the NSB and WA, as well as journalists
from the *Nationale Dagblad: voor het Nederlandsche volk* and *Die Deutsche Zeitung in
den Niederlanden* welcomed him with Gouda cheese and with right arms
raised in salute, crying out '*Heil Eder!*' and '*Heil Hitler!*' One day later,
reporters describe the Nazi boxer as 'Eder, the phenomenal German
champion' and the 'famous Master Eder'; the match is already being
described as 'historic'. Only in the *Rotterdamsch Nieuwsblad* is any reference
made to Leen, 'against whom Eder lost in Berlin'. No other Dutchman
had ever beaten 'Ironside' Gustav, and Bep had been flattened by him
in 1937 – the only time he was ever knocked out.

At eight o'clock an announcer steps into the ring to start 'the boxing
match of the season'. Leen is unable to listen to wireless coverage
because the occupiers have taken his radio. The German chief military
commander in the Netherlands, Friedrich Christiansen, is seated
next to General De Vlieger and Theo Huizenaar in the dignitaries'
box, and windows and ticket counters bear the unequivocal message:
JEWS NOT WELCOME.

IV.

It is late in July 1942 when Bram Sanders – no longer the owner of a gymnasium – receives a registered letter from a Rotterdam police officer. Only three weeks before, Bram had been celebrating his thirty-eighth birthday. On the breast pocket of the left side of his jacket he is wearing a six-pointed yellow star, the black stitching on which reads: JEW.

He lives at 28 Smeetslandschedijk in the IJsselmonde district of Rotterdam, where, in 1940, 515 emergency dwellings were built. Ships ferried rubble from the city centre to Smeetslandschedijk and horses pulled carts to the building site, where a small factory was used as a large-scale stable; labourers worked more than ten hours a day to get the job done as soon as possible.

In the summer of 1941, Bram was able to move into one of these emergency shelters together with his parents, sisters Jetty and Sipora, and his youngest brother; most of the neighbours are goys. The man delivering mail to Bram and his family is an odd-jobber called Koolmees. He is known to the police and sells fox terriers, meat-slicing machines, builder's ladders, carts with tyres, hay and Shetland ponies. He also operates a sideline in selling ration cards and is arrested every so often by the German Reich Inspector for Price Control.

SUMMONS!

You must proceed to the Westerbork transit camp, Hooghalen Station, for personal vetting and health assessment for the purpose of possible participation in a job-creation scheme in Germany under police surveillance.

To that end, you must present yourself at 20.00 hours on 31 July at the assembly point: Warehouse 24, Entrepotstraat, Rotterdam.

You may take with you as luggage:

1 suitcase or rucksack
1 pair of work boots
1 pair of socks
2 pairs of underpants
2 shirts
1 pair of overalls
2 woollen blankets
2 sets of bed linen (a cover with sheets)
1 bowl
1 mug
1 spoon
1 pullover
towel and toiletries
basic provisions for three days

You may not bring: living household effects

Bram's sister Jetty and his youngest brother, Mozes, have received the same letter. Their mother and father do not have to come with them as they are over the age of sixty, and their oldest daughter, Sipora, is given permission to stay at their emergency dwelling on Smeetslandschedijk in order to care for them. Mozes is twenty; his brothers, sisters and parents call him 'Max'. He apprenticed as a construction worker and has had a lot of work since the May air raids; nevertheless, he received a *Berufsverbot* (professional disqualification) in 1942. Jetty is twenty-eight and, until all of the anti-Jewish regulations, was a furrier, just like her eldest brother, Jakob.

Bram, Jetty and Max say their goodbyes to Josua, Saartje and Sipora. It is Thursday evening. A few weeks before, policemen on German orders came and took their bicycles, which is why the summons envelopes also contain travel permits: for this one time only, Jews will be allowed to travel by tram, bus or train again. Bram, Jetty and Max take some money with them, but it amounts to very little, for Bram has been unemployed for some time now. Half an hour later they arrive at an isolated dockside location near Stieltjesstraat in Rotterdam South, where ships lie at anchor in the inner harbour; the nearest residential districts are a good ten minutes' walk away. They walk into a wooden building labelled 'Warehouse 24'.

Two thousand of Rotterdam's Jews have received a summons, and of these, just over 1,100 have actually turned up. The Nazi officials are furious. The friendly approach is not working; tougher measures will have to be taken. However, Bram's thirty-six-year-old brother Meijer has certainly been obedient: until the anti-Jewish regulations, he'd been working in the port of Rotterdam as a porter, but in 1942 he has been left without an income, just like Bram and

Leen. Meijer Sanders is accompanied by his wife, Aaltje, their four-year-old son, Leendert, and their daughter, Saartje, who turned eight only the week before.

Bram, Jetty, Max, Meijer, Aaltje, Leendert and Saartje go to the waiting room. Men, women and children are sitting on just-dusted school benches or else are parked on the floor, their heads resting against their bags or suitcases. Bram's sister Sini is also there. Until her summons, she'd been living with her older sister, Roosje, on Schieweg in Blijdorp. Roosje's husband, Simon, has a temporary exemption from deportation owing to his profession as a tailor. Roosje works as a seamstress and that profession can also be of use to the Nazis, so she has also been declared exempt from deportation until further notice.

Rotterdam detectives are speaking to SS men in Warehouse 24, and German officers are checking to see that Jews are not being given too hearty a welcome. Tables have been laid out with cups, jugs and bottles of lemonade. Coffee is free, but lemonade costs five cents. A sixteen-year-old girl writes later on in her diary: 'I don't think many of them will be coming back. Germany will take revenge on the poor Jews to the very end. That's how it's always been, that's how it always will be for the Chosen Jewish People.'

The rear of Warehouse 24 is sealed off and one Nazi barks out that anyone who has not received a summons must leave the building immediately. Nurses try to calm people suffering panic attacks while a doctor inspects the arrivals in a small office. Even the sick and the crippled are approved. The Jewish Council's typists, secretaries, couriers, coffee ladies, sandwich makers and stenographers submit proof of their exemption from deportation and are permitted to return home. A German refugee is taking her daughters away but is held back by a soldier; she screeches: 'I want to say goodbye to my children! Gertrude! Hilda!' The soldier gives her a shove and tells her he has had quite enough of 'you Jews'.

It is around ten in the evening when Bram and his assorted family hear that they must make themselves ready to go; they walk outside to join the other approved Jews. An eyewitness describes them in a diary entry as 'poor countrymen who are heading for their deaths'. SS men scare off relatives making their farewells. On returning home, a member of Rotterdam's Jewish Council writes: 'Misery, everywhere the same misery.'

Bram and his family members know only that they are to board a train for the north-eastern province of Drenthe. The Nazis have told them that from there they will be transported to their workplace in Germany, but what guarantee do they have that they will not be sent to Mauthausen or some other horrific camp? Aaltje's sister had been married to a Jewish man who had been in the resistance and, after capture, sent to Mauthausen. According to the Nazis, that is where he died on 7 July 1942. Cause of death: suicide by walking into the electrified perimeter fence. Nobody in Aaltje's family can believe such a thing could be true.

It is now ten past one in the morning on a new day, 1 August. Bram and his relatives show their travel permits and enter a carriage, supervised by Rotterdam police officers. Bram's cousin Meijer Spreekmeester is seated in the same train, along with his sisters, Esther, Elisabeth and Saartje, his brothers, Leendert and Nathan, and Esther's illegitimate son, Joseph. Meijer had been Leen's teammate at Janus Riesmeijer's National Boxing Club and had lived a few houses further along in Nieuwsteeg. He had been almost as good as Leen, but he suffered a few successive knockouts and at that point, as Leen would later recall, 'he scarpered out of it *tout de suite*'.

The train passes Delftsche Poort Station and, after a few hours, stops at Hooghalen Station in Drenthe. Once there, 1,120 Rotterdam Jews step out along with their suitcases, flasks, carrier bags, bundles and basic provisions, their rucksacks on their backs, feeling fatigued. It is dark, and they have to walk five kilometres to reach their destination. They trudge across heathland under the watchful eyes of armed Dutch policemen until they enter the main hall at Westerbork transit camp. It's like a miniature village set in half a square kilometre of heath – albeit a village surrounded by barbed wire fencing and seven watchtowers. On a podium there are tables bearing typewriters and draped in white tablecloths, where German Jews are typing out personal data, one prisoner describing the sound as 'the machine-gun fire of bureaucracy'. Male registrars are in their best suits; women are wearing make-up. Kurt Schlesinger, a German Jew nicknamed 'the Jewish SS man', tall, bald and sporting a moustache reminiscent of Hitler's, screams out that everything must be done faster. Longer-term camp inmates know never to cross this man. As Head of Administration, he compiles the transportation lists: failure to mind your step can mean being on a train to the east before you know it.

After a lengthy wait, Bram finds himself the next up. His sepia card provides the following information:

SANDERS, ABRAHAM J.
CARAVAN, SMEETSLANDSCHEDIJK 28, ROTTERDAM
10.7.04 ROTTERDAM

DUTCH

BOXING INSTRUCTOR

UNMARRIED

Doctors inspect the newcomers for diseases and their hair is deloused. The whole family group then has to visit a small room designated as the Lippmann, Rosenthalbank & Co. Bank. Operatives demand to know whether they have valuables with them; if so, they take possession of them. The newcomers are assigned a barrack block and sleep with two or more other people in a bunkbed riddled with fleas. There are constant sounds of coughing, banging, whispering and crying. After a few hours, Bram and his family are required to get up and go outside for the morning roll-call, where Nazis with machine guns look down from watchtowers. Men, women and children are walking along Westerbork's main thoroughfare, also known as the 'Boulevard of Misery'. The sun is shining, the thorn bushes and lupins are in bloom. It's dusty and sultry; sand is blowing through the camp from the heath, and these grains of sand get everywhere: in inmates' hair, noses, mouths and underwear. They try waving away the flies.

The commandant of Westerbork is an SS officer called Erich Deppner. According to one prisoner, he has the look of a murderer. The Camp Police Service consists of twenty Jewish men, virtually all of whom have come from Germany; they come down particularly hard on their Dutch fellow prisoners in revenge against the Dutch politicians who refused to issue them residence permits.

After three days at Westerbork, the lights come on in the barracks and a German Jew enters, holding a transport list typed in blue by an official. This is List A no. 17:

Sanders, Abraham Josua
Sanders, Mozes
Sanders-Droomer, Aaltje
Sanders, Saartje
Sanders, Leendert
Sanders, Sientje
Sanders, Henriette
Sanders, Meijer

They have to get ready for departure. One Rotterdammer writes in a letter home: 'Well, perhaps you'll have heard this already, or perhaps not, but for now I'll just write to you about everything in any case. On the evening of 30 July the city was in uproar. Then you started hearing how so-and-so had done themselves in, then someone else, and someone else again, and so it went on all day long. From Westerbork we're going on the goods train to an unknown destination. Where are we going to? Where are we going? Those are the words on everyone's lips. People are desperate, senseless and despondent.'

It is 3 August, Monday morning. An empty train heads towards the station at the village of Beilen and arrives there at half past nine. The engine driver then departs at 9.48am, still without any passengers. From Beilen the train continues for ten minutes before reaching

Hooghalen, where 1,013 men, women and children clamber aboard into cattle wagons. According to a survivor of Transport 7 from Westerbork, the migrants were 'beaten on to the train'. Some of the doors are standing open and people can dangle their legs over the edge; songs are being sung, and a sense of optimism prevails. They reach the border with Germany at Nieuweschans; the train then travels via Bremen, Hanover, Berlin, Liegnitz (Legnica in modern Poland), Breslau (Wrocław), Oppeln (Opole) and Cosel (Koz´le) to Kattowitz (Katowice). After a few hours they come to a halt. Lights are glowing in the darkness. 'What's that?' 'Where are we?' For hours, nothing happens. The platform is illuminated by spotlights; it is still dark. The train moves on a little way. SS men with Alsatian dogs are standing in the fog. In the same survivor's account it was a scene reminiscent of a *film noir*. Some of the prisoners faint.

'*Los, los, heraus!*' (Go! Go! Get out of there!)

'*Pakete liegen lassen!*' (Leave bags behind!)

Luggage is piled up in heaps, prisoners beaten for any last-second attempts at taking things out. Women must line up to the right, alongside the train; men to the left. SS doctors pass down the line. People with walking difficulties may climb into the lorries next to the platform; from there they will be taken to the bathhouse, where they can have a good shower. Some 316 prisoners get on board.

Leen's cousin Meijer is directed to join those selected for the camps – likewise his sister Elisabeth and his brothers, Nathan and Leendert. Their elder sister, Esther, climbs into a lorry; her son Joseph goes with her, as does the third sister, Saartje. Bram, Max, Meijer, Jetty and Sini must go to the right. Meijer's wife, Aaltje, is directed to a lorry, and her children, Saartje and Leendert, go with her.

V.

Leen leaves his home on Paviljoensgracht for the last time on 18 August 1942. He has taken a decision – one which he'd tried to postpone for as long as possible, but that he, his wife and children must now act on. Resistance fighter Zandbergen has warned Leen that the Germans are on the look-out for him, and he must go into hiding.

Earlier that day, Selli had said her goodbyes to her sister Elisabeth and brother Jozef, who had already received their registered letters. They have to report that very same day for transport to Westerbork 'for personal vetting and health assessment' and thus to be verified suitable or otherwise for a 'job-creation scheme in Germany'. Selli's parents, David and Geertruida, have been allowed to remain at their home in Bierstraat.

The first transports to start leaving The Hague have made Leen and Selli fearful. Should they go into hiding? The question is an academic one for most of the people in the Neighbourhood, who have neither the financial means nor the connections. But Leen and Selli have decided to take the risk. They walk with their boys along Heilige Geesthofje, Spinozastraat and Paviljoensbrug to 7 Gortmolen on the other side of Zuidwal. From 19 August onwards, this is where they will be living – in the utmost secrecy – at the home of Mr D. de Wolff.

In the middle of the night of 9 October 1942, Leen's parents and thirty-two-year-old sister Sipora are picked up from their emergency home on Smeetslandschedijk. They are relieved of their keys, with police promises that their furniture and other possessions will be properly looked after.

Josua, Saartje and Sipora take the tram to Warehouse 24, where there are fifteen hundred other people standing around, sitting down or lying on the floor. Almost all of these travellers are between sixty and sixty-five years old: the Jewish Old People's Home on Claes de Vrieselaan has been part-emptied. Jewish Rotterdammers aged well over eighty are brought to the assembly point in carts or on stretchers.

Leen's father, Josua Jakob, is sixty-nine, while Saartje is three years younger. They've heard nothing more from Bram, Jetty, Sini, Max and Meijer since 31 July. Their daughter Roosje is still living in Rotterdam: like her husband, Simon, she is still exempt from deportation. Josua, Saartje and Sipora get into the train for Westerbork. The transit camp is bursting at the seams: on 1 October, 42 Dutch work camps were evacuated, which meant 5,242 young men travelling to Westerbork or to the concentration camp at Vught, and thousands of Amsterdam Jews were picked up in raids. It was hardly possible to register all of these newcomers, never mind find a bed for them.

Josua, Saartje and Sipora endure three days there. Saartje's sister Sientje is also at the camp. The lights to their barrack block come on very early in the morning on Monday 12 October and a man armed with a transport list cries out: 'Blom-Grootkerk, Sientje; Sanders, Josua; Sanders-Grootkerk, Saartje; Sanders, Sipora.'

A few hours later they are standing with 1,708 others on Westerbork's Boulevard of Misery; the new German camp commandant, Albert Konrad Gemmeker, tells them that none of those departing need worry. Next, they find themselves having to walk the five kilometres to Hooghalen Station, where sergeant De Jong, an Amsterdammer and head of the Marechaussee (Dutch military police), is waiting for them alongside a train with twenty-one wagons. They need to load up faster, so De Jong beats and shoves people on to the train.

The train passes through Beilen, Winschoten and Nieuweschans to reach Bremen. SS men bring a piece of bread, a bit of sausage and a pack of margarine – one hundred people are expected to share this fairly with one another – and there are red cabbages inside one of the last wagons. The migrants get nothing, while the SS men give the bread to their countrymen at rest stops. The train makes frequent stops en route, and Germans on the platform sometimes make throat-slitting gestures with their index fingers.

The small Sanders family group travels via Berlin, Breslau, Cosel and Kattowitz to arrive at Auschwitz on the morning of Thursday 15 October. Birkenau concentration camp is in the distance; it is dark, misty and cold. Anyone lingering is forcibly removed from the train. Men in striped uniforms want everything to be done '*Schneller! Schneller! Schneller!*' They yell: 'Get out! Leave everything behind!' Young men receive the order to carry the elderly from the Old People's Home to the lorries and SS men threaten to set their dogs loose. Josua, Saartje, Sipora and Sientje are too old to work. They must go to the left, and are taken in lorries to Auschwitz-Birkenau.

VI.

On 10 December 1942, Leen, Selli and their sons are still living at Mr De Wolff's home when the doorbell rings: SiPo officers. The Jews-in-hiding have been betrayed and are arrested; David and Jopie, in tears, cling to their father's leg. The policemen grab the children. A family member subsequently relates how Leen defended himself with left hooks and punches.

Policemen bring Leen, Selli, Jopie and David from 7 Gortmolen to the *Polizeigefängnis* (Police Detention Centre) in Scheveningen. They are driven past houses with tall hedges bordering spacious gardens and turn left at Van Alkemadelaan, stopping at a redbrick building with high walls, barbed wire and small cells. The family walks to the corner of a road, a guard calls out '*Vier Häftlinge!*' (Four detainees!) and the door opens. The detainees enter the prison, where soldiers hold them by the arm and lead them along a lengthy corridor to the central hall. They must stand with their faces to the wall; after a protracted wait, they are registered, and have to surrender their belongings in the process. A sergeant leads Leen, Jopie and David down a corridor and into a side passage, the walls and doors plastered in graffiti, such as:

HOE MOEILIJK DE TYD (However tough the times)
HOE ZWAAR OOK DE SCHEIDING (However hard the
    separation)
WE ZIJN WEER EEN DAG (One day we shall be)
DICHTER BY DE BEVRYDING (Closer to our liberation)

and

Orange Will Overcome
God Be With Us

A cast-iron gate is swung open and the sergeant directs them to their cell. The lightbulb goes on and the bolts slam shut. Selli is being taken to another part of the prison; a sign next to her cell reads FRAUENABTEILUNG (Women's Section).

Leen and his sons find themselves in a cell measuring 1.9 by 3.7 metres. The walls have been painted yellow and there are bars in the door's inspection window. An electric light hangs from a few wires. It is cold and draughty, and the sheets are thin and grey. They have to relieve themselves in a bucket with a lid.

In the afternoon they are given a cup of cabbage soup; in the evening a guard slides through the door hatch a few meagre slices of war bread with reconstituted milk. They have to be quick at taking it, or the guard just throws it to the floor.

The Jewish prisoners have to empty their waste buckets once a day. Sometimes they are allowed to sit on a wooden stool – but never for too long. They wash once a day in a tin basin; showering is permitted once every two weeks. 'Aryans' are allowed to shave twice a week, a privilege completely denied to Jews. Talking too loudly can result in floggings;

cells must be kept clean with a dustpan and brush; it is forbidden to sit on beds during the day. Any prisoner caught breaking this rule receives nothing but *kalte Kost* (bread and water).

By now, the Dutch royal family – and its royal House of Orange – has become a symbol around which the Dutch resistance rallies. Many 'Orangist' resistance members are imprisoned in Scheveningen, and thus refer wryly to their temporary residence as 'the Orange Hotel'.

The letter 'U' graces the door to Leen's cell: it means that his case is being *untersucht* (investigated). He has been arrested because of going into hiding; they don't know about the leaflets he's been disseminating, nor about the identity cards he's been stealing; his punishment would be so much the worse if they did. Political prisoners are taken from their cells for interrogation a few times each day. They have to give up names and are beaten for several minutes at a time, or else have their heads pushed under water, known as the 'U-boat technique'. Cell 601 is the death-row cell. Sometimes the door will open, and resistance fighters sing the national anthem as they are taken through the corridors to a van, which drives them to the dunes to receive a bullet to the brain.

Cellmates explain the 'knock code' to Leen: one knock against a wall or door is an A, two are a B, and so on until 26 knocks bring you finally to Z. Your knuckle soon becomes raw from this, so then you move to the next one. British aircraft can be seen through a small window, which can only be a good sign. On some evenings the prisoners hear the sound of a ball striking wood, indicating that the hockey players from Little Switzerland have begun their training session.

*

On Wednesday 16 December a guard calls out that Sanders, Leendert, Sanders, Josua, and Sanders, David are to come with him, and Selli is taken from the women's section. A van then drives them to a train, from which they emerge to find themselves at the Westerbork transit camp. It is night-time when they come into the registration hall. Leen is thirty-four, Selli thirty-two, Jopie ten and David eight. A German Jew types out on a card:

SANDERS, LEENDERT JOSUA
PAVILJOENSGRACHT 11A
GYM INSTRUCTOR
DUTCH
MARRIED TO: SANDERS-PARK, SELLINA
SANDERS, DAVID
SANDERS, JOSUA LEENDERT

Leen hands in his civilian clothes and receives in exchange a pair of red-and-blue overalls with yellow Star of David, a beret, clogs and a white armband marked 'S' for *strafgeval* (criminal case). His back shows his prisoner number, and below his shoulders a red stripe has been stitched on to make him an easier target for the guards to shoot should he attempt to escape. Leen, wife and children are taken to punishment block 67. They live apart from ordinary prisoners, separated by a barbed wire fence, and are given next to nothing to eat; Leen is forced to do hard labour and is under additional surveillance. According to a Rotterdam boxing friend, he was arrested 'owing to his underground activities'. This explains the annotation 'Sch.' on his registration card: an abbreviation for *Schutzhaft* (protective custody) and a sign that he is a political prisoner.

He meets familiar faces, and also becomes acquainted with new ones. He chats with his cousin Sientje Tol-Spreekmeester, whose brother Meijer had been Leen's sparring partner and team member at the National Boxing Club. Despite being in a mixed marriage, Sientje had gone into hiding, only to be betrayed later; SiPo officers had taken her to the Orange Hotel on 8 December that same year. The reason given for her arrest on her detainee's card: Jew.

Rotterdammer Mozes 'Max' Lezer enters Westerbork's prison barracks, accompanied by his wife, Sophie, his parents, Isedoor and Betje, and his uncle, Noach. Leen knows Max and Isedore from when he and Selli were living in Kipstraat; father and son had opened a lamb butcher's shop there. Leen used to get roulades from them and would always have to update them about his next boxing match. Would he be challenging Bep van Klaveren for a third time? The whole of the Netherlands was waiting to see that.

Everyone in punishment block 67 is lucky still to be in Westerbork. Criminal cases are always the first to be sent east, but there have been no new transports since 15 December on account of the *Weihnachtspause* (Christmas break). Nazi soldiers are allowed to spend Christmas Day reunited with their families at home, and the German railways need every train they have to make that possible.

Christmas 1942 in Westerbork. Prominent Germans are arriving from Amsterdam and The Hague and the best musical talents at the transit camp are obliged to sing songs and provide the cabaret. The Christmas tree has been decorated in orderly rows of colourful baubles and the prettiest Jewish girls pass around wine and champagne. SS officers cry out '*Heil Hitler!*' until late in the night, singing *Wir fahren gegen Engeland* (We're sailing to England). They are well fed and toasts are made to final victory.

The transports resume three weeks later. The lists are ready; the first page reads: JEWISH TRANSPORT FROM THE NETHERLANDS — WESTERBORK CAMP. At the top on the right someone has typed: List A – No. 20. Halfway down the page is the word PRISONERS, which means the criminal cases at the Westerbork transit camp. What will happen to them out there in the east? The very worst cannot be ruled out. One of Leen's friends says to him: 'You can expect anything from people: good, but also evil.'

Part IV

All-weights Champion
of Auschwitz

I.

————

The light in punishment block 67 comes on early on the morning of 11 January 1943. A German Jew is holding a list of names; old-timers at the camp call him the 'Angel of Death'. He calls out names in alphabetical order. Some people cry, while others are silent with resignation. After more than a hundred names, he arrives at the letter S.

It is still dark when Leen, Selli, Jopie and David are walking along Westerbork's main thoroughfare to the changing rooms. The SS has designated them an escape risk, so they are monitored by German Jews working in the Camp Police Service. Leen is still wearing a white armband bearing the S for *strafgeval* (criminal case). Ten-year-old Jopie stands a good ten centimetres taller than his eight-year-old little brother; they hand in their red-and-blue overalls, berets and clogs, and in exchange they have their civilian clothes returned to them in a jute sack.

Waiting next to a train with twenty wagons in tow there are 194 other criminal cases; young fathers in knitted caps and gloves cradle babies in their arms, and orthodox women are wearing headscarves.

Snow lies on the ground and people are skating on Drenthe's frozen drainage ditches.

The railway track runs alongside Westerbork's main avenue, where people from the hospital block are carried to the train on stretchers. Jewish porters put bags, suitcases, baskets and cases into the wagons while armed Nazis crack jokes with members of the Camp Police. Often, even the SS will be friendly towards departing prisoners; after all, they do not need to know what awaits them.

Camp Commandant Albert Konrad Gemmeker stands with a whip in hand, a pistol in his holster and the SS logo on his pale green cap; his Alsatian dog lies at his feet. The Jewish *Oberdienstleiter* (Administrative Director) Kurt Schlesinger is cycling alongside the train. He is wearing a black leather overcoat with a yellow star, an army-issue shirt, a green Nazi cap, brown riding breeches and riding boots with steel toecaps. Like the camp commandant, the Jewish leader of the Camp Police Service, Arthur Pisk, is carrying a whip; according to Westerbork prisoner Philip Mechanicus, he looks like a pirate. Gemmeker's mistress, Frau Hassel, is standing next to Pisk. She laughs when transported goods are loaded on to the train heavy-handedly. Crates containing food – sausages, beetroot and turnips – are lifted inside more carefully. A note from transport manager Dr W. Molhuysen reads:

30kg butter for 3 days
250kg sugar
31kg coffee substitute
612.5kg pearl barley
25kg potato flour
120kg jam

62.5kg green peas
1,000 loaves of bread
2,000kg carrots

The doors are bolted. Men, women and children peer through hatches; those left behind call out to friends or family inside: 'Take good care of the baby'; 'Look after yourself, won't you?' Most of the migrants try to stay positive: they are going to Germany to work, either on the land or in a factory; the children will likely be put into hostels. It will not be easy, but you can hardly say it's been good in the Netherlands either lately, and the war can't last much longer. In the words of a popular Westerbork song: 'An optimist's what you need to be, still standing after every round, not letting them go and knock you down.'

Leen, Selli, Jopie and David climb into a wooden wagon high up off the ground at the end of the train. They sit with sixteen others in this enclosed space, with bucket in one corner to relieve themselves in. A guard passes out sheets of paper listing the 'house rules': windows may be opened only if there is absolutely no alternative, and they must never lean outside, never mind throw letters from the window for friends or family.

A *Waggonleiter* (compartment controller) designates the men charged with keeping an eye on the luggage. Five women must comfort crying children; others are given a first-aid kit and a barrel of drinking water, and in emergencies they have to clean. Nazis from the *Grüne Polizei* (*Orpo*: the green-uniformed police force) and Jews from the Camp Police Force quickly board the wagons to confiscate watches, cigarette lighters, fountain pens or jewellery. A steam whistle blows. People down below wave off the train as if its passengers were travelling on holiday to warmer climes.

They stop at Assen. A criminal case has taken Veronal and died; her body is dragged from the wagon by German policemen. At Haren, a man in wagon 13 stands up and declares: 'People, I'm going to jump right now. Do you have any messages to pass on to family?' Prisoners hand him cards and letters with entries such as: 'Don't send post to Westerbork, because I'm not there any more. It's a pity, but what can you do? Byee!'

He rips from his jacket the yellow star and white S-branded armband. The doors open surprisingly fast and out he jumps from the speeding train, whistling to a fellow prisoner who also removes the star from his own jacket. He wants to jump as well, dares not do it at first, then plucks up courage and clambers out of the wagon. Guards sound an alarm and the train comes to a halt. Shots are fired at them. The second man hides behind a wheel, his face turned towards the engine. He waits a few minutes, then gets up and runs.

'Off that transport?' asks a farmer working in a field some distance away. 'So, you've escaped, have you?'

'Yes.'

'Come with me.'

After the train passes the former Dutch border at Nieuweschans, the prisoners see that Bremen is burning, and houses in Hanover lie in ruins. Since the escapes, the guards are now even stricter than before: the train stops time and again, and the wagon doors are opened frequently for repeated headcounts of the prisoners. At night, the train is usually at a standstill. The migrants are given none of the food loaded on board and are allowed nothing to drink either. They try to scrape up snow during stopovers. The train goes through Breslau, Oppeln, Cosel and Kattowitz, passing tall buildings, garden plots and a church. Much of what had once been called Poland consists of meadows, marshland, fields and forest, frozen lakes and streams. The roads in larger towns are crowded with cars, buses, trams, tanks and military vehicles.

Leen, Selli, Jopie and David arrive at the town of Oświęcim/Auschwitz in Upper Silesia on 14 January 1943. They pass by houses with high fences; in some of the gardens there are children's toys scattered about, and it smells of pine trees. The train stops; nobody knows why. It is only after a few hours that the wheels start to turn again until the train comes to another halt next to the 'Jews' ramp', as the Nazis have dubbed the small platform at Auschwitz-Birkenau. Prisoners see SS men in green, insignia-bearing peaked caps and ranked uniforms, pistols in their holsters. Criminal cases quickly pull off their armbands as the doors roll open. '*Raus, raus, raus! Schnell, schnell!*' scream men in striped outfits. All of them have badly shaved bald heads.

It is colder here than at Westerbork, and snow is falling heavily. Mothers hold on tightly to their children, Alsatians bark, luggage is thrown onto the platform; an SS officer tells them it will be brought to the camp later. Photographs and other precious items are taken away.

Leen can see a large redbrick building with a gable roof and a gate tower with a tented roof, and factories behind these. Smoke is issuing from a tall chimney; it smells of burned meat. Behind barbed-wire fencing, prisoners are walking about in ragged striped uniforms, wearing clogs while lugging bricks, wood and building materials to sheds, barracks and storage sites. They are also digging pits and moving earth in wheelbarrows. They look thin and neglected, but all the same, no SS men seem to be in sight. Who knows, perhaps this camp will be all right after all.

The men and women have to stand along either side of the train. Doctors pass down the lines and ask in German: 'Age?', 'Are you healthy?', 'Profession?' They point with a baton or gloved hand. To the right. To the left. Right. Right.

The 43rd transport from Westerbork had carried 750 people. After the selection, 88 men and 101 women were left over. A photographer, an accountant, a bank clerk and an antiques dealer are all too old for hard work and must go to the left. One woman begs her sister to join her line, but the sister replies that she wants to stay with their mother and adds: 'I'll see you soon enough!' A lawyer from the country town of Oude Pekela is directed to the left. Some prisoners lie about their professions – those with the greatest chance of survival are boxers, watchmakers, chemists, locksmiths, dentists, carpenters, electricians, musicians, doctors and tailors.

Right.

Right.

Right.

Right.

An SS officer glances briefly at Leen, who is thirty-four years old and weighs 73 kilograms – standard for a middleweight, thinks Leen. He has broad shoulders and muscled arms. His bag has been labelled: LEENDERT JOSUA SANDERS. BORN 12-06-1908. ROTTERDAM. HOLLAND.

Right.

Leen walks to a row of ostensibly fit men; according to the Nazis they are *arbeitsfähig* (able to work). Thirty-eight-year-old tradesman Jonas Pront is also lucky enough to be allowed to join the line; Asser van Gigch from Rotterdam bids farewell to his teenage son Salomon Joël, another tradesman. Leen's Rotterdam friend Max Lezer is told to go to the right with his wife, Sophie, whereas his father and mother, Isedoor and Betje, must go and join the other line of people and then walk towards the lorries. Raincoat-makers Leo Parreira and Nathan Pels are standing in the same line as Leen, Max, Jonas, pet-shop owner Samuel Blazer and Salomon Joël. Those deemed able to work must go to the main camp at Auschwitz, guarded by Poles and Germans. Almost all women over the age of thirty have to turn to the left. Sellina Park-Sanders is thirty-two. Jopie and David have to go with her. They climb into a cattle truck.

'Every night, I see it still before my eyes,' Leen says later.

II.

It is snowing on 14 January as Leen walks towards the gate to Auschwitz I, with the sign ARBEIT MACHT FREI (Work sets you free) above it. He passes a wooden building with a watchtower and reddish-brown chimneys: this is where the SS keep their records and assault prisoners who are not in line during the roll-call. Musicians in striped uniforms are playing marching tunes. Avenues divide neat rows of redbrick prison blocks, and prisoners sweep snow from the pavements. 'It could have been a model village: a camp of thousands of workers engaged in some great and useful endeavour,' writes a survivor later.

Signboards bear a skull symbol and the words HALT! and STÓJ! (the Polish equivalent); writing on the walls reads: THE JEWS ARE OUR MISFORTUNE. The newcomers are kept in the gunsights of men manning the watchtowers. Surrounding the site there is fencing three metres high with electrical wiring and white warning signs: CAUTION. HIGH VOLTAGE. DANGER TO LIFE! Prisoners who occasionally run towards these fences are shot dead by guards, or electrocuted, which the Nazis record as 'suicide by electric fence'.

Leen and the others have to wait in front of Block 24 of the *Politische*

Abteilung (Political Department), also known as 'Camp Gestapo' on account of the Nazi secret service agents who work there. Compatriots in striped uniforms whisper advice and warnings, asking after people they know. German nationals and Poles ask Leen, Jonas, Max, Leo, Salomon Joël and the other newcomers whether they still have with them any wedding rings, gold crowns from teeth, jewellery, watches, cigarettes or food. These items will be kept in Block 27, which is called 'Canada', a country that symbolizes wealth; they will get their clothes and possessions back if they are released from the camp.

There are many SS men in front of Block 24. They look healthy, their haircuts are sharp and they wear fur coats and fur hats, frequently yelling out 'Move it! Move it!' or 'Keep your trap shut!' They are even more dangerous than usual because of the escape, a few hours before, of three Poles. The SS leave the day-to-day management of the camp to Polish, Ukrainian and German prisoners known as kapos (prisoner functionaries), whose tailor-made striped linen clothing has been recently laundered and ironed. They wear black caps and polished boots and they, too, are well fed; a newcomer describes them as 'moon-faced'. The red armband on their left side gives their camp number. Camp Commandant Rudolf Höss says that ten kapos guarding his camp are more effective than a hundred SS men.

There are beatings with rifles. The newcomers turn right and pass the prison kitchen, the roll-call square and gallows. They walk to the other side of the camp and stop at the Canada warehouse: Block 27. 'Strip!' shout the SS men. 'Quick, quick, quick, Jew filth!' The newcomers may keep only their belts and handkerchiefs, while the rest must be placed on the ground. Leen takes off his jacket, trousers and socks and shrugs off his sweater. It is thirty degrees below freezing and a strong wind is blowing; the street is now littered with pullovers, waistcoats and shirts alongside trousers, socks, vests and underpants. Kapos put the clothes into carts and wheel them away.

The prisoners are kept standing naked outside for hours. They do gymnastics to keep themselves as warm as they can. Kapos beat them every now and then, while SS men threaten to set their guard dogs loose. They have to run to yet another spot, where they receive a piece of paper with figures on it. A Dutchman scores the number 86763 into the left arm of Amsterdammer Jonas Pront. Leen is standing right behind him and subsequently becomes 86764. A triangle is tattooed under their camp number, a form of branding to show that they are Jewish. They must learn their number by heart in German and forget their former names – any mistakes will mean dropping their trousers and receiving twenty-five *am Arsch* (twenty-five strokes of a bullwhip or heavy stick 'to the arse').

Leen and the others are herded to another block. As Jonas Pront recalls in 1946, they then step into a hot bath and have to get out again without drying off. Notices on a wall read: UNCLEANLINESS IS THE BASIS OF DISEASE; CLEANLINESS IS THE PATH TO HEALTH; KEEP YOURSELF CLEAN. They are disinfected with some kind of liquid and are then walked at high speed to the Clothing Room, where there are large piles of well-used clothes. The striped uniforms fit badly, the trousers sag, underwear is heavily stained and full of holes, and the clogs are either too big or too small.

'Quick! Quick! Faster!' And off to yet another block. Seated behind tables there are Polish, Dutch and German *Schreibers* (clerks) waiting to register the newcomers. They ask questions and type out the replies on a *Häftlinge-Personal-Karte* (Prisoner Personnel Card). A *Schreiber* notes down that Leen has brown eyes, brown hair and a cauliflower ear; his parents are called Josua Jakob and Saartje, he is married to Sellina Park, he is designated 'stateless' and his race is Jewish. A block barber removes armpit and pubic hair. According to one prisoner, 'the Russians and Poles are nice enough to tear your hair out, especially from the nether regions'. Stubble or the hair on their heads is removed with clippers.

An SS man looks at Leen's left ear.

'Boxer?'

Leen nods.

'Good.'

Leen, Jonas and the others are led to Block 8, where they have to stay in quarantine to determine whether they are carrying any diseases. Inside there are bunkbeds comprising wooden planks with straw mattresses on top and a small sheet; the cold seeps through the nooks and crannies. The smell is one of sweat, open wounds, delousing lotion and the skin ointment Ichthyol. Filthy toilet bowls are in continual use all day long – diarrhoea is a common entry in prisoner medical records, and a *Scheissmeister* (Shit Foreman) has to clean the latrine daily. The notice on the toilet wall reads VERHALTE DICH RUHIG (Keep Calm).

The block leader gives a welcome speech. He is wearing a striped linen outfit, a black cap and steel-toecap boots; his face is a good deal less emaciated than those of the slaves working outside the main camp. He explains to the newcomers that they are in *Stammlager Auschwitz* (Auschwitz Main Camp): a concentration camp, he emphasizes, and they should never forget that. They will never be able to relax for a moment; it is not a sanatorium. Every breach of the rules is punished with five, ten or more floggings, or will mean standing naked outside in the freezing cold. They will not get any breakfast and there are no maids to make their beds for them. They must work and follow all orders; if they do not, they will be punished, and anyone committing sabotage will be hanged from the gallows on the roll-call square in the presence of all the others.

The newcomers must keep scrupulously clean and watch out for lice. Anyone with lice will be sent to the gas chamber: it is a serious violation. They should keep well in mind that they are filthy swine and not make any attempts at escape; it is pointless, as nobody has ever escaped from a concentration camp; the Poles from this morning will soon be found and killed. The only way out for a prisoner here is through the *Kamine* (the chimney). In any case, within six weeks they will all be *Muselmänner* ('Musselmen' or 'Muslims'): prisoners so weakened and apathetic as to be of no further use to the Nazis. Such walking corpses are sent as quickly as possible up the chimney. On average, most prisoners here stick it out for three weeks. Prisoners assigned to work outside are typically engaged in hard labour, ending in death by exhaustion, or by being singled out for the gas chamber or a bullet to the head. Such work details are described sarcastically by Auschwitz inmates as the *Himmelfahrtskommando* (Suicide Squad); at times, the SS describe them literally as such. Prisoners must always answer *'Jawohl!'* when an SS man barks an order at them, and they must never ask questions or contradict. It is forbidden to stuff jackets with straw or paper when working in frosty weather. Prisoners must remain stripped to the waist when washing, and must wash their feet carefully in the evening. Splashes of paint may remain on their prison uniforms, but mud must be removed; nails must be kept to an acceptable length using their teeth. All prisoners who encounter an SS man must remove their cap and tap it against their thigh. Just as important: *Bettenbauen* (bed-making): they may take no more than five minutes to make the bed and must fold the sheet in the correct manner. This is checked by the *Stubendienst* (room-detail functionary: one of the block leader's assistants).

Leen sews his number and a star onto his blue-and-white striped uniform. The lights go out at nine o'clock, and the quarantine block's newcomers sleep two or three to a bed. They nestle closely together; the meagre sheets are threadbare. Leen, Jonas and the others are woken at half past four and are given water with a hint of tea or coffee flavour. The prisoners must assemble at the kitchen building for the morning roll-call. It is twenty-five degrees below zero and SS men with guard dogs are circling the newcomers. Sometimes bets are placed; Nazis like to guess which of the Jewish legs on show will be mutilated first by their dogs.

The prisoners marshal themselves in rows of ten in front of the kitchen at Blocks 16 and 17. On warmer days, this is the spot where the boxing ring is erected. The *Rapportführer* (Reporting Officer) calls out: 'In rows! Faster! Faster! Move on!' Oswald Kaduk has big ears, black hair and well-polished boots that can land a hefty kick; his uniform bears a prominent swastika. One prisoner describes Kaduk as 'an ordinary, normal fellow who had provided his colleagues with a detailed explanation of how they could torment, bully, harass and degrade the prisoners even more than they already did'. Kaduk is always present if Jews or Poles are being tortured to death, and grins when acting as executioner.

The headcount is lengthy but calm. Once, following a previous escape attempt, the roll-call had lasted twelve hours. Sick newcomers' teeth are chattering, their eyes are bloodshot and they are near to collapse. SS men come up to Kaduk to report the number of prisoners in attendance, and the *Rapportführer* screams out: 'Caps on! Work details fall in!' Dead prisoners are placed neatly in between the living; the headcount must tally. Only afterwards are they dragged off to the morgue basement in Block 28.

The slaves in the details working outside the camp walk towards the gate marked ARBEIT MACHT FREI. Kapos screech: 'Get a move on! Look sharp!', 'Faster! Faster!' The road that passes in front of the kitchen and Block 24 is called the 'Dalli-Dalli-Allee' (Look-sharp Avenue) and also 'Blood Street' because of the number of people killed there. The musicians in the Auschwitz I Orchestra play 'Alte Kameraden', a march about friendship, the only thing that counts. The prisoners file out of the camp and have to sing along while Polish and German kapos yell at them: *'Los, los, alles schnell, raus, raus, dalli, dalli!'*

Leen is permitted to return to his block. Prisoners have contracted fevers or lung infections from waiting in the snow; feet have become swollen; frostbitten toes have to be cut off by a camp doctor. Leen is examined for scabies, dysentery and typhus. Being sick is dangerous; SS men will frequently enter the block to make selections, also known as 'gas commissions': *Muselmänner* near death are loaded into lorries and driven to Auschwitz II-Birkenau.

The newcomers sweep the block and check themselves for lice. A notice on the wall warns: ONE LOUSE – YOUR DEATH. In the afternoon they are given a small bowl of cabbage or beetroot soup, or some potatoes. In the evening, officially, 300 grams of bread; in reality it's usually less than that. This has to sustain them for twenty-four hours. According to the rules, the camp authorities must serve a piece of meat four times a week, but that never happens. In the afternoon, Leen, Jonas, Max, Samuel and the other newcomers take some air in front of Block 8. As far as possible, their talk avoids parents, siblings, wives and children; one Dutch *Schreiber* went mad in two days because of dwelling excessively on his wife.

The work details return in the dark to the *Stammlager* and headcounts are taken again. *Rapportführer* Kaduk barks whether caps must be on or off: he is not bothered about how long the roll-call takes, as long as it's correct. Kaduk is usually drunk by the time of evening roll-call; he kicks and beats in a haze of vodka and whisky. Later, Leen recalled how the *Rapportführer* would laugh after an assault, clearly showing his pleasure. At Kaduk's Auschwitz trial in 1963, Leen declared that he had seen this 'with my own eyes'.

After the headcount, Leen returns again to Block 8, where he has to spend two weeks. A few days later, an SS officer shouts at Leen: *'Achtsechssiebensechsvier, antreten!'* (8-6-7-6-4, fall in!) Leen assumes he is about to be murdered, but the opposite proves to be the case. The SS officer tells him that he had recognized Leen as 'Len from Tulipland' once he'd been clipped and shaved. In the 1920s and '30s, the officer had been a sports journalist; he had seen Leen box in Berlin and admired him. In October 1929 he'd been sitting in the press section at the Spichernsälen when Leen had beaten the many-time European champion 'Ironside' Gustav Eder on points, and fairly easily at that.

'Pity that you're Jewish,' he says, but he promises to arrange a decent work detail for Leen. He intends to tell his superior officer who Leen is, as well as why, for now, he must be kept alive. Boxing matches are often held on free Sunday afternoons at the Old Laundry or, in warmer weather, in a ring on the square used for roll-call. And, who knows, perhaps 86764 can even make his comeback as a boxer at the camp.

Leen returns to the quarantine block to scrub the floor and make the bed. In the afternoon he is allowed to go outside for some air and to talk to friends and acquaintances.

One week after his arrival, he hears that Selli and the boys have been gassed.

III.

Leen is washing and cleaning swastika-encrusted Nazi uniforms, trousers, shirts and underwear, as well as caps bearing the letters SS. The former German journalist had kept his word, and Leen is now allowed to work in the New Laundry Work Detail. He's surrounded by dozens of machines, and there is a disinfection and shower room; it all generates a lot of heat. Working alongside German criminals and Polish resistance fighters, he is one of the few Jews to be included at the SS laundry, where he has to take orders from *Unterscharführer* (Corporal) Clauss Otto.

After the morning roll-call, Leen is sent to a large, low barrack block on the other side of the camp. Prisoners can peer out through its tiny windows onto the Birkenallee, where there are birch trees, watchtowers, electrified fences and the omnipresent signs with their skull symbols and warnings. On free Sundays in summer, the prisoners stroll along Birkenallee as if going to the opera; they sit on narrow benches or lie on the grass. A Dutch prisoner refers to the avenue behind the SS laundry as 'the prisoners' Sunday promenade'.

Every week the New Laundry washes four to five thousand items of clothing. Prisoners hang up uniforms to dry from wooden beams, sheets are folded, army green caps are neatly steamed and underpants cast into boiling water as if they were potatoes. The least favoured prisoners in the work detail push trolleys outside the camp to pick up basketloads of soiled linen. Work in the New Laundry Detail is hard going, but it could be worse; one camp inmate felt it was 'a slightly more favourable position'. Leen receives the consent of Auschwitz Commandant Höss to fetch a cushion, two extra sheets and an extra pair of underpants for himself from the Canada warehouse.

Lice are found crawling in SS underwear; sometimes they jump out onto the prisoners in the laundry. Consequently, at the end of each working day, Leen and the others have to change into clean underwear at the laundry so they don't carry any lice back with them to their block. Other advantages of the New Laundry Work Detail: after the morning roll-call, no. 86764 does not have to leave the camp to dig for coal in a dark mine or build a factory in an external camp at twenty-five degrees below freezing. It is warm and dry in the block and it is relatively easy to 'organize' something there – the camp's euphemism for stealing. Socks, shirts and pullovers are smuggled out under striped uniforms: shirts can be exchanged for butter, freshly washed underpants for cigarettes, a clean, neat uniform for a sausage from the SS abattoir. A second Dutchman in the laundry detail revealed that he, Leen and the others 'always [sought out] the very best items'.

One of Leen's female friends noted the 'great danger' that such 'organization' entailed, 'because this was, of course, a punishable offence from the perspective of the SS'. Organizers would get at least twenty-five *am Arsch* with either a whip or stick – often tearing pieces of flesh from victims in the process – but a thief could also be sentenced to death in the building opposite the laundry: Death Block II, also known as 'the Bunker', where twenty-eight punishment cells had been built into the basement. Cells 8 to 20 had no window, while in Cell 22 at the back of Block II, prisoners could only stand. Usually, four convicted individuals would be squeezed into each of these tiny spaces; dead prisoners would be left standing limply with the living, as there was no room for them to fall to the floor.

Leen sees prisoners entering the Bunker almost daily; he can hear shrieking, singing and gunshots. Prisoners sentenced to death have to undress in the laundry room, and from there are led to the Bunker's courtyard, where SS officers take them to a mobile gallows or place them up against the infamous 'Black Wall', nicknamed by Leen 'the Wall of Death'. Their bodies are then dragged away and carted off out of the camp. A trail of blood is frequently to be seen on the road in front of the New Laundry.

Leen can engage in sports activities on free Sundays. Prisoners of every nationality move pawns, bishops, queens or draughts pieces in their prisoner blocks. Wrestling is permitted under strict conditions and, on warmer days, athletics, football and basketball matches are held; training can be done in a room in Block 7, which is fitted out with weights and other sports or gymnasium equipment. Jews are not welcome there. Most of the camp's German boxers sport a green triangle on their striped uniform to indicate criminality; their crimes include theft, smuggling, pickpocketing and murder, and the Nazi term for them is *Berufsverbrecher* (professional criminals).

There are two types of sport at the camp: the sort that serves as punishment, and the sort that is for pleasure. *Sport machen* (exercise) is punishment: the SS version of gymnastics. For an hour or more, prisoners have to leapfrog and do press-ups or push each other like wheelbarrows through the icy cold. SS men yell out instructions such as 'Squat! Lie down! Squat! Stand up!' Their laughter is uncontained when people drop dead.

Sport is often at a high level; dozens of professional athletes have been imprisoned at Auschwitz I, II and III, as well as in the external camps. The wrestler and many-time Polish champion, Lucjan Sobieraj, is nine years younger than Leen and 15 centimetres taller. After the occupation, he began smuggling firearms, was arrested and arrived in the camp on the fourth transport from Kraków. Sobieraj had weighed 87 kilograms, which was a requirement in his field of sport – at Auschwitz, he lost 30 kilograms in the space of a year. Sobieraj felt his condition had deteriorated when, in 1940, he wrestled for the first time against a kapo in a camp contest held in Block 24. Poles and German nationals had taken the sheets off their beds and placed them on the floor to create a mat. Sobieraj's kapo opponent then undressed: he was muscled, lean and 90 kilograms. This man had been classed a professional criminal in Germany; he had stabbed a man in the neck for staring at him a little too inquisitively. Moreover, this German adversary had tortured Sobieraj several times in the camp, and the idea that Sobieraj might beat him seemed impossible, although he knew that victory would mean getting extra bread and soup. It was that thought that 'gave me strength', said Sobieraj later.

The kapo was disgusted by the badly emaciated Polish prisoner. Sobieraj had pustules on his body and red marks from bedbugs, which is why the murderer ordered Sobieraj to put his shirt back on again. However, the kapo did shake Sobieraj's hand before they started and said they could fight as equals. In his memoirs, Sobieraj wrote: 'I'm fighting against someone who has assaulted and beaten me, and today he shakes my hand and fights me with a mocking smile on his face.

He is stronger than me, but I'm fighting for bread and life, or else the crematorium.'

Sobieraj tried a hip toss, but was too weak. He was wheezing after only thirty seconds or so, continually trying to catch his breath. He knew that with things as they were he wouldn't be able to last the course for long and so, after a few minutes and with full force, he grabbed the kapo by the shirt. The shoulder throw was a success and 'the murderer fell on the floor'. Sobieraj hadn't had the strength to stand up but, nevertheless, he'd won his first contest: 'I was weak and sweating, my head was spinning and the fight had lasted only two minutes. [. . .] I was so dazed and half under that I had no clue about what was going on around me. I didn't take it in at all. It was only once I saw the soup and the bread in the hands of the kapo coming towards me that I realized I had won.'

This took place in January 1941, and Polish historians cite it as the first sporting event at Auschwitz I.

After Sobieraj's victory, the Nazis recognized how sport at the camp might also have its benefits; it provided a diversion on a free Sunday, and it would probably make prisoners less likely to riot out of either rage or boredom. Polish architect and prisoner Eugeniusz Nosal was ordered by the Nazis to lay out a football pitch; he also had a boxing ring made, which, on free Sundays, was placed between Blocks 5 and 6 and Blocks 16 and 17, immediately opposite the kitchen building and the roll-call square. At first the fights were between German nationals, but it was more of a spectacle when a greater element of risk was at play. One afternoon in 1941, SS men and kapos went round the blocks to recruit Polish boxers. The most important requirements were, first, that they had to have fought to a professional standard before the war; and secondly, that they must not be Jewish. The latter eventuality might mean Jews beating Aryans, which would be *Rassenschande* (racial defilement). That rule later came to be amended when it was decided that a Jew fighting against an Aryan could provide blockbuster entertainment.

A boxing contest was held at the kitchen building. Prisoners slid the gallows aside and set out chairs for the SS and kapos. Winners received additional food; losers were not shot. A Polish observer recalled later: 'When I look back on that scene which I saw at first hand from the very front row, I realize that not a single person is going to believe it.' Camp Commandant Höss gave permission for more matches, but they had to be of a high standard. Unexpected visitors might attend at some point, such as Himmler, Goebbels or even Hitler, and that would necessitate entertainment at the highest level.

Polish prisoner Stanisław Frączysty from Chochołów wrote: 'Nearly every Sunday, fights lasting three rounds, and in various weight divisions, were held there under the gaze of referees in a temporary ring usually placed in front of the kitchen. There were quite a few pretty decent boxers in the camp and the fights were attended by all the prominent figures there.' In the words of a former camp boxer: '[W]e fought until one of the two couldn't go on any longer or until the Nazis had had enough of it. They never left before some blood had been spilled.' Nobody knew for certain what might await them following an inglorious defeat; rumours went around about gassing. The best Polish boxer in the camp called the matches *walk gladiatorów* (gladiator fights) and, after the war, he wrote about the most important spectators at these matches: 'Sometimes they would look the athletes over and then you had to watch out that there was no "thumbs down" from this *Übermensch* (superman) by the finish.' Another boxer said that 'the losers had been severely weakened and weaklings were killed'. A Jewish Greek boxer admitted to shaking before his first camp fight, but he did add that 'a boxer couldn't have any compassion and if I hadn't won I wouldn't have survived'.

Boxing was done with bare hands, with mittens stuffed with horsehair, or with the winter gloves worn by the SS. In the event of rain, snow or freezing weather, the Nazis would relocate the boxing ring to a warehouse, bathhouse, barrack block, the camp canteen or the Old Laundry. Most matches were held in the afternoon, but on warm days the camp gladiators would also fight at dusk. The ring was then lit by the electrified fence spotlights, with SS men in watchtowers pointing their firearms at the prisoners, in case they used the event as an opportunity for escape. According to the former boxer and prisoner Kazimierz Albin, it was the fights between Poles and Germans that generated especially 'heightened emotions'. The feared head of the Political Department in Block 24 saw the renewed strength and hope that Poles drew from each defeat of a German opponent, and for that reason, he banned all forms of sport for entertainment in the autumn of 1941.

After only a few months of this break from sports, the camp authorities received a request to resume boxing; the SS were getting bored on their Sunday afternoons. In fact, the head of the Political Department was also missing *Deutsche Faustkampf*. So it was that, from the spring of 1942 onwards, boxing matches were reinstated in the roll-call area facing the kitchen, and Poles fought against Germans, Russians and Ukrainians in boxing tournaments dubbed 'the Olympic Games'.

Boxers were respected at the camp. SS officers would approach

any strong-looking men arriving off a transport: 'Healthy? Boxer?'
On one occasion, an officer had gone inside a block to call out that
he needed 'a strapping Jew', and no. 48307, Aron 'Arie' Pach from
Amsterdam, had stood up to tell the officer who he was. Leen knew
Arie from boxing events in the Netherlands, where he'd won matches
and championships for Maccabi Amsterdam as a light heavyweight.
All of the Dutch at Auschwitz I, II and III knew that following the
occupation, Arie had expelled two German policemen from his house
in Amsterdam using left and right hooks; he'd flattened another two
on the street before being sent to Auschwitz in mid-July 1942.

He had to go to the satellite camp of Jawischowitz, where he was
given kid gloves and pitted against a kapo in a trial bout. Arie bloodied
the kapo's nose and became the pet project of an SS officer; he was
given sports shoes, always won, and one Sunday afternoon had to
fight against an undefeated kapo nicknamed 'Bobby the Boxer'. Arie
recalled how, before the match, the officer who had allowed him
to box had turned to him and said: 'If you lose you're going to the
crematorium.'

Bobby the Boxer and Arie Pach shook hands; armed guards stood
around the ring. The *Lagerführer* (Camp Leader) made a throat-cutting
gesture and Arie punched Bobby the Boxer to the ground as if he had
been a German police officer. The SS men would not credit that this
Jew could be so much stronger than a German Aryan, and inspected
his gloves to check whether Arie had slipped in a horseshoe.

Boxing mania reached its apogee in the spring of 1942. Increasing
numbers of spectators were attending the camp tournaments where, as
well as food, the victors were also able to get better jobs for themselves.
The Italian prisoner Primo Levi wrote about an encounter he had had
with a German professional criminal on his first day in Auschwitz.

That man had told him 'unbelievable, insane things', such as how music concerts were being held at the camp on Sundays, as well as boxing and football matches. The criminal added that the very best boxers enjoyed such high status that they could even become camp chef, perhaps the very best job that a prisoner could get.

SS officers' wives would attend major tournaments, coming from as far afield as Cologne, Kleef (Kleve), Wiesbaden, Augsburg or Berlin. Matches were discussed in detail while marching to and from work; boxers took on the status of camp idols. Every Pole knew the story of Dobrowolski, who had fought every Sunday afternoon against his non-Jewish countrymen or against German nationals. During a roll-call, he lost control and shoved a kapo. The German retaliated, but Dobrowolski brought him down with a right hook, and other kapos punched Dobrowolski until his body was black and blue. He just survived, but was locked up in the Bunker, where he underwent daily torture. Even so, he clung to the will to stay alive, and SS men would visit the Bunker to see this miracle for themselves, leering at him while keeping a safe distance, and throwing bread and cigarettes his way. One day Dobrowolski performed a new heroic act which was still being talked about in 1943: he gave a series of head-butts to the kapos who had been his most frequent torturers in the Bunker, following them up with left- and right-swing hooks, after which he tried to escape. The SS tracked him down, and Dobrowolski was put up against the Black Wall in the Bunker's courtyard; he sang a patriotic Polish song and seemed to be laughing as he was shot.

A Polish boxer in the camp, blond and blue-eyed, often looks out of his block's window to size up the new arrivals as they come into the main camp. He is Kazimierz Szelest and comes from Kraków; the Poles in Auschwitz call him 'Kazik', 'Kaziu' or 'Kazio'. Female members of the SS think he looks like the American actor John Wayne.

On 14 January 1943, Kazik had seen a broad-shouldered but short Dutchman with a cauliflower ear walk through the ARBEIT MACHT FREI gate. Most of the men from the Westerbork transport were emaciated, but this prisoner had a strong, fit look about him. Kazik was not surprised to learn that Leen Sanders had beaten Gustav Eder as a professional boxer in Berlin, and had fought for the European title in 1935; this would mean that this Dutch Jew newcomer could well be the best boxer in Auschwitz I, II and III. Two weeks after Leen's arrival, Kazik approaches him.

'Are you Len Sanders?'

Leen nods.

'Come tonight to kitchen. I have proposition.'

After evening roll-call, Leen walks via Dalli-Dalli-Allee to the *Häftlingsküche* (the prisoners' kitchen), where Kazik is the kitchen storeroom kapo. His status affords him freedom in the camp and he asks Leen whether he would teach him the 'noble art of self-defence'. He is already boxing in Sunday afternoon contests, but he needs to raise his game. With Leen as his trainer, adviser and sparring partner he might have a chance at winning the title 'All-weights Champion of Auschwitz'. In compensation, Leen can be given extra bread, margarine and soup. He treats the newcomer to some sausage to prove that Leen can eat what he wants in future, so long as he becomes Kazik's boxing coach. Leen takes up the offer and at once is allowed to move to a block for prisoners with privileged positions. As Leen said later, 'You wouldn't normally be sent straight to the gas chamber from there.'

IV.

No. 86764 is standing in the kitchen storeroom amid great kettles of soup. He attacks, ducks away, protects his face. His Polish pupil, Kazimierz 'Kazik' Szelest, is fruitlessly trying to break through Leen's double defence. He's a good boxer with much longer arms, but he never touches Leen. Until January 1943, Kazik had not known about the hermetically closed defence technique for which Leen had become famed in the Netherlands, Great Britain, France, Belgium and Germany.

Kazik makes fast progress thanks to Leen's tutoring. They spar for up to ten rounds in the storeroom, where he learns about the 'shell'. Leen is pleased with him: he sees how Kazik can take a lot of punishment, and how increasingly successful he is at being able to emerge from a closed defence when choosing his own time to go on the offensive, just as Leen always did in the past. Kazik tells Leen that boxing at the camp comes with a couple of distinct advantages attached: you can get additional food as a result, and it's the only way in which you can safely 'retaliate against the German kapos who beat us every day'.

Shelves are lined with loaves of bread, bags of sugar and salt, heaps of sausages, jars of jam and packs of margarine; there are barrels full of turnips and beetroot. Men from the *Kartoffelkommando* (potato detail) are sitting side by side, peeling potatoes that they place in large baskets. SS men bark orders into the kitchen storeroom that work must be done '*Schneller! Schneller!*' as the weakest prisoners scrub the floor, sometimes casting surreptitious glances at the boxers. Leen fights in clogs, referred to by the Poles as 'Dutch shoes': not ideal for boxing.

Parked on the road outside the kitchen and at the entrance gate there are cars, lorries and barrows waiting to transport potatoes, turnips, soup, coffee and tea to the blocks or to external camps. Prisoners haul barrels, crates and baskets. Bowls and kettles arrive back in the afternoon and late evening; kitchen staff scrape the last remnants of food from the bottom. Tongues scan bowls in a quest for crumbs of bread or droplets of jam.

Many boxers and other athletes are employed in the kitchen. No. 39551, Henryk Zguda, is Kazik's best friend and, as the chef, is responsible for the soup. Until 1939, Henryk and Kazik used to play sports together in one of Kraków's most beautiful buildings. In 1937, Kazik had come second in the Polish swimming championships; in Henryk's view, Kazik had been better still as a water-polo goalie. Even the best centre-forwards were left stumped what to do when they made a line for Kazik, only to see the goalie seemingly rise up out of the water as if climbing a flight of stairs. Kazik is 1.92 metres tall, weighs over 90 kilograms, has broad shoulders and a perfectly lean physique. Henryk considers him 'one of the strongest men' in Auschwitz; in Leen's view, he has a body perfectly suited to making him one of the camp's best boxers.

As boss of the kitchen storeroom, Chef Henryk had given Kazik a job in the prisoners' kitchen when the man was close to death.

On 30 August 1940, Kazik had been in one of the first transports to arrive at Auschwitz, having been sent from his prison in Kraków following his failed attempt, after the invasion of France, to join the Polish army, resulting in his arrest by the Gestapo. Of the people who had been on his transport there was now virtually nobody else left; most had been tortured and shot in the Bunker.

Since then, Kazik had been using his position to come to others' rescue. In March 1942, nearly one thousand Jewish women arrived at Auschwitz I from the women's camp of Ravensbrück. They were housed in a block behind electrified fencing punctuated by watchtowers every fifty metres. Kazik had approached carrying a basket filled to the brim with boiled potatoes, given a signal to a watchtower guard and then used a rope to hoist the potatoes upwards. 'I don't know how he was able to do this,' Henryk said later, 'but Kazio managed to get things like that arranged.'

Kazik is also making sure that his boxing coach is well looked after; after the war, Leen referred to him as 'my saviour'. 'After hauling the cooking kettles about I could fetch extra soup from the kitchen and I got extra bread. It was up to me to transport it by myself, and I was able to share it all out. That food meant I was able to save a lot of human lives.'

Leen is yelled awake at half past four each morning, and then works until four or five o'clock in the afternoon at the New Laundry. After evening roll-call, he and Kazik are able to resume training for a while, and they spar with each other almost every day. Leen improves his physical condition by skipping and shadowboxing; Kazik gives him even more bread together with sausage and jam, as well as soup with sauerkraut. Leen feels his strength return as he becomes fitter. 'Two buckets of nasty soup are worth more than gold,' commented one camp boxer.

Both Leen and Kazik keep their ears to the ground to find out what's happening in the camp; who is coming through the gate, and who is going outside? Which SS officers treat the prisoners acceptably, and which ones are the worst sadists? At times prisoners are nailed up at the entrance gates with sign boards stating things like: I RAN AWAY THREE MONTHS AGO, BUT THEY STILL TRACKED ME DOWN. Every few days lorries come into the camp to pick up *Muselmänner* and the gravely ill; *Rapportführer* Kaduk is always present when loading up these men in response to a gas commission; Leen sees him laughing, shoving and beating. SS Sergeant Scheffler steals sausage, bread and margarine from the kitchen storeroom nearly every day, loading it into carts and transporting it along Dalli-Dalli-Allee to the SS kitchen.

SS officer Karl Egersdörfer is in charge of the prisoners' kitchen. He has a puffy face, sagging red cheeks and moles to the right of his nose. The Polish prisoners at the kitchen call him *Wujkiem* Karl (Uncle Karl). For strategic reasons, Leen and Kazik get along well with Uncle Karl, but they always have to be on their guard, particularly when he comes in accompanied by kapo Franciszek Nierychło, a Pole from Łódź, usually called 'Franz' owing to his love for Nazi Germany. Franz screeches and kicks like an SS officer. 'His specialism was drowning Jews in water tanks,' said Kazik later. During the Christmas of 1941, seven prisoners had broken into the prisoners' kitchen storeroom. They were caught, each receiving a bullet to the head; Franz and Uncle Karl had their bodies placed under the Christmas tree as if they were presents.

In 1942, Egersdörfer appointed Kazik as the kitchen storeroom kapo; in Henryk's opinion this was because of his 'Aryan beauty'. Since then, Uncle Karl has had no idea that Kazik is simultaneously undermining the Nazis at the camp as leader of the Auschwitz underground resistance. They arrange clothing, bread, sausage, sugar, margarine, jam, soup and medicine for the sick in the infirmary, or for the condemned in the Bunker. Moreover, should no. 86764 stroll into the storeroom to steal food, Kazik often turns a blind eye.

It is not uncommon for Egersdörfer to come and watch the training sessions; he is well versed in the sport and can see Leen's level of expertise. For quite some time the best boxer in the camp has been a Polish resistance fighter, no. 77; might Leen be capable of beating him? The whole SS would want to see that match. 'Don't *you* want to be boxing too?' asks Egersdörfer one evening.

Leen is hesitant at first. As a Jew, he knows his death sentence will be carried out sooner or later; the camp system is set up to that end, and any fault can meet with punishment. An SS officer might be angered by the result of a match at the camp; winning could be as hazardous as losing. SS officers *might* want to exact revenge with twenty-five *am Arsch*, but it could just as easily take the form of the Black Wall.

Leen returns to his block and discusses the matter with fellow Dutchmen. His opponent is a camp legend; should he really risk it? His friend Max Lezer says: 'Look, old boy, go ahead and box anyway, because then we can see it too.' Leen considers the benefits: he's already getting extra food, but as a camp boxer he will get still more privileges. At the moment his working day can sometimes stretch out to eleven hours, but boxers are often given free time and almost never have to work outdoors in the bitter cold. Kapos will treat him less badly and it could give him the chance to get compatriots added to his relatively benign New Laundry work detail.

Early in February 1943, Leen tells Karl Egersdörfer that, after a gap of more than two years, he will make his comeback to the ring. After the war, he noted that this decision had also been 'for my own self-preservation'.

V.

The All-weights Champion of Auschwitz strolls along Birkenallee. He is wearing an ironed camp uniform and his head has been neatly shaved; he is fit and muscled. His arm bears the number 77. SS men, kapos and fellow prisoners greet him and make small talk. Tadeusz 'Teddy' Pietrzykowski is the undisputed boxing champion at Auschwitz I: a Carpentier-like legend, the Jack Dempsey of concentration-camp boxing and the Gustav Eder of the main camp. He is nine years Leen's junior, comes from Warsaw and loves literature, drawing and painting. His mother, Sylwina, had been a teacher from a wealthy family; she had taken her son with her to museums, the cinema and the theatre, but never to sports matches. In 1933, Tadeusz appeared in his first boxing contest under a pseudonym because of his mother's loathing of the sport. He decided on 'Teddy' in tribute to the Polish-American world champion Teddy Jarosz. Tadeusz made his breakthrough as a bantamweight at the Warsaw championships of 1937, and boxing experts predicted a golden future for him – unanimously so after he became vice-champion of Poland. Two years previously, Teddy had already created a sensation when he beat Antoni Czortek, the Polish boxer ranked second in Europe.

In 1939, Hitler gave his brutes the order to invade Poland. Teddy had graduated from the Technical University that same year as an architect, afterwards entering the air force. In September 1939 he defended his city of Warsaw as an officer in the Polish army; after Poland's capitulation he joined the resistance. He was arrested in Hungary and Gestapo officers tortured him in prison. Teddy was then put in a fourth-class carriage and, along with 727 others in this first transport from Poland, walked through the gate of the newly built *Konzentrationslager*, Auschwitz, on 14 June 1940.

On the first Sunday of March 1941, he and five other Polish resistance fighters were sitting on a pile of bricks next to the prisoners' kitchen. Teddy's memoirs reveal that their work shift had just finished and they had been 'tasked with looking for lice in our striped uniforms'; they carried out this assignment naked. Noises were issuing from the kitchen building, with raised voices in German: 'Kill him!' A German professional criminal, registered as camp prisoner no. 2, approached the Poles out on the pavement, telling them that he was looking for candidates to fight against the best boxer in the main camp: Walter Düning from Bielefeld.

No. 2, also known as Otto Küssel, looked at the skinny, naked Poles and sighed: 'Listen, we've heard that one of you lot can box.' The sculptor and resistance fighter Bolesław 'Bolek' Kupiec pointed to Teddy, whereupon Küssel asked him whether he fancied earning some bread. Bolek warned him to say no, but Teddy stood up regardless because he just could not get that 'one insistent thought' out of his head: being given bread for fighting. His memoirs describe his decision to box against a much heavier adversary as 'an uncommon, never previously imaginable need to satisfy the irritable feeling of emptiness in the stomach'. Teddy was hungry, his friends in the camp were hungry, and boxing would give him an opportunity 'to procure a higher position in the camp's community'. He was not a doctor, chef and or carpenter; instead, he was an architect, making it next to impossible for him to get a decent work detail. Boxing could radically improve his life at the camp, and it was only in the ring that a few prisoners could get the chance to settle some scores with their kapo tormentors.

No. 77 passed through the wooden door into the kitchen to confirm that, yes, he was indeed a boxer. Kapo Walter Düning took one look at Teddy's body and said in German: 'Pity.' The other kapos in the prisoners' kitchen just laughed at this virtual *Muselmann* from Warsaw: that emaciated Pole would be beaten to death. Moreover, Düning had been the undisputed middleweight boxing champion for Hamburg and district before his arrest. Teddy and Düning sparred for a little while, and the virtual *Muselmann*'s standard proved to be surprisingly high. Düning then turned to fellow kapo Küssel and told him to give Teddy extra food and let him train. A date and place were agreed upon; the winner would be the All-weights Champion of Auschwitz.

The match took place in March 1941 on the roll-call square in front of the kitchen building. Polish prisoners were permitted to watch, but they could not cheer Teddy on or encourage him. Teddy was issued mittens that the external detail workers wore in winter. He filled these with damp rags and walked into the ring with his second, Otto Küssel. The Polish challenger was nervous: losing could mean death.

The referee was Bruno Brodniewicz, who had arrived in Auschwitz in May 1940 along with twenty-nine other professional criminals from Sachsenhausen concentration camp; his left arm bore a tattoo of the number I. No other prisoner was as feared as Brodniewicz, and even the toughest boxers did not dare talk back to him; the Germans called him 'Black Death'. He introduced the camp's boxers as Pole, Warsaw, Algerian, Paris, Poznań, Vienna or Berlin; Teddy was 'Warsaw' and Düning was 'Bielefeld'. Kapo Düning looked at the Polish prisoner and said: 'Never fear, lad.' But Teddy was not in the least fearful; he had nothing to lose apart from, perhaps, his life, but that was not such a terrible thing for him. Dying in the ring would be the perfect death.

Referee Brodniewicz brought the gladiators together. He announced that Warsaw weighed 49 kilograms, while his opponent, Bielefeld, was 22 kilograms heavier. In Teddy's eyewitness statement after the war, he recalled that 'I knew one thing: that I had to win the fight.' Given the weight difference, that appeared virtually impossible. His friends Bolek and Kazik were begging him right up to the very start of the match: 'Don't do it, Teddy; Walter will kill you.'

After the gong died away, Düning stepped towards his opponent. Teddy punched him with left and right jabs to the jaw. Düning's head flew back. The kapo recovered in the break following the first round and was able to continue, but Teddy had scored a clear lead. There was some tentative cheering from his compatriots. It seemed, according to Teddy, that 'to my astonishment, the German prisoners were looking at me with greater warmth'. Düning was quicker and more agile in the second round, but Teddy went on the offensive whenever he could, dishing out uppercuts and stomach punches. Düning expertly blocked Teddy's attacks and the challenger had to 'employ [all of his] technical skills not to take any punches himself'. Teddy was becoming rapidly fatigued and knew he could not stand the pace much longer.

He went for a desperate attack: a hard left punch followed by a series of right jabs and a few swing hooks to Düning's ear.

A German second wanted to throw the towel into the ring, but the Bielefeld kapo wanted to carry on. Teddy tried yet again to end the game in a knockout. By his own account, he caught Düning 'on his nose or lip; in any event, blood appeared under his nose, above his top lip'. The favourite wavered again; Polish prisoners cheered. Teddy moved in on Düning, appearing capable of punching him to the floor; his fellow Poles forgot about having to keep silent and started yelling out: *'Bij go, bij Niemca!'* (Bash him, bash the German!) Several German kapos had learned Polish and the referee also understood it. They proceeded to silence Teddy's fans 'by means of their fists and legs' and stopped thumping and punching only once Teddy 'signalled to his compatriots for silence'.

Bruno 'Black Death' Brodniewicz halted the match and declared Teddy the winner. The Poles tried not to cheer. According to an eyewitness, it had been the most sensational victory at the camp up to that point and served as an 'uplifting boost for the starved Polish prisoners'. Bleeding profusely, Walter Düning took off his gloves to congratulate Teddy: 'Good, lad! Very good! Come with me!' He led Teddy to the first floor of Block 24, where the 'VIPs' lived.

'When did you last eat?'

'Yesterday.'

'Do you want some food?'

Teddy nodded and was given half a loaf of bread and some butter. He broke it into pieces, took it away with him and shared it among his Polish friends. Düning had even more good news; Teddy could start work in an easy-going detail as an animal keeper. According to Teddy, his new life afforded him 'unlimited rations'; he milked cows, always pouring himself full mugs of milk, and could eat beef steaks to recuperate and become stronger. After work, behind the stables, he would do an hour's training for new matches at the camp, and the other Poles in the detail protected him. The horse belonging to Camp Commandant Höss was housed in a separate section of the stables where Teddy worked. Her name was Fulwia, and Teddy would sometimes eat her food, as well as stealing mashed turnip and potatoes from the pig trough. He soon put on weight, and after a year he weighed in at 66 kilograms. He had become once again the boxer he'd been before the war. Expert opinion had it that he actually fought better at Auschwitz than he had done in freedom, and he won admiration from Nazis, making a great impression on them thanks to his style and speed. They dubbed him *Weiss Nebel* (White Mist).

However, there was one occasion when it might all have gone awry. In the summer of 1942, Teddy boxed against a renowned professional boxer and convicted murderer who was 15 kilograms heavier than him, and quite certain of his victory. Teddy brought him down in the second round. After the war, he admitted: 'In all honesty, for the first and final time in my life I was fully aware of taking pleasure in knocking out an opponent.'

Teddy did not know that an SS doctor called Entress had placed a thousand marks on the murderer's victory. Entress seized his arm, muttered 'Come with me', and proceeded to lead Teddy to the infirmary, where he took a syringe, laughed, and said: 'This is your reward for that victory. Multivitamins. It'll give you the strength to box even better.'

Teddy was laid up in bed for a month. He was delirious and on the verge of death. Entress had given him 'Vitamin T': typhus. Rumours circulated about a gas commission; Teddy was sure to be selected.

Kazik and other Polish friends got him out of the typhus block and hid him. After a week he was feeling better, and he recovered so well that he continued to win matches held afterwards at the camp. One Pole said that he gave 'comfort to those who had no hope'.

In the space of two years, Teddy had only drawn once in a boxing match, and that was against a German Jew known as Bully. That aside, he had been hailed the undisputed boxing champion of Auschwitz. He wrote in a letter to his mother, Sylwina:

> Today, I am *Mistrzem wszechwag KL Auschwitz* [All-weights Champion of Auschwitz Concentration Camp] after defeating Janowczyk, Dexponko, etc. Yes, mateńko [mama], for that I have received 10 loaves of bread and 10 blocks of margarine – I gave it away to the poor at Christmas so that the others could also have something. You see, boxing was of use to me, wasn't it? Do you remember what everyone told you? 'Sylwina, what's to become of your son? He won't do all right in life, boxing is brutal.' [. . .] Were they right, mateńko? I'd do all right even in hell.

'Out of the kitchen! Fight!'

Karl Egersdörfer, head of the prisoners' kitchen, is standing in the storeroom and looking on as Kazik spars with Leen, who is no longer wearing clogs, but sports shoes instead – shoes that Egersdörfer has procured for him. Meanwhile, Kazik has been arranging nutritious meals for Leen. Keeping kosher is a thing of the past now for no. 86764, but the Almighty is sure to be merciful.

Leen also spends time during the day preparing as well as he can for his debut as an Auschwitz boxer. His fellow prisoners at the SS laundry spar with him, and when the kapos aren't looking and there are no SS officers around he is able to rest. He has a brief window of time in the afternoons for stretching, breathing and pull-up exercises, as well as push-ups and abdominal crunches. He shadowboxes in the drying loft, with a trusted lookout warning him in the event of an approaching kapo or SS man. Kazik spars with him in the kitchen, and the storeroom head explains to Leen about the things he is allowed to do, as well as the things he must avoid doing at all costs. The ringside Nazis will try provoking him, but he must never react. After the war, a former boxing pupil of Leen's brother Bram summed it up: 'In our boxing ring in Rotterdam the blows came from either side. In Auschwitz it was always one-sided. Anyone daring to defend himself was a dead man.'

Looking from the kitchen window, Leen can see his forthcoming adversary standing every day in front of Block 24, the VIPs' block, where Teddy lives in excellent conditions. Leen calls him 'the officer' on account of Teddy's resistance history, but until his deportation Leen had never heard of Teddy. In February 1943, that now seems almost impossible to imagine. The officer had boxed at Auschwitz I in thirty-nine matches, winning thirty-eight of them. According to Poles and Germans, nobody can defeat the All-weights Champion of Auschwitz; even Max Schmeling and Joe Louis would stand no chance against him, never mind Leen Sanders from Rotterdam, the man who had beaten Gustav Eder, and who was soon to be Tadeusz 'Teddy' Pietrzykowski's fortieth challenger.

His ear has saved his life and now here he stands, just as in the past, inside a boxing ring on a Sunday afternoon. Outside it is twenty-seven degrees below freezing; inside it is stifling. The bunkbeds have been shoved aside at one of the barrack blocks in Auschwitz I; snow is melting from boots, and prisoners quickly mop it up from the floor. The ring is furnished with a stool for each combatant, as well as towels and drinking flasks. A pall of smoke hangs beneath the ceiling, smelling of blood, sweat and ethanol. Outside, beyond the misted-up windows, armed guards stand in their watchtowers.

Obersturmbannführers (lieutenant colonels) come in together with *Scharführer* (sergeants), *Standartenführer* (colonels), *Rapportführer* (reporting officers), SS-*Sturmmänner* (lance corporals), *Kommandoführer* (labour-group supervisors), *Oberkapos* (head kapos), *Rottenführer* (senior lance corporals), *Postführer* (post-office leader) and the *Schutzhaftlagerführer* (camp-compound leader). As Auschwitz champion Teddy 'White Mist' Pietrzykowski put it, they were 'the masters of life and death over us', 'petty lords of the world craving amusement'. Concentration-camp boxing was 'a spectacle to break up their bloodthirsty monotony'.

The highest-ranking Nazis have been assigned the best seats in the first four rows. Camp Commander Höss, a large, tubby man, is hated, even by most in the SS, but the head of Auschwitz I is one of Himmler's inner circle. Political prisoners sit a little further back from the ring alongside professional criminals, block leaders, room-detail functionaries, room leaders and block clerks. Nazis are smoking cigars, pipes and cigarettes, betting on the result while swilling down whisky, beer or vodka, with their Alsatians, Great Danes and Doberman Pinschers at their feet. VIPs are brought to the main camp in lorries or army vehicles. Some of the SS and camp guards are unable to find seats and are obliged to stand to watch the Auschwitz All-weights Championship.

No Nazi loved boxing quite as much as SS-*Hauptscharführer* (sergeant major) Gerhard Palitzsch, who could often be found at the entrance gate seeking out boxing candidates. Teddy admitted in his memoirs that in 1942 he had still been 'Gerhard Palitzsch's pet', a special favourite treated by the *Hauptscharführer* just as a manager would treat his most successful boxer. Teddy called Gerhard Palitzsch 'one of the greatest criminals in the camp', 'the biggest bastard', 'the most brutal of the SS brutes' and 'a blackguard who finished off Jews like rabbits'. When his wife died of typhus, Palitzch became even more violent and was transferred; as a result he missed the camp fight that was about to take place.

Another absentee was the professional criminal Otto Küssel, camp prisoner no. 2, and until recently Teddy's second. Küssel had given his favourite prisoner food and advice, and had defended him against SS men indignant about Teddy's popularity. Together with three Poles, the kapo had escaped from the camp on 29 December 1942, leaving behind a letter which revealed that Bruno 'Black Death' Brodniewicz, the camp's usual referee, was a thief who had hidden gold and other 'organized' items in his private oven at the VIP block. An SS officer found the loot, leaving Black Death now in fear of his own death by way of execution at the Black Wall.

The camp orchestra conducted by Franz Nierychło is playing marching music. Meanwhile, a German cabaret artist is trying to raise laughter among the spectators with salacious anecdotes. It is forbidden to make jokes about Hitler, Himmler, Goebbels or other Nazi leaders, and it is life-threatening to refer to the poor progress of the war on the Eastern Front or any other current news topics. As is ever the case at this time of day – three o'clock in the afternoon – *Rapportführer* Oswald Kaduk is dangerously drunk.

Leen and Teddy enter, towels draped around their shoulders, boxing kit on. Proper boxing gloves have been sent over from Germany. Four matches have already been held; eight to ten boxers compete at an average camp event. None of those present seems to have the patience to take any real interest in the preliminary bouts; everyone is waiting for the main-event duel between the Jew and the Pole.

The gladiators bounce about on their toes as a warm-up. Leen is four centimetres shorter, six kilograms heavier and nine years older than his opponent. Poles call him 'Leu', 'Len' or 'Leo Sanders'; Germans call him 'Der Holländer', 'Rotterdam' or '86764'. He is bald, his hands large and coarse, his arms and legs muscled. He talks to his Polish instructor, confidant and sparring partner, Kazik Szelest. What is the strategy, how should he start off? Is a Jew actually allowed to beat an Aryan? And if he is, would he be taking a risk by doing so? Or would losing be the fatal option? Following Otto Küssel's escape, the kapo Walter Düning is now Teddy's sparring partner and second.

Leen steps into the ring; the spectators jeer, scream and curse.

Nazis hand Reichsmark banknotes to bookmakers, while clerks
keep track of the placed bets in notebooks – and never before have
so many bets been placed on one boxing match. Most SS men put
down a hundred-mark stake, but some stretch to five hundred or
even a thousand. Teddy is the clear favourite. SS officers drawn from
the camp sports command sit behind a long table alongside three
adjudicators who will keep the score and announce the winner at the
end. A professional criminal with watch in hand will soon be calling
out 'Time!' at three-minute intervals, while another kapo will be
throwing talcum powder into the ring during the breaks to keep the
floor dry; a third will be hitting a tin can to substitute for the gong.

Leen pulls on his gloves and shakes out his arms to loosen up. 'Len
from Tulip-land', the 'Mobile Wall' from Rotterdam, 'the Benny
Leonard of the Zandstraat district' – is he still just as good? Despite
not being allowed to see the match, the Dutch in the camp know for a
fact that Leen is going to win.

Teddy waves at the spectators, to the cheers of most of the Poles and
Germans. He is looking good: neatly shaved head, properly laundered
boxing outfit, professional boxing gloves, muscled legs and lean yet
strong arms. Leen and Teddy wait for some time before the referee
steps hurriedly into the ring with a suitcase showing on one side
the names of his most recent travel destinations: Mauthausen and
Gusen, concentration camps infamous even among Nazis. As one Pole
recalled: 'The situation was so comical that the whole room burst into
laughter.' The referee approaches the boxers and explains the rules
of the match: punches below the belt will result in disqualification;
firm action will be taken against clinches. After the war, one prisoner

described camp boxing as 'violence restricted by rules in a place where excessive, open violence was in use every day'. The fight is to last for no more than ten three-minute rounds.

Leen and Teddy extend their arms towards each other, briefly tapping their gloves in greeting. Leen's second, Kazik, stands in Leen's corner with a sponge, a bucket of water and a towel; Kapo Düning whispers some final advice into Teddy's ear. An *Unentschieden*, or draw, could be perilous, and both boxers know it. The SS must not be led to think that a behind-the-scenes deal has been struck; the suspicion of a scam could result in death.

Leen is introduced as 'Rotterdam', while Teddy is, as ever, 'Warsaw'. A German bashes a tin can and the referee shouts: 'Seconds out! Round one! Box!' Warsaw versus Rotterdam is finally about to start – and about time too. One Pole describes 'two things' uppermost in the minds of nearly all the camp's inmates in recent days: 'The German military's first defeat at Stalingrad and the duel between Teddy and Len Sanders.'

An eyewitness account describes Teddy and Leen in the first round as being 'in complete balance' – a state of affairs quite at odds with previous matches fought by White Mist. Leen does indeed appear to be just as good as predicted by Kazik, Karl Egersdörfer and Leen's SS protector. Teddy boxes well at a distance, but he is also prepared to clinch, and engages in man-to-man combat straightaway – one of his specialities is the side-step taught to him by Felix Stamm, a legendary Polish boxing coach from Warsaw.

The tin can is bashed and the boxers retire to their stools. Kazik massages Leen's neck, handing him a flask of water, and Kapo Walter does the same for Teddy, waving a towel above his head in the way that seconds do.

'Seconds out! Round two! Box!'

Warsaw and Rotterdam continue to be well matched. The eyewitness describes Leen as 'a master of evasion, unexpected twists and turns, and deadly counterattacks'. Teddy's famed right hooks come to grief like 'a scythe against a rock'; Leen is 'just as fast as Teddy' and 'technically even better', so landing a punch against such an experienced, capable boxer is 'a serious problem'.

'Seconds out! Round three! Box!'

Rotterdam seems better than Warsaw, but the difference remains slight because Teddy is also a master of the 'noble art' and his style is similar to Leen's own: Polish articles written before the war described him as 'the king of the dodgers'. A Polish fellow prisoner calls him 'no picture of physical strength', but 'nimble and cunning'.

'Time!'

'Round four!'

'Round five!'

As befits professionals, they continue to gauge and test each other for weak points; are there any? The majority of the SS want to see blood flowing and have absolutely no interest in seeing a perfect demonstration of the 'noble art' on their free Sunday afternoon, and boredom is beginning to take hold among the first of the bloody-nosed proletariat. Fans of *Deutsche Faustkampf* they may be, but only when it involves brawlers in the ring: men with split eyebrows who neglect their defence. Occasionally, a German kapo or SS man shouts out: 'You stupid Polack!' or 'Filthy Jew!'

'Seconds out! Proceed! Round six!'

Leen is conserving his energy, as is Teddy. The Polish spectator calls it 'a duel between two technically perfect boxers, each of whom is waiting for his opponent to make a mistake'. The frustration builds, with SS men and kapos screaming out that they should stop hugging and stroking each other, clamouring instead for punches to the stomach or liver: noses should be flattened and cauliflower ears could do with being made even bigger.

'Round seven! Box!'

Warsaw appears to be breaking through the stalemate. He attacks and, according to an eyewitness, performs 'a series of powerful punches, both left and right'. Rotterdam seems to be in difficulty. Polish kapos have taken to their feet, while the SS are crying out that Warsaw must finish off the 'Jew pig'. Leen has never been knocked out, and this cannot be the moment when that happens for the first time. He retreats behind his famed double defence, calmly soaking up the blows and waiting for the moment when he can launch a counterattack: his assailant is often unprepared for that. The eyewitness then sees Leen counter 'with lightning speed'. His quick left hook gets Teddy's jaw; the All-weights Champion of Auschwitz collapses, then scrambles back to his feet but stands there 'in a daze'. 'Murmurs of astonishment' ripple through the block; White Mist has never been vulnerable like this and he is now clearly behind on points. Will Kapo Walter throw the towel in the ring? The referee is already starting to count, but fortunately Teddy is able to continue: at last, the SS are getting their entertainment. Connoisseurs are calling Teddy v Leen I the best camp boxing match ever, as if they were at a packed Sportpalast and watching from a few metres' distance a title fight between Max Schmeling and Hans Breitensträter during their glory days.

'Round eight!'

'Round nine!'

'Round ten!'

Teddy has recovered again just a little, partly because Leen has been toning it down a bit, perhaps intentionally; the 'officer' could stand to lose everything if knocked out. One Pole later observed how Nazis from external camps were yet again 'loudly goading the boxers in order to see greater aggression', while the spectators 'with some knowledge of boxing were, by contrast, spellbound; never before had they seen a match of such quality at Auschwitz'. The title fight was 'less bloody than usual, but it is far superior'.

The kapo with the tin can hammers at it for the last time as if it were a proper gong. The referee lifts up Rotterdam's arm and says: '*Sieger nach Punkten*' (Victor on points).

The new All-weights Auschwitz Champion is ambling along Dalli-Dalli-Allee. His camp uniform is ironed, his underwear is clean and he has a neatly shaved head. He is greeted by SS men, kapos and fellow prisoners from Poland, the Netherlands, Ukraine, Russia, Algeria, France, Italy and Belgium. Poles are calling Leen 'the beast of Rotterdam', while German fans of the 'noble art' feel that Len from Tulip-land is 'the rightful winner of an unforgettable battle'. *Der Holländer* is capable, brave, powerful and confident: qualities prized by any 'racially pure' German.

He puts his new status to use by 'organizing' a great deal more extra food in the kitchen storeroom and distributing it among sick and debilitated prisoners. He smuggles even more clothes out of the SS laundry, and he barters underpants, uniforms and caps for sausages from the abattoir. Later, he will write in a letter to a Dutch civil servant that it 'was not without its dangers', but that he 'was able to help my fellow man and by that means was able to save several people from the gas chamber'.

Part V

The VIP

I.

___

It is the summer of 1943. Since his win against Teddy Pietrzykowski, and thanks to *Unterscharführer* (Corporal) Karl Egersdörfer, Leen has been promoted to the status of 'VIP' and *Funktionshäftling* (prisoner functionary: a useful prisoner who enjoys a degree of protection). He is dressed in a fresh-smelling striped jacket, striped woollen trousers and a cap. Fully serviceable socks – no holes – are keeping his feet warm, and on cold days he can pull on two or three pairs, one over the other.

At four o'clock in the morning it's his task as room leader to check that all the forced labourers in his room are up and ready. The roll-call is about to begin, and everyone knows that any prisoner arriving late will meet with punishment from *Rapportführer* Kaduk's whip, carbine or fists. Leen checks that beds have been made correctly and that the room is being kept clean. As a reward he receives even more food and, for the time being, will not be in line for review by the gas commissions. He also enjoys more freedom than others – one of the few Jews to have that privilege. According to a fellow inmate, virtually all kapos, whether block leaders or fulfilling some other role, are exclusively concerned with their own survival and are just as complicit as the SS guards. In contrast, Leen always tries to use his position to the benefit of others.

Since his victory over Teddy, Leen has been in charge of the drying loft at the SS laundry. After the evening roll-call, he usually heads to the kitchen for training with Kazik or to the basement of Block 8a to give his boxing classes, where the camp's best boxers come by for advice. Block leaders get a private session with the champion and Polish kapos have wanted to spar with him ever since Teddy 'White Mist' Pietrzykowski's transfer in March 1943 to Neuengamme concentration camp. Leen and Kazik say their goodbyes to him at the gate. Teddy's first opponent at the camp – the kapo Walter Düning – gave the former Auschwitz champion a farewell pair of boxing gloves, a gift that he had 'organized' at the Canada warehouse.

For his own safety, Leen no longer takes part in the Sunday afternoon boxing matches. Kazik had advised him to pull back from that: the Nazis would never allow a Jew to remain the title holder for long.

The twenty-two-year-old Leon Greenman is lying seriously debilitated in the infirmary at Auschwitz I. A doctor had come to his barracks, taken his pulse and simply said: 'You're sick.' In the event of a gas commission, he would certainly be picked out at once.

Leon was born in the East End of London, but his grandparents had come from the Netherlands and, before it was anglicized, the family name had been Groenteman. Leon had moved to Rotterdam's Helmersstraat, where he was nicknamed 'the Englishman', and now, non-Dutch fellow prisoners also call him 'the Englishman'; to the Nazis he is 98288.

Leen knows Leon from his brother Bram's gymnasium on Gedempte Botersloot. Before training sessions, Leon would sometimes eat at Leen's parents' place and, because of Leon's knowledge of English, he was offered a secondary job as gymnasium secretary. In 1937 he'd corresponded with English promoter Bella of Blackfriars on Bram's behalf to report the latter's discovery of a marvellously good boxer: Nol Lagrand, a combination of Bep van Klaveren and Len Sanders.

In 1942, Leon, his Rotterdammer wife, Else, and their young, fair-haired son, Barnett, were sent to Westerbork. On 11 January 1943, while standing on the Boulevard of Misery, the 'Englishman' had seen Leen, Selli, Jopie and David boarding a train and presumed he would never see them again. Leon, Else and Barnett arrived at Auschwitz a month later and were separated. As Leon was walking with forty-nine other men towards the ARBEIT MACHT FREI entrance gates, they had had to make way for a passing lorry filled with women and children. It was still dark, but he recognized his wife by the hooded cape she had fashioned from their Rotterdam home's thick, plush curtains. She was carrying Barnett in her arms. He called out her name, but the lorry engine was making too much noise.

Leon had to go to Auschwitz II-Birkenau, where, on his arrival, he was struck by an SS officer and fell to the ground like some 'one-punch-and-he's-out' boxer at the Arts & Sciences Building. He got up swiftly, behaving as if nothing had happened – something that pupils of the Bram Sanders boxing school were taught. Leon was instructed to turn to the right.

The day afterwards he was told that he, along with fifteen hundred other men, had to run at the double to the main camp, where they would be working in a construction detail: digging, hauling pieces of barracks buildings, unloading trains, and lugging bricks, coal and cement. By then, almost all of the Dutch from his transport had already died.

It's at the infirmary that Leon hears from a nurse about a famous boxer from Rotterdam who is also a prisoner at Auschwitz, and who, after an unexpected victory over a Polish champion, has been awarded a prestigious position in one of the best barracks. Leon guesses that this must be Leen, the 'Mobile Wall' from Rotterdam, the man who perfected the 'shell'. He can scarcely believe his ears on hearing how much status his old friend has acquired at Auschwitz I.

He looks out from the infirmary window and asks a young prisoner whether he could organize pen and paper for him in exchange for a scrap or two of food. Leon writes to Leen that he is that skinny secretary from the Bram Sanders Gymnasium for Ladies and Gentlemen, making it clear that he has become seriously ill while at Birkenau and must have extra food fast, otherwise he will not survive selection. Could Leen perhaps help him?

A few hours later, the young prisoner-messenger is standing once again at Leon's infirmary bed, his prison cap firmly clenched in his hand. He glances quickly left and right, and then extends his arm to Leon. The cap contains six large, superb boiled potatoes: Leon gives two of them to his young intermediary and eats the rest in measured doses. Over the days and weeks that follow, he receives via Leen yet more food 'organized' from Kazik's kitchen storeroom. His strength builds and his will to survive returns.

Leon Greenman has more or less recovered when, on 3 August 1943, the next sick young Jew from Rotterdam comes through the camp's

gates. Sebil 'Bill' Minco is twenty-one and has been sent from the
notorious concentration camp of Mauthausen. In peacetime he'd had
blond hair, but now, after delousing, he is bald. The blunt blade used
to shave him has left cuts all over his head, his legs are covered in
infected spots, and bandages are wrapped around his swollen belly
and its festering wounds.

He is standing at Block 24 with his head to the wall when Dutch
clerk Rob Beckman from Zeist approaches him and asks Bill his name.
The newcomer has forgotten. Date of birth? He can't recall that either.
Beckman walks to Block 8 to fetch Leen, telling him that an arrival
from Mauthausen is a Rotterdammer unable to remember his own
name and hardly able to keep upright. Leen goes back with Beckman
and also asks the newcomer's name, but to no avail. Well, is he hungry?
He nods. It's the first time someone has asked him that since the start
of the war.

Leen crosses the road, goes into the prisoners' kitchen and comes
back ten minutes later with a whole loaf of bread. The newcomer stares
at it, disbelieving. He tears the loaf into pieces, eating it in one go, and
his memory slowly returns. What just happened? Is he dreaming?

Bill had been nineteen when, in the autumn of 1940, he joined
the resistance group known as De Geuzen. Until his arrest in
January 1941, he would cut telephone lines, deliver pamphlets and
pass on the addresses of occupied buildings to the British. Two SS
officers had interrogated, kicked and beaten him. Bill had denied
everything, saying he had no idea what 'Geuzen' were. The krauts
hurled him down the stairs, after which he was driven in a van to the
Orange Hotel in Scheveningen. He then stood trial at the Supreme
Court in The Hague along with forty-two other suspected resistance
fighters. Eighteen of them, including Bill, were sentenced to death

on 4 March 1941; his friend Sjaak was tortured to death in a death-row cell. Thanks to his youth, Bill's sentence was commuted to life imprisonment in a penitentiary; other members of the Geuzen were informed of their execution by firing squad on 13 March 1941, and Nazis from the *Sicherheitsdienst* took them away at half past four that afternoon. The Geuzen resistance fighters were brought in vans to the Waalsdorpervlakte in the dunes, where they sang Psalm 43:4. Bill wept in his cell.

Bill spends two days in Block 2. The tattooist gives him the number 136862. Each morning, the newcomers may take some fresh air between Blocks 8 and 9, which is when Leen passes by to give Bill some extra nutrition. He brings with him not only turnips or other things he can do without, but also items in very great demand at the camp, even among the SS.

When Block 2 becomes too full, Bill is moved to quarantine block 8a, where he has to share his bed with two others. Leen lives in a comfortable room on the floor above, and it's thanks to him that Bill does not have to work in an onerous work detail outside the camp. He is able to conserve his energy somewhat, as his sole duty is to keep the block clean throughout the day. He is given ten weeks to recuperate, and his extra provisions are increasing his chances of survival.

According to the clerk Rob Beckman, Auschwitz is home to small groups of 'fellow diners': prisoners who share as much food with one another as possible, enjoy mutual trust and do their utmost to keep one another alive. At the main camp, the Beckmans are just such a group, consisting mainly of non-Jews from the Netherlands; Leen is their leader.

Detained in the block opposite Leen, there are three Dutch female prisoners from the 14 January transport: Lien, Bep and Hanna. Dr Clauberg, originally a barber, is now conducting medical trials in that block because the Nazis could find nobody else. The doctor performs peritoneal injections on women to produce infections and glues their fallopian tubes shut, disabling them from ever having children again; another doctor will sometimes cut out a part of the uterus. Bep often voices her fears, to which the ex-barber replies: 'You lot aren't guinea pigs for no reason.'

Leen refers to Lien, Bep, Hanna and the others as 'the Dutchwomen from Block 10, the Experiments Block'. He talks to doctors and kapos allowed entry to the block and drops off potatoes and jam from Kazik's kitchen storeroom. Lien distributes this among the Dutchwomen in the block and hands the doctors packages and letters in return. Leen receives these and delivers them to friends, acquaintances or any family in the camp. On one occasion he is apprehended; his exceptional status does not spare him a beating.

Lien asks Leen if he could also send them clean clothes, so at the New Laundry he 'organizes' socks, pullovers, bras, towels and underwear taken from female SS personnel. In thanks, Lien, a seamstress, patches up worn socks, shirts and underpants. Leen regularly assists the women at the Experiments Block with other items as well, such as medicines. Very often, these goods first have to be taken from SS wards, then smuggled back into the camp afterwards. As Leen said after the war: 'It was very much a risk, of course. If you got caught then . . . then . . . then you were punished to such an extent you never came out the other side. I was enormously lucky. I was never caught. There's no way of knowing how you'd cope with that.'

II.

On 16 September, Eliazer 'Eddy' de Wind and one hundred other Dutchmen walk through the entrance gates to Auschwitz I to the sound of a German marching tune played by the camp orchestra. The newcomers must wait in front of Block 24 and the kitchen; block leaders and kapos ask whether they have any watches, jewellery or cigarettes with them. They just want to put them into safe keeping for the prisoners; there's no need for alarm. Eddy hands cigarettes to a Dutchman, which results in an SS man knocking Eddy to the ground.

However, one sprucely clad prisoner *is* allowed to talk to the newcomers. Eddy describes him as short, but with a herculean build, and the SS men and kapos clearly have some respect for him.

'When did you lot leave Westerbork?' Leen asks Eddy.

'Three days ago.'

'What news do you have?'

Eddy whispers: 'Have any of you heard yet about the Allied landings in Italy?'

'Of course, we read the papers. How are things in the Netherlands?'

Eddy has no idea how to answer that. He'd been studying in Amsterdam to become a doctor when the deportations started, and had been in hiding in his native city of The Hague when his mother, Henriëtte, was picked up. The Jewish Council was on the look-out for doctors who would go to Westerbork voluntarily, which motivated Eddy to sign up on the condition that his mother would be freed; a civil servant duly gave his word. On Eddy's arrival in Westerbork he found out that his mother had just been sent east.

'Who are you?'

'Leen Sanders, the boxer.'

Eddy looks him over. He is better kitted out than the other prisoners and looks well-nourished too. 'How long have you been at Auschwitz?'

'Over six months.'

This is reassuring news for Eddy: it means that it's possible to survive this place.

'Are there many from your transport still here?'

'You shouldn't ask so many questions here, you'll see for yourself,' says Leen. 'Look, listen and keep quiet.'

'But you seem in great shape, don't you?'

Leen laughs. 'That also comes of being a boxer.'

'What are we going to have to do here?'

Leen explains that they will be divided up into work details. There are the good work details, such as the laundry, where he himself works during the day, and there are the external work details, which are far more severe. Eddy will have to become a doctor at the camp; as a privileged profession, it means his chances of survival will be much better than those of other prisoners. For that matter, boxing is also a good way of obtaining a privileged position, but Eddy doesn't look the sporty type.

'What'll be happening to the old folks who went off in the lorries?'

'Don't you ever listen to British wireless broadcasts?'

'Of course.'

'Well then, you know all about it already.'

Eddy is thinking about his mother and brother. He is also greatly worried about his wife, Friedel. He'd met her at Westerbork, where they fell in love and got married. A few hours earlier Eddy had lost sight of her on the platform; he went looking for her, inadvertently ignored an SS officer's orders, had received a blow and then lost his balance.

One of the other newcomers from Eddy's transport is Elie Aron Cohen. He'd been a doctor in the village of Aduard near Groningen until, in August 1942, he tried to flee to Sweden aboard a cargo vessel with his wife and young son. Instead of heading for the harbour at Delfzijl, the driver of the car took them to the police station. On their arrival at Auschwitz his wife had fainted; the SS threw her into a lorry, with their son following on behind.

Leen gives a signal to indicate that it is safe for Elie, Eddy and another Dutchman to be introduced to other VIPs such as Berthold Krebs and Elkan Speijer. The Jewish (and German) dental technician Berthold Israël Krebs is thirty and wears black-rimmed spectacles; it's thanks to his profession that he also enjoys privileged status. Elkan Speijer has dark blond hair and blue eyes, is eight years Leen's junior and was born in Lemmer. Elkan had arrived in the main camp one month after Leen. His friend Velleman had screamed when a blunt blade scraped off his pubic hair; a kapo slapped a clump of it in his face and popped an eye out of Velleman's eye socket. Two days later he was dead.

Elie studies Leen and Elkan. Their faces look plump to him; Eddy calls them moon-faced. Leen takes Elie, Eddy and other prisoners along with him, gives them something to eat and drink and questions them about the situation at Westerbork, asking for information about their families, place of residence and arrest. The congratulations that Elkan offers Elie – which imply his survival – meet with the reply that he is not feeling particularly overjoyed; to Elie, Auschwitz appears a good deal worse than Westerbork.

'That's true,' says Elkan, 'but the rest of the transport you lot were on has already gone up the chimney.'

'What do you mean, "up the chimney"?'

'For heaven's sake, you're telling me you haven't heard?'

'No.'

'Good grief!'

Eddy wants to know what has happened to the women in their transport.

'They're now in Block 10.'

'Is that a good block?'

'Yes, that's one of the best, but it's an Experiments Block.'

'What's that?'

'Well, see . . . they're guinea pigs there. All sorts of tests are done in that place and that's why those women are there.'

Eddy, Elie and the other newcomers then pass along Dalli-Dalli-Allee with Leen, towards the SS laundry. They linger outside the Canada warehouse and Leen explains how it came by its name; Polish prisoners think that all Canadians are rich, and the Canada stockroom is stuffed to the rafters with looted items. Eddy and Elie cast their gaze upwards, where, visible behind barred windows, they see sacksful of clothes, jewellery, sports equipment, food and other property previously owned by prisoners sent off to be gassed.

The newcomers undress between Blocks 26 and 27. Men in striped uniforms put their clothes on a trolley; kapos yell out that they must get into rows on Birkenallee. Hours pass by, waiting in the bright autumn sunshine, before they are registered by clerks seated behind tables. Men with clippers and blunt razor blades remove hair from their heads and nether regions. The prisoners are then handed a scrap of paper with a number on it and proceed naked inside Block 26, where they have to shower, be disinfected and then go quickly to Block 27, the Clothing Room, where they get their striped attire for the camp. Prisoners from the prisoner's kitchen bring large kettles of soup with beech and elm leaves floating about in it.

Dr Elie Cohen is now sitting in Birkenallee alongside Eddy, who says: 'I'll never see her again.'

'You don't know that.'

'Haven't you heard how things are at Birkenau?'

'What is Birkenau?'

'Birkenau is a truly huge camp. It's part of the Auschwitz complex. When they arrive there, all the older people and young children are crammed together in one large room and told they're getting a shower. Their bodies are burned afterwards.'

'That just can't be how it is.'

After a few hours, Eddy, Elie and the others are herded into the New Laundry, where most of the newcomers learn that they will have to work at Monowitz-Buna concentration camp next to the IG Farben rubber factory. The positions of main camp nurse and doctor are assigned to Eddy and Elie respectively, but before that they must go into quarantine in Block 8. Leen advises Eddy to stay there as long as he can: quarantined prisoners get as much food as in a work detail, plus you can build back your energy there – something the newcomers are going to need in spades. Eddy listens and passes the message on to Elie.

After the quarantine period, they are assigned a bunkbed in Block 9. Leen lives in the block next door and often comes in, bringing food and clothing with him. Eddy's wife, Friedel, is now living opposite in Block 10; sometimes he catches sight of her standing at a barred window and they wave to each other.

On 25 September, while Eddy, Elie and the others are on their ninth day of quarantine, Leen's regular sparring partner, saviour and protector, Kazik, is apprehended. SS men from the Political Department torture and interrogate him in Block 24. The charge against him: membership of a secret military organization. Kazik refuses to supply any names and denies everything. A Nazi judge declares him guilty. He is led along Dalli-Dalli-Allee in handcuffs and leg irons to Death Block 11. A Polish executioner takes him to Cell 8 (standing only); Kazik can neither support his own weight nor sit. From the darkness of his cell he can hear Polish songs; just before they die, his compatriots will often cry out: 'Long live Free Poland!' He is given almost nothing to eat and during the first few days is taken out of his cell only to be subjected to assaults. The Polish executioner used to box before the war, and it's through him that Leen is able to smuggle food into the Death Block.

Kazik is ordered to throw the bodies of executed prisoners into lorries, and there are days when he is forced from the Bunker to toil with other rebels in the cruellest of the work details: the punishment company. After the morning roll-call they have to go to a quarry, where they are beaten with whips and pickaxes, guard dogs biting at their legs. The working day is longer for them, the breaks shorter, and their further punishment is to receive virtually no food at all. The SS goal is to mete out death by way of extreme hard labour.

Kazik maintains his silence, which is why, on 11 October, the Death Block executioner conveys him to the Black Wall in the courtyard. Soldiers from the firing squad take up their rifles. A German cries out: 'Halt!' An SS officer is seen standing at the gate to the courtyard with an order from the secret service in Block 24: Karl Egersdörfer, the head of the prisoners' kitchen, has come to Kazik's rescue.

Leen sees the newcomer from the SS laundry window on 27 March 1944. The lad passes by Block 21 and the New Laundry, walking through the snow towards the Clothing Room; his head has been badly shorn and he's wearing clothes that do not piece together. The newcomer explains to a Clothing Room kapo why he is there. A prisoner fetches sheets for him; he has to wait at the entrance.

'Dutch?' asks Leen.

Louis de Wijze nods. He is twenty-one and, until 1942, lived in Nijmegen, where he had played football to a high standard at the Quick 1888 club. Leen introduces himself, and Louis asks whether Leen is the famous boxing champion from Rotterdam. Leen nods. Louis guesses that Leen must be around fifteen years older than him; his kindly eyes and open face inspire confidence.

Louis grips the sheets under his arm as Leen takes him off to a quiet spot where they can swap information. Louis says that he arrived at the main camp two days earlier – his arm bears the number 175564 and the tattoo is still weeping a little. He's in quarantine on the attic floor of Death Block 11, and there are roughly a hundred people left from his transport of eighteen hundred. Up until now they've had only a small piece of bread and some watery coffee. They are suffering from the cold; there were no sheets, and it's only after three days that he has finally been allowed to fetch some.

His parents, Sarah and Jakob, and his sister, Inge, had left for Auschwitz a month before; Louis has not found them yet. The journey from Westerbork to Auschwitz was an unnerving experience. The Jewish asylum Apeldoornsche Bosch had been emptied, with hundreds of its residents travelling in Louis's transport to Auschwitz. By the time the train reached its final destination and the wagons were opened up, they were all mired in excrement, without any idea where they were, continually shrieking. During registration they had crawled along the floor, unable to understand the questions, ignorant of their own names, snapping at the SS officers and laughing at them.

Leen indicates the injuries to Louis's face and asks what happened. During a roll-call he was dragged indoors by the Polish kapo from the Death Block. Camp inmates whispered that 'Bunker Jakob' had been a boxing champion in Poland, and Max Schmeling's regular sparring partner. Bunker Jakob then put Louis in a device that just prevented his feet from touching the floor; this had made the beatings by whip and stick especially brutal.

Leen tells him that they are lucky to be at the main camp and not Birkenau. Louis's lot are sure to be put to work in one of the external work details, such as the IG Farben rubber factory at Auschwitz III-Monowitz-Buna or, say, the road-building detail. But all of that would still be a while yet; newcomers first have to spend a few weeks in quarantine because of the risk of infection. Leen cautions Louis to make good use of that time: get some rest, build your strength up; you'll be needing it later, however fit you all feel at the moment. In other words, keep calm and prepare yourself for what is to come.

Meanwhile, Leen will be trying to organize some extra food or warm clothing from the SS laundry. Leen asks Louis whether he has friends in his block, then asks him to wait where he is for a bit while he goes off to sort something out for them.

He walks to the kitchen building, emerging from it ten minutes later. He looks all around, then pulls food from his jacket and trousers. There are even some apples in the haul; it has been years since Louis ate an apple.

Louis asks Leen how he has managed to get hold of the food. 'Simply a matter of organization, lad, simply a matter of organization. Now, no questions; just promise me that you'll share everything honestly with your friends.'

Louis conceals the food inside his clothes and, shaking hands in farewell, thanks Leen for everything. He drops off the sheets at Death Block 11 and takes the stairs to the top to tell his friends about Leen. They wait until nightfall, then proceed to eat their banquet in a corner of the Bunker. With their bellies now fairly full, the three of them are able to drop off to sleep. Years later, Louis de Wijze would write: 'I crawled under my sheet with the image of Leen Sanders still fresh in my mind. An incredibly wonderful man! For the first time in this foul place, I had encountered some shared humanity again . . .'

The next day, Leen calls on Louis and his companions in the attic in order to share out some more food and warm clothes. While he's there, he sees a friend from Rotterdam. Jacob de Wolf is six years older than Leen; he has three gold teeth and a deep scar on his forehead. His son, Harry, one of Rotterdam's greatest boxing talents, is in hiding at his trainer's gymnasium (Wetemans) in Schilderswijk, The Hague.

Jacob was arrested in 1943. He had tried hanging himself in his cell, but the rope had snapped, landing him on his head. He'd come round a few days later with a reinvigorated desire to fight, and put up a photograph of his son Harry in full boxing kit on the wall of his cell.

After two weeks of quarantine, Leen arranges a job for Jacob at the SS laundry. He is allowed to bring his three companions with him: the Theebooms (father and son) from The Hague, and Juda Kattenburg, a mechanic from Rotterdam, all of whom had always hung around together at the Vught transit camp. Leen also succeeds in getting jobs at the New Laundry for another four Dutchmen. Consequently, they no longer have to perform gruelling forced labour in the bitter cold.

Thanks to Karl Egersdörfer, Kazik is reinstated to his former job in the prisoners' kitchen and is seeking a sparring partner because he wants to be champion of Auschwitz; extra bread and butter can be earned as a reward. Leen passes on the proposal to Jacob and arranges boxing gloves, shorts, a T-shirt and sports shoes for him; after work, they go to the kitchen storeroom. Jacob's first impression of Kazik is of a big Polish storeman with the look of someone who has eaten well on the back of it. Straightaway, Kazik lands Jacob a punch so hard it gives him a stiff neck for the next three days. Kazik rewards him with food.

After three weeks of working at the New Laundry, Jacob hears word that he, the Theebooms and Juda Kattenburg are to be transferred to Auschwitz III-Monowitz-Buna. Leen feels that Jacob must be allowed to remain and promises to put in a good word for him with the camp authorities so that Jacob can continue to box in the main camp. However, Jacob wants to stay with his friends and stresses: 'You can say what you like, Leen, the four of us are sticking together.' They shake hands, hoping to see each other again soon in Rotterdam or The Hague.

It is 8 April 1944 and a new transport is pulling up to the platform at Auschwitz. Leen's eldest brother, Jakob Josua, is on board. His sister, Rozette, steps out with her husband, Simon Ossendrijver, and their eleven-year-old son, David. They had been in hiding in Rotterdam when, on 9 November 1943, policemen raided the house from both sides. As the family was being ushered into a police van, the heavily pregnant Rozette suddenly went into labour. A German policeman said: '*Wir kommen bald zurück*' (We'll be back shortly). A doctor advised them to give up the newborn baby, so Rozette wrapped the little boy in a scarf and left him behind with her best friend, Annie, and her husband, Henk, who named Leen's youngest nephew Klaas.

Jakob, Rozette, Simon and David fled Rotterdam and went into hiding again in the village of Molenschot near Gilze-Rijen in North Brabant; it was there that they were apprehended in February 1944, probably betrayed. After two months in Westerbork's punishment block, they boarded a cattle wagon at the Boulevard of Misery along with 106 men, 122 women and 22 children; three days later they were in Auschwitz.

The men are immediately separated from the women and children. Jakob and his brother-in-law, Simon, have to turn right; Leen's sister Rozette and his nephew David have to turn left. In his statement taken in 1947, Jakob Josua Sanders declared as follows: 'I suspect, although there can be no doubt about it, that the men who went to the wrong side with the women and children were gassed.'

IV.

It is a Sunday afternoon and the SS want some entertainment. The great laundry barracks at Auschwitz I is completely packed, with a queue of people at the entrance. The boxing ring is illuminated from above. The *Lagerführer* (Camp Leader) has a place of honour just a few metres away from the boxers; prisoners have to stand. Top-tier Nazis from Auschwitz I, II and III, as well as from the external camps, are seated next to German kapos on chairs arranged around the ring. They are placing wagers, screaming and swearing, while Jewish girls top up their glasses: everyone is fired up for the greatest boxing match since Teddy 'Warsaw' Pietrzykowski versus Leen 'Rotterdam' Sanders in February 1943.

The Polish boxer Antoni Czortek is the first to enter the ring. His countrymen cheer on the twenty-nine-year-old from the village of Buśnia, who in 1939 was ranked number two in Europe and has been national champion several times. Polish prisoners are convinced he'll be even better than Leen. Before the war, he would appear every week in the sports magazine *Przegląd Sportowy*, and actors clamoured to be associated with him. In 1935 he had boxed in front of 30,000 spectators; even Teddy had never managed that. Czortek's arm bears the number 139559.

Polish prisoners could scarcely believe their eyes when they saw Czortek standing on the platform at Auschwitz in August 1943, and an SS man recruited him as a camp boxer immediately. His first match was against his best friend and fellow boxing professional Zygmunt Małecki, and took place in pools of blood amid the corpses of murdered prisoners.

Czortek's opponent steps through the ropes: Walter Düning from Duisburg, the German kapo who, three years before, had lost in the legendary fight against Teddy Pietrzykowski; Leen is his second and coach. Czortek and Düning are introduced as 'boxers of international fame'. Just as in 1941 against Teddy, Düning is a good deal taller and heavier than his adversary, and virtually everyone in the SS is betting on and toasting his victory. Czortek is being assisted in the ring by kitchen assistant and camp boxer Andrzej Rablin from Warsaw, against whom, just a few weeks earlier, Kazik had boxed to a draw.

An SS man bangs on a real gong. 'Seconds out! Box!' Polish spectators bellow out the strictly forbidden phrase: 'Punch the German!' and Czortek hits Düning hard. He falls to the concrete floor and is counted out in the third round. Responding to the match afterwards, one Polish spectator sneers: 'That Walter, just look at him. In the detail he'll punch a prisoner to the ground whenever it suits him, and here he is with absolutely nothing!' Another Polish observer sees the winner taking a post-match walk to the ARBEIT MACHT FREI gates 'like a hero [. . .] surrounded by prisoners all shouting out his praises'.

Leen moves on to Block 24, where a concert by the camp orchestra is beginning. Thirty musicians just fit inside the small space and the audience is packed together as closely as possible; SS men are holding back any latecomers because it is already too full. The conductor, Franz Nierychło, has the members of his Polish camp orchestra play the overture to the opera *Tancredi* and compositions by Berlioz. On days like these, any visiting outsider might be fooled into thinking all was well at the main camp; one person present at both the Czortek v Düning boxing match and the concert writes in his diary that Auschwitz is a *Betrugslager* (a camp of deceit).

A few days later, Leen is celebrating his thirty-sixth birthday. He is living in the VIP room in Block 4 and still working during the day in the drying loft at the SS laundry. He wears a black jacket and proper leather shoes, freshly polished and of excellent quality, as if purchased from the fashion department store Gerzon on De Dijk. He is tanned, muscled and well-fed, even to the point of developing a slight belly. After evening roll-call, he trains Germans, Poles and Dutchmen in Block 8a, and takes the additional food received for this to prisoners in the very worst condition, handing over potatoes and clean clothes to the block leader at the Experiments Block. From out on the street he asks the women about their health, whether there is anything they need, and which of them was taken away during the most recent selection.

Prior to all of this, early in 1944, his protégé, Bill Minco from Rotterdam, had become seriously ill again, ending up in the infirmary just as he had on his arrival at Auschwitz, but surviving a number of gas commissions. He received food from Leen, recovered, and was allowed to leave the infirmary one day after his twenty-second birthday on 21 May 1944. Leen arranged things so that Bill could come to live with the VIPs in Block 4 and ensured that he was assigned relatively light duties during the day in a job outside of the camp at the Union munitions factory. This meant he had a roof over his head in inclement weather, which could make all the difference between life and death. Leen often provided food and clothing for the women and girls working there.

In the summer of 1944, Leen also becomes a block barber. Prisoners are shaved once a week according to strict guidelines; tufts of hair must be left to make prisoners more easily identifiable if they attempt to escape. VIPs are treated to shaving soap and a sharp blade, and after a few minutes they walk outside bald and spruce, without any scratch marks. One fellow prisoner notes how Leen's job as a block barber makes it possible for him to extend his 'organizational skills' even further.

Leen socializes a good deal with Dr Elie Cohen, dental technician Berthold Krebs and a Protestant called Max. They smoke real cigarettes and read the *Krakauer Zeitung*, the *Völkische Beobachter* and the *Oberschlesischer Zeitung*. In the afternoons, Leen and the other VIP prisoners eat white bread with real butter and salami; in the evenings, they sometimes have baked potatoes with meat, accompanied by vodka; their fresh white bread can mop up any gravy.

On Sunday mornings Elie, Berthold, Max and Leen stroll along Birkenallee and lie out on the grass in the sunshine or relax on the benches. Prisoners bend over backwards to impress the women in the Experiments Block; they wave, make witty remarks and blow kisses. In the afternoons, Leen organizes boxing matches in front of the kitchen building, a Czech professor gives gymnastics classes, international football matches are held and VIPs are given entrance tickets to a camp orchestra performance in Block 2.

Leen keeps running into familiar old faces, such as his second cousin Levie 'Lou' Sanders. Lou had walked through the gate on 6 June 1944 with the singer Hijman 'Bob' Scholte, forty-two and even more famous than Leen thanks to hits such as 'Vriendinnetje', 'Breng eens een zonnetje' and 'Ik heb een huis met een tuintje'. In Tilburg, he'd had to abandon his hiding place when his helpers' young son told people at his school that the great Bob Scholte was living with them. He had spent a long time imprisoned at the Vught transit camp, where members of the Dutch SS would shout out 'Hey, Bob!' when they saw him.

Lou and Bob's wives were, respectively, Eef and Miep. They had already been waiting for hours on the platform at Auschwitz when all at once they saw a jet of flame reach several metres into the sky above the camp. Miep turned to Eef: 'There's such a strange smell here.' They were inspected by a man with dark hair – 'not unattractive,' according to Eef. This proved to be Dr Josef Mengele, the German doctor with the nickname 'Angel of Death', who experimented on some prisoners and selected others for the gas chambers. After their arrival, Eef and Miep had to go to another camp straightaway and waved goodbye to their husbands with the words: 'See you soon.'

Lou was stunned when he saw who was walking towards him from the direction of the kitchen building, but Leen had been alerted to the arrival of some Dutch people in the camp. The two of them caught up on recent events: where was Eef; was she still alive? Where had he and Bob come from; what had Vught been like? Lou was hungry; his clothes stank of sweat and diarrhoea, so Leen organized some extra bread and clean clothing. Lou asked how he managed to do it. 'Cousin Leen', as Lou called him, explained about the SS officer Karl Egersdörfer and about the kitchen storeroom manager, Kazik.

Because of that Nazi and that Pole, he had been able to box, and things had got much better ever since. Leen advised Lou about the work details he should avoid; in his experience, an average prisoner doing hard outdoor labour would last, at most, three to four months. 'Then it's all over.' Lou was shocked.

Bob and Lou have the misfortune of having to work in an aggregate loading detail. There's nothing Leen can do to prevent it, although he does ask the work unit's kapo if he will go easy on them. They turn out every morning in a group of one hundred men, with the camp orchestra playing marching music at the gate, and after walking for over one and a half hours, Bob and Lou arrive at the site. Lorries and wheelbarrows are filled with sand, which then has to be tipped out a little further on. Lou quickly deteriorates, so Leen supplements his food and arranges support and protection for him. On a few occasions Lou is able to build back his strength when Leen conceals him in his block, which is known in Auschwitz as 'work suppression'.

Leen does all of this for others as well. The lawyer Herman Boasson from Drachten arrived at the camp on 24 August 1943 and was soon having to work at Auschwitz III, where he developed a leg infection that resulted in being sent off to the main camp. During the spring of 1944 he was lying gravely ill in the infirmary, where Leen succeeded in gaining entry to bring him a bowl of soup filled to the brim. It seemed only a matter of time before Herman would be selected for a gas commission, but on dozens of occasions Leen hid him in the drying loft above the SS laundry.

Another camp inmate became seriously ill and feared he would have to work in one of the lethal external work details. Leen smuggled him out of the infirmary, then walked him as nonchalantly as he could to the SS laundry, guided him up the narrow stairs to the drying loft and hid him under piles of washing. Of all Leen's activities, this 'work suppression', otherwise known as 'hiding people', was possibly the most dangerous. Concealing prisoners when 'raids' – as Leen called them – were in progress was viewed as the worst expression of sabotage in the camp, and was met with the severest punishment.

One summer's morning in 1944, Leen wakes up at four, as on any working day, but to a nose that is twice as large as usual. He doesn't dare see an SS doctor; it could mean ending up in the infirmary and review by a gas commission. During roll-call, Leen keeps out of sight of *Rapportführer* Kaduk and, at the end of the day, pays a visit to Dr Cohen in Block 9. Elie examines Leen's nose and diagnoses the bacterial infection erysipelas, a serious problem that needs urgent attention; Leen had assumed as much. Elie agrees that a hospital admission would be too risky, for a mild illness at Auschwitz can have fatal consequences, even for VIPs.

Elie visits a German SS pharmacist, comes up with a ruse and takes away with him a sulphate treatment. Leen rubs this into his nose, trying to keep out of the way of the SS for a few days. The swelling reduces and his nose returns to normal, albeit a little squashed, but that's nothing new– he makes a full recovery. After the war, Elie calls Leen 'one of my trophies from my time in the concentration camp'.

V.

It is an August evening when thirty-five of them come through the gates of Auschwitz I. The newcomers cannot be registered straight away and have to wait in a barracks for twelve hours. SS officers in the camp leadership consider it too late at night to give them food. They're not allowed to speak to anyone; armed guards with dogs are stationed at the doors, and sometimes they go in and beat a few of the prisoners with their rifles.

The Dutchmen are lying down on the floor. They have spent days walking and are starving; dozens of their fellow prisoners have already died en route, collapsing with exhaustion, then shot and left behind in the ditch like roadkill. For the briefest of moments they had hoped Auschwitz might improve their situation, but instead they find themselves in an unusually bleak environment and their hunger is overpowering.

The door opens and a short, broad-shouldered man enters. Most of the men from South Holland recognize him as Leen Sanders; they used to go to the matches held at the Arts & Sciences Building or at the De Doelen events hall on Rotterdam's Coolsingel. Nobody is allowed inside the barracks, so why is he? And a Jew to boot!

'How many of you are there?'

'Thirty-five.'

'I'll go and see what I can do for you lot.'

A quarter of an hour later, Leen returns with three other people: Dr Elie Cohen, nurse Eddy de Wind and dental technician Berthold Krebs. The short, stocky man is carrying in his burly arms and big, coarse hands a large mess tin of soup, several loaves of bread, real butter and clothing. Elie, Eddy and Berthold pass out medicines. Leen reassures the newcomers, promising to bring more food – and perhaps even cigarettes.

Leen and the others then tell the newcomers about Auschwitz, and in their turn the new Dutch arrivals try to describe their previous camps. According to a former member of the De Geuzen resistance, Ilse Koch, wife of the former camp commandant at Buchenwald, had lampshades made from human skin. Being non-Jews, the newcomers had had things better there than their Jewish fellow inmates. On Sundays they had been allowed to play skittles or tennis, and there had been a library containing all the works by British comic writer Jerome K. Jerome.

In February 1944, they'd been told they had to be moved from Buchenwald to another camp because of the Russian advance; they had still been in good condition at that time. SS men had yelled at them to 'Fall in!' at half past five in the morning, after which they walked to the station at Buchenwald, where 157 people had to get into a train with five wagons; there was no room. The SS guards had brought two days' worth of food with them, but the journey to Lublin had lasted almost a week. By the end they were being given virtually nothing to eat; it was only at the Polish border that a little soup and slivers of sauerkraut were doled out. From Lublin it had taken them forty minutes to walk to

Majdanek concentration camp, and a sign on the main thoroughfare had stated WER SICH HIER AUFHÄLT WIRD ERSCHOSSEN (Anyone stopping here will be shot). Shaven-headed, desperately emaciated women were dragging a large cart forwards.

At Majdanek, Jews had to march past the crematoria, keeping two metres' distance from the prisoner in front. SS men would shoot them in the back of the head and guards would push the bodies into the incinerators. Shooting began at five in the morning and lasted until well after midnight; the murderous SS relieved one another every few hours, and the Nazis had named the operation *Erntefest* (harvest festival). Camp orchestras from Majdanek and external camps gave the loudest possible rendition of *The Blue Danube* by Johann Strauss in order to overpower the sound of gunshots and screaming. A former De Geuzen resistance fighter heard that, in late 1943, some 18,000 Jews had been exterminated in one night. When the incinerators were full, the SS would push and kick the victims into huge concrete pits, throw petrol over them and set light to the corpses.

Leen's office-bedroom comprises a desk, a small kitchen, an oven, a stove and more than enough coal; his bed is roomy and lice-free. The Dutch often ask one another for favours: who has connections with a kapo or SS officer; can some 'organized' items be bartered? Dr Elie Cohen, a fixture in Leen's office-bedroom, is always on the receiving end of the same question after a gas commission: 'Have any more of our countrymen been taken away?'

The women from the Experiments Block have been moved to a barracks behind the barbed wire, right next to villas built for SS officers. Eddy de Wind is eager to see his wife, Friedel, again – can

Leen do anything for him? It is strictly forbidden for prisoners to come anywhere near the new development; one prisoner wanting to see his sweetheart has already been riddled with bullets. Leen is giving boxing lessons to a kapo nicknamed 'Bloody August' and, through talking to him, manages to get Eddy smuggled into the road-building detail as a 'guest'. Eddy is given a shovel, has to lug bricks at the new women's camp and is able to catch up with Friedel in relative safety.

The Majdanek newcomers are finding it hard to adapt to life at Auschwitz. SS men go on the rampage just as they had experienced them doing in their first months at Buchenwald; sometimes they are thrown out of bed in the middle of the night and have to go outside on the double while their room is searched for contraband. At the morning roll-call, *Rapportführer* Kaduk is already drunk; his brother has just been killed on the Eastern Front and he screams at the prisoners that he will be taking his revenge. Hamburg Annie works at 'Puff', the camp brothel for non-Jewish VIPs, where she shouts out one afternoon that Hitler is not in fact winning the war. She is murdered in the Bunker.

Leen also strikes up a close friendship with newcomer Jo Hoek. He is thirty-five, blond and blue-eyed, tall and fit, and speaks good German. Until his arrest, Jo had lived next door to Feyenoord Stadium, then became no. 5416 in Buchenwald owing to his membership of De Geuzen. His brother Leendert, six years his senior, had been murdered in that camp on 11 January 1943 – the SS had thrown him into a mass grave somewhere near Bremen. Jo and Leen are more or less equally matched in terms of strength, share the same Rotterdam sense of humour, and chat easily about Bep van Klaveren, De Dijk or Max Hakkert's legendary salt beef and chopped liver rolls in Westewagenstraat.

Leen spars with Jo and gives boxing lessons to still more Dutchmen. After work, they go to the basement of Block 8a, where Leen hands out sports clothing, tells his new pupils about the importance of a double defence technique and advises them on how best to take any punches dished out by the SS. The newcomers regain their mental and physical strength.

The Dutch meet up almost every night at Leen's Block 4 to sing Dutch songs and reminisce about Amsterdam and Rotterdam. The Russians are getting ever closer and the Allies are in Sicily. Leen has heard all of this from fellow prisoners who have been able to listen to British wireless broadcasts, and there's also news about it in the *Krakauer Zeitung*.

Most of the talk in Leen's office-bedroom is about music. No. 139829, Max Rodrigues Garcia, recalls how at family get-togethers in Amsterdam he loved singing German, French and Dutch songs; he'd imitate the French singer Maurice Chevalier and sometimes donned a boater, took a walking stick and tried to create a convincing Charles Trenet. Max treats everyone to the hits by Trenet and Chevalier that he used to sing, but the SS must not get wind of it – French is forbidden at Auschwitz. Twenty-year-old Max was introduced to Leen by his friend, Samson 'Lex' van Weren, four years his senior; they both often go to Block 4. Max says that the place rings with laughter centred, more often than not, on their predicament – for him, humour in such an environment works like medicine.

Lex van Weren, Max's best friend at the camp, had arrived at Auschwitz in November 1943 and had been assigned to work in the coal mines at the external camp of Janina. He became ill at the beginning of 1944, whereupon an SS man put him into a lorry filled with corpses and then had him driven to the main camp. Lex recovered in the infirmary. The Dutch women in the Experiments Block called out his name when he first walked past Block 10: alongside Leen and singer Bob Scholte, he is the most famous Dutch prisoner at the main camp , thanks to his pre-war performances as a trumpet player.

In Max's view, his own story is a dull affair compared with that of his best friend. Lex had played with black jazz heroes such as Cab Calloway, Louis Armstrong and Coleman Hawkins. They had all come to Rotterdam to play with the Rhythm Five, made up of Louis Bannet, Lex, Jack de Vries, Maurice van Kleef and the goy Dick van Heuvel. They were even popular in Germany until 1933, and band leader Louis Bannet was hailed as 'the Dutch Louis Armstrong'; he's now the star player in the Birkenau camp orchestra.

Leen is standing to attention at a morning roll-call in October 1944 when he hears explosions and sees fire reaching into the sky above the camp at Birkenau. Nobody knows for sure what's going on – there are mutterings about an attack on the crematoria and rumours abound about a revolt; perhaps there's an actual uprising. Forced labourers in outside work details have to return to the main camp at a run. Leen's block companion and protégé Bill Minco calls it a state of siege. Barracks and rooms are searched; if the SS find so much as one weapon in Block 4, then both Leen and Bill are likely to be going up the chimney.

After a few days, Leen gets to hear what actually happened: prisoners had smuggled explosives into the camp, and crematoria were blown up; shots were fired at SS guards, some of whom had died. The saboteurs were surrounded and killed.

The camp authorities fear more resistance, and as a result the majority of the Polish prisoners, including the camp orchestra, are put aboard trains for camps such as Mauthausen and Dachau. According to Elie Cohen, following the attack on the crematorium the main camp has been all but cleaned out of Poles. Thanks to SS officer Karl Egersdörfer, Kazik is permitted to stay at Auschwitz I, as is the Polish conductor and orchestra leader Adam Kopiciński: after all, the SS must not have their musical entertainment interrupted.

Protective Custody Camp Leader Franz Hössler tasks Kopiciński with putting together a new camp orchestra and on 15 October 1944, notices are posted on the walls of all the blocks: 'Tomorrow evening, after their work, all musicians can report to Block 24 for auditions!' Jews are also allowed to take part this time. Trumpet player Lex van Weren talks to Leen about the auditions – it's been a long time since he last played and he's worried about possibly poor embouchure (whereby his lips might no longer shape properly around the mouthpiece, resulting in dud notes). Leen finds his way to the Music Room, where the shelves and floor are crammed with violins, wind instruments, guitars, drum kits and microphones; he stuffs a smart-looking cornet under his prison jacket and leaves. Lex then practises for as long as it takes to get back to his pre-war standard of play.

When the time comes for Lex's audition, he finds a long queue waiting outside Block 24. Hössler is evaluating the candidates together with orchestra leader Kopiciński; some of the men have never played an instrument before. A Dutch saxophonist is in front of Lex, but it has been too long since he last played and he is unfamiliar with the instrument he is given. He fails to get any sound from it and is dismissed. Filled with anxiety, Lex drops his place in the queue a few times, but his turn comes in the end. He takes up the cornet, plays perfect scales and Kopiciński is pleased; he follows this up with a march, which also pleases Hössler. The upshot is that Lex is hired, and from then on the cornet is his constant companion wherever he happens to be. His admission to the orchestra is a turning point in his life at the concentration camp and, after the war, he cites Leen as having been his saviour.

VI.

The upper room at Block 2 is full to capacity, as if a boxing match were about to commence. The first rows of chairs have been reserved for the SS, and guards use whips and fists to keep order. Former De Geuzen resistance fighters are wearing frayed striped uniforms; one Rotterdammer calls their style 'zebra'. As a VIP, Dr Elie Cohen is wearing a tailor-made reefer-style jacket and fur-lined gloves.

Amsterdammer Max Garcia gets the proceedings off to a start in the manner of an MC at a boxing event, telling jokes in German and announcing the Jewish Dutch performers. Lex van Weren is introduced with his cornet and his camp number embroidered on his striped uniform.

Rotterdammer Jack de Vries is playing tuba and double bass, while Maurice van Kleef is beating on the drums as if he were performing with the Rhythm Five at Café Restaurant Pschorr on Coolsingel. Meanwhile, lawyer Herman Boasson is trying to get sound out of a cello, and Bob Scholte is singing songs that he sang in Germany in the early 1930s.

Like the other VIPs, Leen has a seat with a good view of the stage. He's wearing a black cap, a striped linen jacket, perfectly tailored trousers and boots with steel toecaps; the red band on his left arm shows his camp number. He has been promoted to block leader and, as such, is in charge of more than a thousand prisoners, but also spends a great deal of his time in his office-bedroom. In general, the SS leave the block leader to his own devices, as long as he does his job effectively. The kapos have to heed his words, room-detail functionaries carry out minor tasks for him and keep the barracks clean, and the block clerk does the administration. On Sundays, Block 4's Jewish leader gives boxing demonstrations, which, according to a camp inmate, are also attended by the SS.

Without Leen, this first cabaret night at Auschwitz I, provided by Jews, would never have taken place. It was regular visitors to his office-bedroom Max and Lex who, when brainstorming after work, had come up with the idea of organizing a jazz show for the prisoners. Against the background of a Russian advance, the SS seemed eager to show their goodwill; it was the perfect moment to ask their permission. Moreover, it would lighten the mood, at least temporarily, and might possibly give the SS a chance to relax as well. Max and Lex set out their ideal programme to Leen: a variety show with jazz features. Leen felt enthusiastic about it and, on their behalf, paid a visit to the camp authorities. An SS officer rejected the plan out of hand: jazz remained both decadent and proscribed. Goebbels had ruled on that very shortly after Hitler's takeover. Next they'd be asking to play Jewish numbers as well! The officer had an alternative proposal – a show with German hit-parade songs, German cabaret or songs from UFA films might just be permissible.

Leen returned to Block 4 and discussed the alternative with Max and Lex. The jazz numbers were replaced with German songs, and Max and Lex wrote sketches in German. The new plan was approved and a trial show was given the go-ahead, with some provisos. Song lyrics had to be submitted in advance; political satire was strictly forbidden; jokes about Hitler, Himmler, Goebbels, *Rapportführer* Kaduk or Protective Custody Camp Leader Hössler would result in assignment to a *Himmelfahrtskommando* (suicide mission).

Lex pulled together a group of people who rehearsed on the first floor of the Music Room in Block 24. The girls at Puff, the camp brothel, lived one floor above and threw down bread in appreciation of the music. Leen 'organized' potatoes and jam from Kazik's kitchen storeroom for the performing artists, and they would use Leen's office-bedroom to talk over the material they needed to present at the first variety show.

The trial show was held in the attic at Block 2. There were no prisoners in attendance, only high-ranking Nazis. Max addressed his audience in German, cracking jokes, and the SS applauded and laughed. Lex played popular German hits on his cornet and had the SS men whooping in their seats when they heard the number 'Ich wollt' ich wär ein Huhn' by Willy Fritsch and Lilian Harvey from 1936. Nazis also sang along to 'Lili Marleen' from the UFA film *Der Blaue Engel*. This was followed by a section of slapstick, then some yodelling and a prisoner playing a musical saw.

The trial run was a success, and Max, Lex and the others were allowed to proceed with further matinee performances in Block 2, which even Jewish prisoners were permitted to attend, although they did have to stand. As Max recalled, they did not mind very much because, for a brief moment, some normality was back in their lives. They seemed happy: Jews and SS men sharing entertainment in the same space. The wind section of the Jewish and Dutch camp orchestra would sometimes play a German-language version of the prohibited jazz hit 'Alexander's Ragtime Band', composed by a Jew.

Just like Leen, Lex became a VIP and had permission to move into the same block; Protective Custody Camp Leader Franz Hössler was his protector. On occasion, he would arrive straight from the gas chambers and in need of hearing his favourite song, 'Bei mir bist du schön'. Lex was allowed to put together the new camp orchestra – one that was drawn from Dutch Jews in particular. He might teach prisoners a couple of tones on the trumpet and then take them on, and during performances, some of them needed to do no more than beat on a drum a few times.

Each morning they would play military marches at the gates, and as a reward they would be given bread, cigarettes and a lenient job as potato peelers in Kazik's kitchen storeroom. Sometimes they would be given permission to rehearse in the middle of the day at the Music Room in Block 24. In good weather the windows were wide open and the Puff girls would sing along. Forced labourers returned at five o'clock, when Lex and other members of the camp orchestra were expected to play for a two-hour stretch; on Sundays, they might have as many as five concerts in a day. They played pieces by Wagner, waltzes by Strauss, minuets by Beethoven, arias by Bach and quintets by Schumann.

A Christmas tree decked out in coloured lights and baubles stands in front of the prisoners' kitchen. The camp orchestra is about to start playing. Lex, Jack de Vries, Herman Boasson and the other musicians are standing in the same spot as during the morning and evening roll-calls, wearing specially tailored white uniforms with shiny buttons. There is to be no boxing or football afterwards, nor any variety performances. Today, instead, there is a public hanging on the agenda.

For days now, Auschwitz I has been swathed in clammy mist. It is freezing and they are forced to stand for an hour and a half in their threadbare striped uniforms. The first eight rows of seats are taken up by the most important Nazis in Auschwitz, and just as for the Leen v Teddy and Czortek v Düning fights, there are visitors from Birkenau, Jaworzno, Monowitz-Buna, Gleiwitz (Gliwice) and other external camps. The mood among the prisoners has been at a low ebb ever since hearing the news of a surprise German offensive in the Ardennes; Leen and other VIPs had read about it in the *Krakauer Zeitung*. The Führer was fighting on to live another day. 'You lot will soon see us back in Antwerp again,' says an SS officer.

The gallows stands opposite the kitchen. Lex is the successor to Adam Kopiciński as orchestra leader and, at Protective Custody Camp Leader Hössler's command, has the musicians play 'Stille Nacht, Heilige Nacht' and 'O Tannenbaum'. Under Lex's direction, the orchestra has expanded to include more than seventy members; they journey from block to block and from camp to camp, receiving nearly as many privileges as Leen. Almost everyone in the SS wants to see and hear the camp orchestra; from Herman Boasson's point of view the orchestra is playing for a bunch of dancing, screaming louts.

SS men fetch those sentenced to death, four of whom are Poles. As a block leader, Leen is in full view of the gallows, and Kazik is one of the few Poles to be present. Thanks to Leen, he is no longer imprisoned in the Bunker. An SS officer called Kraus had hated Kazik with a passion and accused him of being a drunkard; Kazik tested sober but had to go to Death Block II all the same. Leen supplemented his rations and notified Karl Egersdörfer, who went to Hössler and, owing to Kazik's indispensability in the kitchen, saved the Pole for the second time.

The camp orchestra spends a quarter of an hour playing marching songs with titles such as 'Germanentreue' and 'Deutschlands Waffenehre', as well as numbers from Verdi's *La Traviata*. An SS officer reads out the charges and the sentences. Two kapos lift up the first victim and thrust his head into a noose. His hands and feet are bound and the kapos then hang a sign from his neck: I TRIED TO ESCAPE. NOBODY TRIES TO ESCAPE FROM AUSCHWITZ. I DESERVE TO DIE. The Pole shouts out: 'Death to Hitler! Death to Germany! Long live the Allies!' A kapo kicks away the stool and a hush descends. The next Pole insults *Rapportführer* Kaduk, who exacts revenge by first knifing him and then having him hanged. The other two Poles' stools are kicked away in succession. Most prisoners try not to look.

The last person sentenced to death is a French Jew called Sim. A year before, he had been standing naked in the queue for the gas chamber when he asked an SS man with a flat nose whether he was a boxer. When the officer answered 'yes', Sim had told him that he was also a professional boxer.

'Where did you fight?'

'Parc des Princes, Japy, Central and once at the Vélo d'Hiv.'

The SS man had laughed and hauled Sim out of the queue. A few months later, he decided to escape with the four Poles. If the camp was to be evacuated, they did not believe that the Nazis would leave any eyewitnesses behind once they heard the Russians were almost at their door.

Sim's stool is also kicked aside. The rope snaps; the public hanging is over. The SS officers return to their cosy rooms or villas, the prisoners to their blocks. Sim is taken back to Death Block 11 – once

there, Bunker Jakob is sure to have him put up against the Black
Wall. His co-escapees are left behind on the gallows; camp cellist
Herman Boasson sees 'lukewarm corpses, dangling in the chilly
Polish evening air'.

On New Year's Eve 1944, virtually all the members of the Jewish
Dutch band have assembled in Leen's office-bedroom, where they
are playing familiar old songs. Nurse Eddy de Wind pitches in on the
clarinet, and the talk is of music, the Netherlands and the war. A few
days earlier, a large transport had arrived containing rebels from
Warsaw. Leen, Lex, Max and the others had witnessed jets of flame
above the crematoria in Birkenau.

A young Jewish Amsterdammer comes into Block 4, goes up to the
block leader and asks whether his cousin, Bill Minco, is also there.
Leen points to him. The young man has been a prisoner at Auschwitz
for eight months, but has only just learned that Bill is here as well. A
prisoner had told him that Bill was living in the VIP Block 4 under the
protection of the famous Rotterdam boxer Leen Sanders. Bill's cousin
is given something to eat and relays to Bill the news that his parents
had managed to go into hiding just in the nick of time.

It is nearly midnight; the lights in Block 4 flicker off and on. The
air-raid siren is often going off now, and in the distance they can hear
artillery fire. This has to be their last year in the camp – how can it
be otherwise? The papers say that Warsaw has been recaptured; the
Russians are coming. What is to become of them now?

Part VI

The Death Train

I.

On 18 January 1945, Leen is standing at the gates when he sees Protective Custody Camp Leader Hössler in discussion with other SS officers. The camp orchestra's players are in the Music Room preparing for the military march. Usually an SS officer would be shouting '*Musik vorbereiten!*' (Music ready!), but not now; nor is there any roll-call – peculiar. *Rapportführer* Kaduk seems agitated, and the work details are not turning out. Prisoners are on quick march through the main camp, ordered back to their blocks where they must pack up their things. Barrels containing soup are brought in and, quite exceptionally, the prisoners may take whatever they want. Equally noteworthy, the Clothing Room is open, and from its windows prisoners are throwing down to others all manner of items: knitted caps, mittens, shirts, pullovers, shoes, spoons and much more besides.

SS men are lifting boxes and cabinets out of the blocks; motorcycles race through the camp; Nazis are yelling at one another. In front of Block 24 – the Political Department – paperwork is being thrown onto bonfires: registration papers, *Sterbebücher* (death-sentence inventories) and other incriminating material; the smoke can be seen from far and wide beyond the camp. The SS announce the evacuation, and everyone who can walk must go with them. Nobody tells the prisoners where they are going. Rumours do the rounds that, at the last, a special unit has been set up to finish off all the Jews. The war against the Allies is likely to be lost, but the war against the Jews must be won at all costs.

Leen says farewell to Eddy de Wind, Berthold Krebs, Bill Minco, Max Garcia, Elie Cohen, Kazik and other friends and acquaintances, then walks along Dalli-Dalli-Allee to the kitchen building and joins a lengthy queue. Thanks to his boxing practice and the additional food, he's still in reasonable condition after two years of Auschwitz. After a long wait he reaches the kitchen storeroom, where prisoners are handed two loaves of bread each. That is a great deal more than on a regular day. SS men and kapos are doling out margarine and tinned meat – another thing they don't see every day. Carts with KL AUSCHWITZ on the side are laden with food that Kazik and other kitchen staff have taken from the prisoners' kitchen, and prisoners are trying to snatch things off. Leen has managed to acquire a rucksack, a spoon, a bowl, additional clothes and other useful items; he's also bringing along a cigarette box made for him in the camp. The front of it shows him in a boxing ring up against a much larger man, while protecting his face with his famous left. The furniture maker Sander Turksma from The Hague has burned into the back: 'KL Auschwitz. Leen Sanders. 86764.'

In the afternoon *Rapportführer* Kaduk barks out that it is time to leave, and it's almost dark when Leen walks through the gates for the last time. The guards in their watchtowers are shining searchlights on the prisoners, their rifles poised. Leen is at the front, with thousands of prisoners following on behind him. Most are wearing clogs, with sheets tied around their heads. Prisoners are ordered to carry SS luggage stuffed full of looted goods; some of the SS have even handed over firearms for them to shoulder. Dr Elie Cohen is wearing quality British shoes 'organized' by him the day before from the Canada warehouse. For him, leaving Auschwitz alive counts as a victory, but his colleague Eddy de Wind has decided to take the risk and is hiding out in Block 9.

It is twenty-five degrees below zero, and snow-bound country lanes are now being tramped by men, women and teenagers in striped uniforms. Balls of fire and flashes of light can be seen on the distant horizon. Elie Cohen senses the prevailing good mood among prisoners – the Russians have never been as close as they are now, and British and American aircraft are making low passes every few hours. One hundred kilometres away, towns and villages have already been liberated; Hitler could surrender at any moment. Leen tries to keep up at the front as best he can. SS men are walking to the left and right of the procession at intervals of ten metres. Suddenly, a gunshot rings out: the first person has tried to flee, and in the hours that follow a good many more gunshots are heard. People are moving to the front because stragglers seem more likely to be killed. Trumpet player Lex van Weren is walking not far from Leen, his cornet hanging from his belt, and there are four others from the orchestra with him: a saxophonist, a Hungarian pianist called Lajos, a violinist and an accordion player who had often used to play 'O sole mio' together, as well as forbidden compositions by black jazz artists. Lex and the other musicians – just like Eddy – had weighed the pros and cons of staying behind at the main camp, ending up hiding behind piles of coal in Block 5 where nobody would be able to find them. However, they dared not hold out – the Nazis would be sure to destroy the camp.

'Schnell, schnell, schneller!'

'*Los, los!*'

'*Wollt ihr laufen, ihr Hunde?*' (You want to *walk*, you dogs?)

The SS appear panicked, and that gives people courage; motorcycles and cars carrying officers occasionally drive at speed up and down the column. The Russians have already passed Kraków, some sixty kilometres from Auschwitz, and at that rate they will soon overtake the exodus. Thousands of prisoners from external camps join the procession, and Dutch prisoners from Birkenau recount how over the past few days more people than ever have been sent up the chimney. Groups of people are led in different directions, passing villages where Poles are standing in tears. A tailor walks past his home and asks an SS man if he might quickly let his wife know; he's gone for scarcely a moment before he is back again and resuming his place. An order is shouted: a rest break. Hunks of bread are broken; tins of meat have frozen solid and cannot be opened; prisoners attempt to steal from one another. The SS open baskets of fresh bread, butter, jam and sausage. They are wearing balaclavas, winter coats and thick woollen gloves.

With every passing hour it becomes more and more difficult to put one foot in front of the other in the thick snow. Prisoners fall asleep as they march, falling by the wayside, never to wake again. Clogs are falling apart, and hundreds of prisoners' feet are clad only in rags. *Muselmänner* cannot keep up the pace; even stronger prisoners give up on account of hypothermia and frostbite. Stragglers get a bullet to the head, and escapees are shot in the back. One Pole says in Yiddish: 'Come now, dear friend, your son has been freed from his suffering.' The mittens of dead VIPs are pulled off, and people towards the rear step over the corpses.

*

Leen spends the first night in a hayloft at a Polish farm. He takes some bread from his rucksack, drinks something and attempts to sleep, but that is hampered by the rats, mice, lice, aircraft and explosions. Other prisoners quickly seek out private spots where they can eat without being robbed, and Leen cannot get up to relieve himself for fear of losing his own spot and having to resort to his fists to get it back.

After only a few hours their march resumes, and Bill Minco now joins Leen in the procession. He had still been at work in the Union munitions factory when, at three o'clock in the afternoon, he was told to pack up his things in the main camp for the evacuation. He took loaves of bread with him from the kitchen and then left with his cousin and a sixteen-year-old boy. After a few hours, he heard that Leen was in front somewhere and told his cousin and the boy that he was going to look for him. He picked up the pace, constantly walking faster than most of the others, but it still took him a day to get to the head of the procession. Thousands upon thousands of people were trudging forwards; there were times when the way was so constricted that he was unable to pass people.

Leen and Bill plod ahead together. All the while SS men are screaming: 'Keep it up, Jew pigs, you bastards, you sons of bitches! Move it! Move it!' Relieving yourself by the wayside is hazardous; the SS are likely to shoot you dead on sight. Trousers then become the repository for this 'uncomfortable ballast', as Leen's friend Herman Boasson would later recall in his memoirs. Every few minutes there's another gunshot; fathers and sons lie side by side in ditches, their bodies not covered up, their blood freezing or already frozen. Leen sees prisoners putting their hands in the air and the SS lodge bullets in their heads at only a few metres' distance. At thirty-three years of age, Victor 'Young' Perez, Birkenau's best boxer and a former professional champion, is just one such victim among fifteen thousand others.

They walk through forest and past lakes, through fields and meadows, the SS often losing their way. Feet are covered in blisters, flesh-wounds and sores. Leen and Bill scrape away snow to find grass to eat; from a stable they steal feed for pigs and horses, and they stuff their mouths with snow. Flasks of tea that Poles have set alongside their route are poured away by the SS. Prisoners take the risk of ducking out of the column when they have diarrhoea; Leen and Bill no longer dare eat the tinned meat. Bill is feeling light-headed and can barely walk any more, and has to stretch out his arms to keep his balance. Leen supports him. As Herman Boasson puts it, that thick layer of snow starts to look more and more like 'an inviting feather bed'.

Darkness has almost fallen when, on their second day since evacuation, they are once again permitted to rest for a while. There is no more food. Leen tries giving words of encouragement to any of the Dutch on the brink of giving up, lifts people up who have gone to lie at the wayside, and wakes them up when they're on the verge of falling asleep in the bitter cold – one fellow inmate calls him a pillar of strength. Leen also helps Bill 'time and again' to get back on his feet.

After three days of walking, Leen sees Lex again at a small station, his cornet dangling securely from his belt. He exchanges a few words with his friend Jack de Vries, Rotterdam's jazz idol and former member of the camp orchestra. Jack has brought a saxophone with him in its case, thinking it might help save him later. Nathan Vuijsje, the former orchestra trombonist, is wearing a striped uniform, the mittens from his cousin Janny at the Experiments Block and clogs without socks.

Lex and Jack are trying to protect their fingers from the cold, and Bill collapses. A locomotive boiler is leaking hot water; Leen collects some and sprinkles it over Bill, pouring some of it into his mouth, and he comes to. Lajos, the orchestra's Hungarian pianist, falls to the ground right beside Leen, Bill and Lex. Dead.

They are in the small town of Wodzisław Śląski in Silesia, very close to the border with Czechoslovakia, and twenty-five kilometres from the city of Ostrava. The Nazis call it Loslau. Local residents try throwing packages and bread from a bridge, but they are shot at by the SS and blood drips down from above, turning the snow into scarlet ooze. It is in Loslau that the SS decide on the camps to which prisoners will be sent; freight and cattle wagons are stationed in a large train yard. Although the high spirits of three days earlier have, in the words of someone present, 'dissipated to quite some degree', laughter is still eked out here and there; Bill calls it gallows humour. They are looking forward to the train journey and finally being able to sit. According to Lex, Leen is a focal point for prisoners at the station, and is the proxy leader of the Dutch. Bill is reunited with his cousin, and the sixteen-year-old boy is still there too. Harry Prins and Maurice van Kleef, drummers in the orchestra, group together with Lex, Nathan, Jack, Bill and Leen. The Dutchmen decide to stick close to Leen, otherwise they will never survive; the Poles are hardier.

They get into the wagon with Leen, but another hundred prisoners have to join them. There is no room, and the SS kick, shove and beat. Most of the prisoners are lying one on top of the other; there are fights for space. Leen makes sure his Dutch friends get places at the sides of the wagon. The destination: Gross-Rosen concentration camp, also known as 'Ninety Days', because the average prisoner lasts no longer than that.

II.

The cattle wagon takes its time going through occupied Poland. Leen, Lex and the others pass bullet-ridden houses, factories missing walls, collapsed viaducts and ghost villages. Most of the wagons are open to the elements; only the SS have roofed transport. The temperature is minus twenty, and the Dutch are trying to rub some warmth back into one another.

The train pulls up to the small platform at Gross-Rosen, where the bombing and shelling of nearby Breslau is clearly audible. They have to wait for hours in the wagon and, afterwards, must walk a further three kilometres. Local residents study them with curiosity. It is still snowing when Leen, Bill, Lex, Jack and the others arrive at a large gate, where SS guards in watchtowers fix the prisoners in their gunsights, and familiar words greet them: ARBEIT MACHT FREI. Gross-Rosen is a camp where prisoners must be worked to death, die from exhaustion or take a bullet to the head.

The newcomers walk past SS buildings, a clothing room, a kitchen and prisoner blocks. Emergency barracks have been built on a rise visible behind barbed wire. Under normal conditions three hundred prisoners would live in the barracks buildings, but they must now cater for seventeen hundred. The newcomers – Jews and non-Jews alike – are assigned a number stitched onto jackets and trousers. Leen, Bill, Lex and the others have only just stopped to sit or lie down when the block leader starts calling out names and numbers and yells that they have to stand up to eat. It is only after an hour that they bring out a thin soup: one in every ten of the prisoners is handed a small bowl, while the others look on.

The block leader is tall, strong and well-nourished; one prisoner calls him 'the bloodhound'. Taking up his stick, he runs through the room, kicking the newcomers with his heavy boots, beating them until they are all lying flat on the floor. His beady eyes glisten and droplets of perspiration break out across his face and neck. There are no beds in the barracks, just a scattering of straw, and in one corner there are hefty, overflowing barrels: the *Scheisskübel* (shit tubs). Leen's friend Jacques Furth comments that Auschwitz was a picture in comparison to this place. Weakened prisoners are compelled to pile one on top of the other; Bill has a fat Pole sleeping on top of him, leaving him scarcely able to breathe. Complaining about it is out of the question, as it serves only as an invitation to the block leader to return with his stick. As he wrote after the war, Leen received 'the beating of my life'.

The Polish block leader screams the newcomers awake at half past four, takes his stick and drives them out into the freezing cold. Leen, Bill and the others dress quickly. They're in quarantine and do not have to work, but the barracks must be kept clean. The camp inmates stand for hours in the snow until they are allowed to go back indoors again. Diarrhoea is running down their legs: it's impossible to stop it and next to impossible to reach the *Scheisskübel* in time. The barrel is too high, and you lose your sleeping place if you get up.

On the third day the block leader makes a speech. He tells them that Gross-Rosen is called the '*komische Lager*' (comical camp) and the newcomers are nonplussed. The block leader promises that the prisoners can have a good life at the 'comical camp' only if they behave. He can tell them nothing about their length of stay there or about what the SS are planning, but comes back a quarter of an hour later to bellow out: 'All Jews fall in!'

Leen and fifteen hundred other prisoners walk outside. Rumours fly that they are going up the chimney. Jack de Vries's saxophone case is taken from him; however, Lex is able to smuggle his cornet out of the camp. Ary Berti Turksma is not on the list because at seventeen he is too young, but he wants to go with Leen, and climbs out of the barracks window.

The Jews march to Gross-Rosen's small station. Walking is difficult for Leen since the beating. Another rumour starts doing the rounds, that Hitler is dead and the Nazis have surrendered, but if so, it is not reflected in the demeanour of the SS guards.

The train's cattle-wagon convoy consists of twenty vehicles, eighteen of which are open-roofed, and out of them emerge prisoners who have been working in a Gross-Rosen external detail. Their air-raid siren had gone off and they'd had to get back to the main camp at the double because the Russians were coming. Leen helps Lex, Bill and eighteen other Dutchmen get into a covered wagon, where there are also Hungarians or Poles. The wagon is twelve square metres in size. The final twenty prisoners are beaten into the train. On either side of the wagon there is a small, barred hatch; one corner contains a *Scheisskübel*, but for the Dutch it is impossible to reach.

Prisoners steal one another's bread – what there is left – and fights break out for sitting space; at times, the Hungarians will simply beat someone to death. Leen is well-known for his left hooks, including among most of the Hungarians and Poles. After the war, one Dutchman recalls how Leen had an 'extremely hard head' and his fist 'always found its target'. In Lex's words, an international battle 'for living space' ensues.

The engine driver sets off. It is dark, and Leen can barely see where he is standing. They get almost nothing to eat or drink and the train seems to make barely any progress. Sometimes they stop for hours at a platform somewhere, hearing only the stamp of German boots and the familiar shouting. Most people think they are on their way to Dachau in Bavaria where resistance fighters and actual VIPs are imprisoned. In the best of all outcomes, they will be exchanged for German prisoners of war, or the Russians will finally arrive.

In Bill's words, the Dutch 'are grousing, without mincing their words', while Poles and Hungarians are tackling people by the legs or have arms flailing in all directions. Clogs come off to bash in neighbouring skulls; some prisoners are stabbing people with knives. Bodies are thrown out at rest stops. Harry Prins notes how Leen keeps 'order' in their corner, from time to time delivering a punch or two; Lex calls him 'our guardian angel'.

Some twenty of the Dutch are either standing or lying down in a corner. They take turns in letting some of their party sit against the wall for a few hours, and Leen affords special protection to former members of the camp orchestra. After all, musicians can be useful in a concentration camp when it comes to 'organizing' food and provisions. Sleeping prisoners are allowed to let their heads rest in a countryman's lap; after a little while, the decent spots are given up to someone else. An old man becomes sick and tries to support himself on others, but loses his balance, colliding against Poles and Hungarians, who push him from left to right. He ends up in the Dutch corner, where Leen makes space for him, finding the old man a cramped spot on the floor.

Two days pass, perhaps three. People are dying of cold or hunger and in fights. The bodies are shoved into a corner and used as beds or cushions. At rest stops, shouts come from the SS: 'Corpses out!' One prisoner is wearing a woollen Norwegian pullover purloined by him from the Canada warehouse before the evacuation. An SS man standing outside on the platform waves a slice of bread in front of the prisoner's nose for just as long as it takes him to give up the pullover in exchange. The SS laugh. Another man swaps his mountain boots for a piece of sausage; some prisoners hand over medallions or other jewellery, receiving cigarettes in return.

Leen knots sheets to a belt to make a hammock. The weakest or most useful prisoners take it in turns to be suspended in this way. As a musician, Lex is classed as a special case in the wagon, and Leen lifts him up into the hammock; he's the only one of them still capable of doing that. Lex lies back in the sheet, his cornet in his arms, looking for hour after hour at the outside world through the small, barred hatchway. Bill is next to take a turn in the hammock; he closes his eyes and imagines himself sleeping in a clean bed with feather pillows. His long legs are poking fellow travellers, but they forgive him; this youngest-but-one from among the group of Dutchmen needs his rest far more than most of the others in their wagon.

The SS refuse to bring them anything to eat on the fourth day. The thirst is worse than the hunger, so Leen uses his spoon to scrape snow from the roof of the wagon. At rest stops he lowers a food bowl on a piece of string, asking railway employees if they'll fill it with snow, water or food. A more hazardous venture is tying a tin can to a belt or rope and then letting it drag several metres along snowy ground to reel it in again afterwards. Sometimes the rope will get caught, and there is the possibility of scooping up excrement or something equally unpalatable.

There are times when the Jewish prisoners are brought to a halt for hours because of the aerial bombardment, with RAF aircraft making low passes overhead. In the meantime, the landscape is becoming less hilly. Leipzig has been partially destroyed. The train stops and the prisoners are permitted to stretch their legs for the first time since their departure; they are handed a small cup of soup and a small piece of bread before reboarding and continuing onwards. Dresden looks like Rotterdam after the 'Fateful Day'. The hillsides and fields of Bavaria are a rolling sea of white; farmers are busy chopping wood and sweeping snow from their barnyards.

After five days and nights the train stops in southern Bavaria. Lips and eyebrows are split, throats are sore, ears and noses frostbitten, legs swollen, and almost everyone has diarrhoea. Ary Berti Turksma estimates that in their wagon 'give or take forty-five men died en route', and of those who remain, most are injured, starving or dying.

The train keeps moving on until it is only a short distance from their new camp. The Dutch feel relief, but the SS continue to beat and kick them here as well, shouting, as ever: 'Get out! Get out! Hurry up! Hurry up!' Guard dogs strain on leashes and bite. Leen steps out and stretches his legs, walking a few laboured paces. Munich is twenty kilometres away, and the Allies are bombing it. Leen lifts Bill out of the train, and as they walk past the wagons they see for the first time how many are lying dead in the filth. Bill is unable to find his cousin; they probably had to throw him out somewhere along the way.

III.

The stone gateway to Dachau concentration camp is just a few hundred metres from the track. Its great iron gate opens with, at its centre, the familiar words: ARBEIT MACHT FREI. Leen, Bill, Lex and the others pass a large white building with small windows. The SS shout: 'Caps off!' and they are lined up on the spacious, windy roll-call square. Guards are carrying pistols and whips, guard dogs restless at their feet. The sick and dying from Leen's transport are carried on stretchers to the barrack blocks.

Leen marches to the *Wirtschaftsgebäude*, a squat building with a kitchen, a room where clothing is passed out, a washroom, a laundry and work stations for forced labourers. The roof bears a quote from Himmler: 'There is one road to freedom. Its milestones are: obedience, diligence, honesty, order, cleanliness, sobriety, truthfulness, sacrifice and love for the Fatherland.' The Dutch have to line themselves up in rows of ten and an SS officer bawls out: 'You are all lawless, dishonourable and helpless. You are all a *Haufen Scheiße* [pile of shit] and that's just how you'll all be treated.' After hours of waiting in bitter cold, Leen enters the *Schubraum* (prisoner transport room): a large space where prisoners are being registered by men seated at tables in striped uniforms, whose heads have been badly shorn and who wear brown armbands labelled CAMP CLERK. Bill jumps the queue; he needs to get inside quickly before he collapses. Leen's turn comes at last after a long wait. Jack de Vries is in front of him and tells the camp clerk that he is a musician. Leen is asked whether he is married: 'Yes.' Next, he is asked about his profession: 'Masseur.' He is handed a registration card and becomes number 139396. The clerk stamps a large 'J' on his card and adds 'Sch.' for *Schutzhaft* (protective custody), a reference to Leen's resistance past and his status as a political prisoner. Jack and Leen are advised not to drink the water; thousands have already died from it.

They have to go to the bathhouse, with SS guards screaming out: 'Forwards! Move it! Faster! Get undressed!' They remove their clothes and are allowed only to retain their belts. Their rags are thrown on to a vast heap and cleaned as quickly as possible. Polish kapos are seizing valuables from the newcomers, and Lex conceals his cornet as fast as he can. The men have to wait naked for hours before being allowed into the bathhouse; Leen's feet are bleeding, covered in corns and blisters. His hair had just started to grow out, but is now shaved off again. He has some disinfecting agent rubbed on to him and for the first time in ages is permitted to shower; according to a concentration-camp friend the water is 'deliciously hot'. Most of the Dutch take the risk and drink some of it. Lex smuggles his cornet with him under the shower; he cleans the mouthpiece and washes out the tubes and valves.

Kapos dole out uniforms and caps. Leen has had to hand in his worn-out shoes and now receives in return clogs like the ones he wore during his first days at Auschwitz. It's the coldest winter since the start of the war, but their striped uniforms are threadbare – summer garments at best. The Allies are flying overhead towards Munich on a fresh bombing raid; one Dutchman calls it 'the sweetest music I ever heard'.

The newcomers must go in groups of one hundred to quarantine block 19, where a litre of soup is being shared out. Prisoners are racing to get there, pushing others out of the way. Poles fight with Hungarian and Dutch prisoners in a re-enactment of the train to Dachau. The block leader warns them about typhus, the first case of which came to light a month before; now, an average of 150 prisoners are dying from it every day, the typhus barracks are full and the SS are not providing them with any medicines. A little further on there is a special death barracks, where the sickest prisoners spend their last hours. There's a shortage of coal, which means that the dead can no longer be incinerated in the crematoria. Corpses now lie between the barrack-block buildings, where they are set alight to burn in deep pits.

A block consists of four *Stuben* (rooms). Usually, each room would accommodate fifty-two people, but many more are now living in them because of the evacuations from other camps. Leen sleeps with two others in his bed, and is awakened at four o'clock. The camp commandant attends each roll-call with his wife standing alongside; he has a riding crop with him and from time to time uses it to strike prisoners at random.

After roll-call, the newcomers must return to their quarantine block. They hardly dare drink any of the water because of the risk of infection, and the overcrowding means that they are getting even less to eat than they did at Gross-Rosen. Leen spends much of the day sweeping the floor, making beds and squashing lice between his fingernails. The block shudders during each air-raid, with bowls and cups falling to the floor and breaking; meanwhile, the sun shines on corpses lying in the small thoroughfares between the blocks. Posters show the Grim Reaper attacking an insect with his scythe; the text below reads:

> *CAUTION!*
> *Eine Laus dein Tod*
> *Een luis uw dood*
> *Un poioio la morte*
> *Un pou, ta mort*
> *One louse your death*
> *Egy tetü, a haladod*

Newspapers are being smuggled into the quarantine block, and Leen reads in them about the Allied advance at Nijmegen. He meets the socialist politician Wiardi Beckman from Block 25, who explains the camp to him: clergy and ministers live in Block 26; room 4 at Block 15 is filled with patients suffering from diarrhoea and, according to Bill, they are dying there 'like rats'. German prisoners had been sent to the front a month ago; since then, most of the kapos have been Polish. As elsewhere, the Dachau policy is to work Jews to death, and strong prisoners such as Leen usually have to work in horticulture or farming details. He cannot be a boxer or boxing coach at Dachau because sports have been prohibited here since 1944. Punished SS men are recognizable by their white overalls; they are treated just as badly as the Jews. Beckman manages to get Red Cross packages for Leen and the others, which contain sugar cubes, margarine, hardtack biscuits, milk powder, Ovaltine, cheese and corned beef.

Lex loses consciousness and becomes delirious; it's typhus, and he has to be sent to the typhus barracks, where he revives and recovers after nine days. As he says in his memoirs: 'With typhus there are two outcomes; you die or you stay alive. Well, I stayed alive.' Leen is sleeping in the same room as Bill, the Rotterdam mechanic Alexander van Gelderen, saxophonist Sally van der Kloot from The Hague, painter Simon Zilverberg from Amsterdam, the Auschwitz orchestra's former drummer Harry Prins and the Amsterdam diamond worker David Frank. Their block also contains typhus patients.

When the block leader sees that Lex has a cornet, he is sent to play in the camp orchestra, which means his transfer to another block; this now enables him to share out extra food among the Dutch. The block leader protects him and in return Lex has to play 'O sole mio' for him for a good part of the day.

After a couple of weeks, Leen and Bill have to leave quarantine to go outside and, together with three others, put up fences for new typhus barracks. They are not given any mittens or gloves and it is almost impossible to hold on to the shovels and crowbars. The earth is frozen, but they have to keep hacking away at it until they make an impression, with the skin on the palms of their hands splitting open in the process. Bill and Leen try digging a hole together, while the three others pace up and down to keep warm; after quarter of an hour they swap. Sometimes the *Lagerführer* will come to watch, at which point the forced labourers behave as if all five of them had been hard at it the whole time. On one occasion the *Lagerführer* takes his riding crop and beats Bill's back black and blue.

After a month in Dachau, Leen undergoes inspection for a work detail, whereupon a camp doctor determines him fit, and an entry is made on his card: WORKER. He is to be sent to work at the Mühldorf external concentration camp. Lex, Jack de Vries and Ary Berti

Turksma remain behind in Dachau, while Leen's friend Herman Boasson is also selected along with Bill, Alexander van Gelderen, David Frank, Simon Zilverberg, Sally van der Kloot and Harry Prins. It's late February when the group marches through the Dachau gate to its small station, from which they travel in cattle wagons to the small town of Mühldorf am Inn, seventy-eight kilometres away. They disembark at the main station and, after a few hours, reach a forest path. Snow keeps sticking to their wooden soles and it is nearly impossible to keep their balance, so Bill and Leen walk arm in arm, their clogs getting heavier with every step they take; prisoners stumble, then give up and are left behind in the forest. Leen, Bill and the others search for stones along the way to help scrape off the snow, but it makes little difference. Bill falls, Leen lifts him back up and on they trudge again. After four kilometres, an SS guard opens a gate in a barbed-wire barrier. The newcomers turn to the left and see prisoners in striped uniform, SS cabins, guard posts and the residence of the camp commandant. They pass through another barbed-wire barrier and arrive at the roll-call square where, lining either side of a long avenue they see *Erdhütten*: turf-roofed wooden huts, the bulk of which lie underground; the roofs serve as camouflage. The men are subjected to a headcount, and Leen recognizes Poles, Greeks and Hungarians from Auschwitz. He asks whether any Dutchmen are also there: perhaps his second cousin Lou has made it to this place, or one of his brothers.

The camp is called Waldlager 6 and is governed by the Organisation Todt, which builds motorways and war-effort factories on the initiative of Albert Speer, Minister of Armaments and Munitions. Now, there are just seven hundred men and youths living here, plus a few women working in the kitchen. At one time there had been many more, but thousands of forced labourers had died of hunger, infections, exhaustion, typhus, tuberculosis, diarrhoea or cold. In summer, the average prisoner at Mühldorf will last it out for a couple of months; in winter, a good deal less than that. The dead are picked up in barrows and tipped into a mass grave amid the trees outside the camp.

Leen descends a small flight of steps into the hut. Bill describes the place as a filth-ridden slum, and thirty prisoners have to live there. Leen's cot has a smattering of straw. At the back there is a small, unglazed window open to the elements; it's usually dark because the air-raid siren keeps going off and then the electricity cuts out. The sanitary facility is outside and a twenty-metre walk; it amounts to a hole in the ground with two planks either side. Three quarters of the prisoners have diarrhoea, and some lack the strength to go outdoors, relieving themselves in the hut instead. Visits to the toilet while dressed are forbidden; any transgression is taken as an escape attempt, and the guards use live ammunition.

On Leen's first morning at the Waldlager he is woken at three o'clock. There is no water for washing. Half an hour later he is given coffee and 250 grams of bread, after which a kapo shouts out that they must fall in, and Leen goes to line up with the other twenty-nine prisoners from his hut. The midday soup consists of water with a little barley. In the evening, eight men have to try to share one piece of bread, some margarine and a small piece of sausage. The Dutch do not have any important posts at the camp and as a result Leen is unable to obtain any additional food. The prisoners' camp leader kapo, a Czech, says in a speech that the war cannot last much longer – kapos and the SS are using the expression 'five minutes before midnight'.

Although the camp leader tells the newcomers they may spend the first three weeks in quarantine, they actually find themselves enlisted for work detail after only three days. Since the summer of 1944, a subterranean aircraft factory has been in operation for the production of Messerschmitt Me 262s, the world's first operational jet fighters, for the Luftwaffe. Leen has to lift fifty-kilogram sacks of cement and empty them out into a tall concrete mixer. For extra warmth, he tries wrapping his legs with paper from the cement sacks, but it rips and creates fresh wounds. He is working twelve hours a day. There's no boxing on Sundays, nor any cabaret or music; there is nothing except the hauling of sacks of cement. Prisoners sometimes lose their footing and slip into the mixer; guards are not permitted to make any rescue attempt. Herman Boasson observes that life in Auschwitz was paradise compared with their new camp.

The air-raid sirens are sounding continually now; the British are flying ever lower over the camp and dropping bombs on Munich and Mühldorf am Inn. Air-raids are accompanied by shouts from the SS of 'Fliegerdeckung!' (Take cover from air attack!) Warehouses storing bread burn to the ground in Mühldorf town centre, so Leen, Bill and the others receive nothing to eat for four days; their bread is being sent in lorry loads to the town. Prisoners are also sent to the town centre to clear rubble and sweep the streets. The SS use the butts of their rifles to beat prisoners caught attempting to loot food or tobacco from shops and the prisoners are frisked on their return. The Lagerführer has a machine gun aimed at them, threatening to finish them all off; SS men enter the huts to search cupboards, sheets and cots. It is twenty degrees below, and that day the roll-call lasts for six hours. Diamond worker David Frank dies of exhaustion. The Greeks have a song that they sing nearly every day: 'After every December there comes a May.'

*

In the third week of April, the camp commandant issues an order that all Jewish prisoners must fall in. A kapo tells them that the Americans are in the area, while others contend that Hitler has surrendered. Leen, Bill, Harry Prins, Herman Boasson, Alex van Gelderen, Simon Zilverberg and their fellow Jewish concentration-camp inmates are marshalled into groups of 120 men. They march through the forest, pass through a gate and stop at a railway track where forty cattle wagons are awaiting them. The Allies are bombing Mühldorf's main station and airfield, and rumours spread that the departing prisoners are to be shot within a few days. Why else would they have selected only Jews?

IV.

Leen is at gunpoint as he boards the train along with 3,600 other Jews;
Bill climbs into the same wagon. It is late on the night of 25 April 1945.
A *Hauptscharführer* (sergeant major) is in charge of the transport, and
the train is a kilometre in length, consisting of sixty-three wagons.
Leen, Bill and the others barely have any room to move their arms or
legs and are given nothing to eat and no bucket to relieve themselves
in. Only their SS guards know where they are going. Their boss,
Himmler, had wanted initially to bomb the concentration camps of
Dachau and Mühldorf, but it had proved too challenging. Instead,
he issued an order that the Jewish prisoners be taken on foot and by
train to the Tyrol for the purpose of murdering them, either en route
or in Austria.

Early the next morning the train stops at a small station. Black
lettering stands out against the small white-painted station building,
giving the locality's name: AMPFING. SS men hurriedly alight, pacing
up and down the platform. Bombers are flying over the Bavarian
hillsides while the engine driver proceeds at sluggish speed, passing
stretches of beech and spruce trees and crossing meadows. The
engine is on its last legs; none of the SS is able to repair it under these

conditions. The first of the sick begin to succumb, but they may not be thrown from the train; one German Jew has typhus and becomes delirious. Where are they going to? Why are they going so slowly? Herman Boasson comments that they are on a journey of the dead into limbo.

To the side of the track at a rest stop there is a cart containing provisions. German nationals head to the front wagon, where they serve food. They then return to the food cart, bringing soup to the second wagon. The idea is to carry on until every wagon has been dealt with in turn, but most of the prisoners from the first few wagons are trying to force their way into the wagons behind and the provisions are almost exhausted by the time anyone gets to Leen and Bill. The prisoners in their wagon receive a saucer and have to ensure that the soup is shared fairly between them. The soup urn is placed on the ground while Poles and Hungarians resume fighting the Dutch, with Leen protecting his friends. Around sixty prisoners make a run for the urn. Saucers tip over, and men try to fish out the biggest vegetable chunks from the urn; most of the soup has gone on their clothes and almost nobody has eaten anything. More arguments, more fighting. After much waiting, one lad at last has some soup in his saucer but is pushed from behind; he tries spooning up the soup from the ground, then licks it up. Leen and Bill watch from their small corner, trying to conserve energy.

It's dark by the time the prisoners and their guards reach a town. Leen, Bill and the others are given a small ration of bread with nothing else and manage to peer outside through an opening to see buildings missing roofs; pavements shelled to destruction; German civilians looking apprehensive. The *Hauptscharführer* inspects the train. Bill asks him what their destination is and receives the reply that the prisoners have no need to worry; they are going to a Swiss refugee camp, where they can shower, have plenty to eat and rest. The *Hauptscharführer* is in contact with the Red Cross and everything has been arranged to make the transfer of prisoners go as smoothly as possible. Bill and Leen simply have to let the others know about this.

'Has the German army surrendered?'

'Not yet, although some localized divisions have.'

The train continues onwards. At around six in the evening on 27 April, Leen and the others reach the Bavarian town of Poing; it has taken them two days to travel seventy kilometres. The doors open onto a large field of potatoes and the prisoners are allowed out to relieve themselves. As Leen crouches down, he hears prisoners cheering; guards are saying that the war is over; SS men are running off with suitcases filled with loot; people are shouting out: 'We're free!' Some former prisoners abandon their wagons and go into Poing in search of food. They walk through the gardens of white Bavarian cottages and farmsteads to find the barns and kitchens of Bavarian workers, taking with them chickens, potatoes, bread and milk as they go. They start spreading out: men, women and boys, reeking of filth, milling about in their ragged striped uniforms in people's front and back gardens, begging for bread. They plead for still more food and are given jam, soup and meat.

A few of the SS have remained behind at the train. Bill asks whether the Germans have really lost the war; an SS man says they have, and the *Hauptscharführer* confirms it. The prisoners are allowed to go where they want; none of the SS will be shooting them any more, and the train will not be going any further. The door to the provisions wagon is broken open and there are still a lot of provisions left; the SS had wanted to hold on to them for their own people. Leen, Bill and the others grab cheese, bread, sausage and jam until others get to hear of the food and start to storm the provisions wagon. With their last remaining strength, men and boys try to push one another out of the way; fights break out again and some Hungarians use scrap iron to smash a way into the back of the wagon and snatch a few Edam cheeses. Leen and Bill see the hole, grab a cheese and look for a quiet spot next to the platform. They break the cheese into pieces, hide the rest for later and rest a while before deciding whether to head into Poing as well.

An SS officer next to the train has been in contact with a superior and tells the *Hauptscharführer* that Hitler still intends to win the war, which he believes is possible; the SS must withdraw only temporarily, to enable them to retake Western Europe later. Although there had been an insurgency by a Bavarian resistance group, the rebels have been arrested; right now, rebels are being shot dead throughout Germany. Members of the Bavarian Luftwaffe have been alerted and are forming a cordon around the fugitives. Harry Prins is walking with five Dutch lads alongside the railway tracks towards Munich when they are apprehended by Nazis toting machine guns and marched back to the train with their hands clasped behind their heads; their friend Mikkie van Coevorden is walking with a limp and is shot. Harry and the others drag him to a farm, where an SS man tells the residents that the Jew had tried to escape. Mikkie is badly injured and a commanding officer shoots him in the neck. Harry has to bury him next to a shed. Gunfire can be heard in the distance: former camp guards from Mühldorf and members of the Luftwaffe are herding together hundreds of prisoners in Poing town centre. They shoot into the air first of all, then use live ammunition on them, and fleeing people take bullets to the legs, head or back. Fifty people die in Poing.

The train does carry on after all. Dozens of prisoners have remained behind in the woodland surrounding Poing, or have hidden in a farmer's house or barn. Leen, Bill and the others are given nothing more to eat because the provisions wagon is bare. Two open-roofed wagons have been coupled together, with both the dead and the wounded placed inside.

On 28 April the engine driver pulls into Penzberg. The day before, democrats had deposed this small town's Nazi mayor but the SS had fought back, stringing up twenty-eight of the rebels from trees lining the main thoroughfare. They remain dangling there as the train pulls in.

On the following day, 29 April, Leen, Bill and the others arrive at the small station that serves the village of Beuerberg. The wounded are carried to a convent, where nuns have offered to care for them, and farmers' wives are bringing meat and vegetable soup to tables set up alongside the chapel organ. The wounded are given tea and water. Aircraft are making ever lower passes overhead, but Bill and Leen have grown accustomed to it. The Americans think the train is carrying German soldiers; bombs explode and shots are fired. The SS are screaming at the prisoners to get out fast. The doors to Leen and Bill's wagon slide open and they seek cover beneath, while Harry Prins ducks under the engine. The SS are ditching their weapons by the railway tracks, leaping over fences and running in the direction of the woods. Hundreds of prisoners take advantage of the chaos and flee. The sound of the aircraft fades, replaced by the cries of SS men:

'Everyone back in the wagons!' They comb the area; fugitives are being killed again; twenty bodies are laid out on the platform; the rest of the dead are brought back on the train. Bill assesses the subsequent mood as 'below rock bottom'.

The train sluggishly sets in motion. Spring should have been in full sway for some time now, but once again it is starting to snow. At four o'clock in the afternoon, the engine driver stops at a three-storey station building painted pale yellow. Its nineteenth-century windows are shuttered, and Gothic lettering announces the name of the stop as SEESHAUPT. The locomotive has broken down again. The prisoners spend the night in their wagons until, at eight in the morning, the doors slide open once more and an SS man tells them that the Americans have arrived. Nobody can believe it. A soldier peers inside a wagon: 'Are you Jews? Can you understand me? Can you hear me? Can you get out?'

Leen is one of the few who can speak a little English, and he talks to servicemen in General Patton's army. German Jews are shouting out: *'Amerikaner! Amerikaner!'* and *'Hitler kaputt!'* Dozens of men, women and boys have died at the very last from exhaustion, typhus or bullet wounds; the dead lie in the wagons amid the living and dying. Two young women are laid out on the platform. A soldier has tears in his eyes. Former prisoners are handed chocolate, bread, water, tinned meat and cigarettes. It is 30 April 1945, and Leen is free. This time for real.

V.

___

For a long time Leen remains sitting next to the *Mühldorfer Todeszug* (Mühldorf death train), as it comes to be known after the war. The Americans force Seeshaupt's inhabitants to go to the train and witness for themselves what their countrymen have wrought. They come up to liberated prisoners and ask: '*Ist es dann doch wahr?*' (Is it really true, then?) The strongest among the Jewish men want to wreak revenge on the SS, but are restrained. Soldiers bury the dead in the woods.

Leen goes to the emergency centre: the NSDAP Adolf Hitler School. His bed is clean and he sleeps long and deeply; in the morning, he drinks strong coffee and for breakfast he has ham, eggs and marmalade to go with his bread. He is given soap and is able to shave, disinfect his wounds and stick plasters on his blisters. The front page of the army newspaper *Stars and Stripes* proclaims: HITLER DEAD.

At the end of May, following a month of recovery, Leen boards a train and, via a place called Cernon, arrives in Paris, where awaiting him on the platform there are baguettes and wine, with a band playing the Marseillaise. He is given fifty francs and then travels, via Calais, to Brussels, where he has a meeting with the editors of *Het Laatste Nieuws*.

'The SS guards were mad about boxing matches and that is why I received special treatment,' he tells the journalist. 'It is that treatment I have to thank for the fact that I am one of the two Dutchmen to have remained alive out of a group of two thousand prisoners.' When asked what he is going to do now, Leen shrugs his shoulders and says he might well start boxing again. He has already arranged to spar with the Flemish boxer Anneet.

He travels on to the Netherlands. While inside the train at Centraal Station in Amsterdam, 'displaced persons' are inspected for diseases; meanwhile civil servants verify whether they do indeed have a right to return. Leen goes to live with his cousin Elisabeth 'Beppie' Blom-Taubman and her husband in Rotterdam's Abraham Kuyperlaan district. He is reunited with his eldest brother, Jakob, also known as no. 179694, who had ended up, via Auschwitz, in Blechhammer. There, he was liberated by the Russians and, in Odessa, boarded a boat for Marseille, arriving in Tilburg on 30 May. In a statement to a Red Cross worker, Jakob says: 'My mind is messed up.' He asks the Red Cross for information about his parents, brothers and sisters 'deported as Jews during the occupation and not as yet returned'. Apart from himself and Leen, only their younger brother Joël appears to have survived the war; he had been a soldier in the Dutch East Indies and is living in Bangkok.

After a few months, Jakob and Leen move to the confiscated house of a former member of the NSB, on Schieweg. Their sister Roosje had lived a few houses along the street with her husband Simon and son David – all of them killed. 'Whenever I walk or drive along Schieweg, I'm always drawn to look at my sister's house. She was gassed,' says Leen to an interviewer.

Leen gives boxing lessons at a gymnasium on 's-Gravendijkwal, attends boxing events in Rotterdam and catches up with Bep, Luc, Theo and other old-timers in the ring. Before and after matches he wanders through the city centre: bridges are still in ruins, the Zandstraat neighbourhood has been devastated, and Sint Laurensstraat no longer exists. Scarcely anyone wants to look back on the war and the dead are seldom commemorated; instead, people are engaged in the rebuilding of Rotterdam. The 'noble art' provides some distraction and, just occasionally, comfort.

Leen talks about Auschwitz only with those who have shared the same misfortune. Had his boxing amid the fumes of the crematoria been the right thing to do? A Polish former concentration-camp boxer describes the feelings of guilt as being 'like a festering sore'. Leen tries to work out how many prisoners there were in Auschwitz and Birkenau. In Birkenau 'in the final year, at least, something in the order of around 60,000 or 65,000' and in the main camp '25,000 or 28,000, and it could also have been 30,000 or 35,000, as there were three or four to a bed in many blocks'. He concludes letters to fellow former concentration-camp inmates with: 'from your Auschwitz friend, Leen'. In an interview, he says: 'I have nightmares three times a week about those experiences at the camp. I'll dream that I'm fighting krauts, etc.'

He often meets up with Jack de Vries and Maurice van Kleef, who form a jazz band with another Auschwitz survivor, Louis Bannet. Jack and Maurice have already remarried, Lex has a girlfriend and Bill is engaged. Leen starts looking around like a *meshuggener* (a crazy man), as he puts it; a new wife might just give meaning to his existence.

He corresponds with Leon 'the Englishman' Greenman. Leen had saved his life at Auschwitz, and in tribute Leon has hung up on his wall a photograph of Leen in full boxing kit. Leon's wife, Else, and his son, Barnett, were murdered in 1943; his brother Morry dies a few months after liberation. Leen writes:

> Dear Friend,
>
> Received your letter and was shocked about your brother Morry.
>
> Oh, mate, as if we hadn't had enough woes already and on top of that something like this has to happen to you. Our paths have not been a bed of roses in recent years.
>
> Via this path, my condolences, and, Leon, we'll just keep soldiering on. Leon, perhaps you won't believe me but there are times when I'm sorry I came back and that I didn't take the same path as my wife and boys, as the world feels so rotten and ruined to me that it's hard for me to feel at home in it.
>
> Anyway, we'll just make the best of it that we can, won't we?
>
> Stay well and hold your head up high. Best wishes from me, your 'old friend',
>
> Len Sanders

In the spring of 1946, just as in the past, Leen is training every morning, seven days a week, in the Kralingse Bos. He writes to a former boxer how 'peculiar' it is that his boxing style should be different from how it was before the war. Between 1922 and 1942 he had been the textbook example of a practitioner of the 'noble art', but in 1946, he can 'be so foul that I could well chew them up'. It comes of 'those horrendous years'. 'It's still a wonder to me that I *did* come out alive and others didn't.'

He wants to start boxing again professionally in England. The Ring was destroyed by German bombs in 1940, but other venues are sure to want to see Len Sanders again. His address books were all burned on 14 May 1940, so Leen asks his British friend Leon if he will speak to 'the Yiddish boxing promoter' Jack Solomons from the East End and to Isidore Colson, a 'Belgian manager with a lot of contacts in the boxing world in England'. Leen wants to be back in touch with them, 'given that I feel so much back on form that I'll soon be making a comeback to fight matches again'. In another letter he writes: 'My weight is virtually back to normal, just as it was before the War; when I'd just arrived back in Holland I weighed in at 80 kilograms and now I've been training so regularly I weigh 73 kilograms, so within a few days I'll be back to a normal middleweight.'

Leon becomes Leen's contact in England. He calls managers and promoters, and he writes letters:[1]

In regards to Len Sanders, a very close friend of me, having been with him in the German camps.

---

[1]   Leon Greenman's various letters to British promoters contain certain inaccuracies and inconsistencies with Leen's account of the camp, the Death March and the liberation. Whether these occasional errors of exaggeration (the length of time Leen was in Auschwitz; British soldiers liberating him, not American) were attempts to garner more sympathy for Leen from British readers is not clear, but they have been retained here as they reflect Greenman's sincere attempts to help his friend get a new start in British professional boxing. The issue of survivor's guilt and the reliability of memory seems to have been common to many who came back home after the war.

Len Sanders, well known international boxer, was sent to German concentration camps after his title was taken away from him by the Germans. He spent over 3 years at Auschwitz concentration camp, returned to Holland, after being liberated by the British troops. He is fit and well, feeling better than ever before, and ready to fight anywhere, especially eager to fight in England.

RECORD OF LEN SANDERS
Ex Welter and Middleweight Champion of Holland from
    1932 until 1940
England: won on points from Billy Bird, Kid Brooks
won on KO 7 rounds from Jimmy Hunter
draw with Stoker Reynolds
won by KO from Jim Shipper
draw with George Rose
Germany: won on points from Gustave Eder, Hans
    Kracht

Leen wants to box in a few Dutch matches first, before travelling to England, and he makes his comeback on 8 April 1946 in The Hague, where his opponent, Jan de Pauw, is younger and taller. A journalist writes in a preview article that Leen 'will be boxing in a contest for the first time since the concentration camp'; another newspaper writes: 'His fame was of no avail to his own family.' He steps into the ring and takes off his bathrobe; his concentration-camp number is clearly visible. The public shows him that 'after all those years of misery, they have not forgotten him'. Leen wins with superior strength, and a reporter notes that 'nobody would have guessed that he had been imprisoned for many years in the Polish camp of Auschwitz. On the contrary, his punches had become harder, he had lost none of his flexibility, and his famous closed defence had remained as solid as ever.'

Eleven days later, he is fighting again. Two thousand spectators look on from the grandstand at Amsterdam's Apollohal. Leen wins. He is praised for his endurance and speed, and for his abiding ability 'to hide behind a sort of shell at all times, the same defence mechanism that Leen Sanders employed before the war'. Who could forget the fights between Leen and Bep from that time 'in which Bep was able to break through his opponent's defence only very sporadically?'

Despite the ovations, Leen stops boxing after that. He is sleeping even more badly than usual, is too anxious to train and gets the shakes just thinking about having to step back into a boxing ring ever again. In an interview he says: 'During the matches I had visions. That I'd be beaten to a pulp, as happened a few times in the camp.'

On 3 November 1946, Leen boards a DC-4 with four engines. It can seat twenty-six and the name on its side states: THE FLYING DUTCHMAN. In his own words, he 'cannot live with all those terrible memories' and has to leave. Bill's fiancée, Ada, wishes him 'a good journey and a safe arrival in your future country'. She writes to Leen, saying that she owes him 'no small measure of thanks'; without him 'I'd probably never have met my man'. 'Lots of luck and success on your future path through life, dear Leen.' 'Look to the sun and the shadows will be left behind you!! Happiness is bound to find you, it can't be otherwise!'

Leen's wife, Henriette 'Jetty' van Creveld-Sanders, is flying out to

Aruba later. She comes from Rotterdam, has brown eyes and is a little taller than her husband. In September 1945 she'd been invited over by Beppie Taubman on Schieweg and Leen had sat opposite her. Jetty had been a friend of Leen's sisters, and during the war she'd gone into hiding, first in Jan van Loonstraat and then with a married couple living on Binnenweg. There, she had her own small room and kept the house clean, but was unable to venture outdoors for two whole years. Ever since the war she stammers and is always nervy; she has stomach aches and, like Leen, is unable to sleep without sleeping pills.

Leen and Jetty had married on 4 July 1946 in Rotterdam. The bridegroom wrote to Leon: 'You must simply not dwell too much on the past because it just won't help you any more; what you want to have back will not *come* back, and you just have to start all over again; anyway, that is the path that I have come to choose, because there are only two paths for people like us and you have to choose one of them in the end: do away with yourself or find a new wife to give you your sense of purpose again; it got through to me late in the day, but in any case it is the only way.'

The Flying Dutchman takes off; Leen flies over Rotterdam, Prestwick in Scotland and Gander, Newfoundland. He transfers at La Guardia, New York, and lands in Paramaribo, Suriname. After three hours, he flies on, and lands at twenty to five in the afternoon in Willemstad, the capital of Curaçao. There, on 5 November 1946, he boards a small aeroplane seating twenty other passengers. After one and a half hours he lands at the Dakota airfield in Sint Nicolaas, Aruba, and drives to the house where he and Jetty are to live. The sun is shining, the sea is blue, and he is going to begin a new life in this place, with or without boxing, far away from Germany, far away from Auschwitz, and far away from Rotterdam too.

EPILOGUE

Initially, Leen had wanted to popularize the 'noble art' on Aruba, and so started off his life there as a boxing coach, but not enough people seemed interested in learning. In the wake of that, he bought a café-restaurant, smartened it up and had a signboard made: WINTERGARDEN. LEEN-SANDERS-BAR. In 1947 he threw a party and placed an advertisement:

> Reopening
> of the Café-Restaurant
> WINTERGARDEN
> in San Nicolas, Aruba
> Intimate and Welcoming
> Now under the management of Leen Sanders

Leen served beer and Dutch gin to Dutch sailors and Americans from the Lago Oil & Transport Company, while Jetty played the piano, accordion or harmonica and sang songs for the customers. On Saturdays, people could dance out on the patio until two in the

morning. The bar and restaurant were downstairs, with Leen and
Jetty living above.

He took pills to ease his rheumatism and wrote 'little letters' to
Dutch and Polish survivors. Bill was married, Lex was in love, and
Jack and Maurice had little work because nobody seemed to like jazz
any more. Leon went from school to school to recount his time at
Auschwitz. Since liberation, Kazik had been fighting yet another
dictatorship; this time it was the communists who were intent on
curtailing freedom. He was tortured, and in Kraków's prison he met
the former camp commandant of Auschwitz. The German had held
out his hand, and Kazik had punched his lights out.

In 1949, Jetty gave birth to a son. Leen called him Josua David in
tribute to his lost children; he would be the boy to make all things
right again. Among family and friends he was 'Jopie'. 'Well now,
Leen, I think it's terrific how well things are going for you and that
you have a happy and peaceful life with your wife and child,' wrote
a concentration-camp friend. 'You've earned it many times over for
everything that you did in Auschwitz for your countrymen and fellow
prisoners. Yes, Leen, we still haven't stopped talking about that;
wherever I go and whenever people speak about that dreadful time,
throughout Holland it's you we all mention. You see, every good deed
meets its reward!'

After the birth, Jetty cried a great deal and suffered from chronic
stomach cramps and homesickness, but Leen did not want to go
back. Café-Restaurant Wintergarden was usually full, and he was
able to jog across the beach, swim amid the coral and attend boxing
matches at the National Arena. In 1952, because of Jetty's health,
he and she went on a long holiday to Rotterdam and Antwerp. Leen
was honoured at a boxing gala, but confessed to a columnist that he

wanted to get out of Rotterdam as soon as possible. It had reopened old wounds.

By 1953 fewer Dutch sailors were visiting Aruba, and Café-Restaurant Wintergarden was almost never as full again as it had been. All the same, Leen refused to look for work in Rotterdam, and on 8 April 1954, he, Jetty and Jopie flew to the United States, obtained visas and began life in a detached house in Culver City, a quiet Los Angeles suburb, where he taught Jopie English and started calling him Joe. Leen had no wish for his young son to be a professional boxer, but he did introduce him to the 'noble art'. Los Angeles was a dangerous city and the possibility of a new *shoah* (holocaust) could never be ruled out. Leen was strict with Joe, and huge fits of temper could flare up out of the blue, quite unlike how he had been in the past. 'Indeed, Auschwitz has left quite a mark on us,' he wrote to a fellow survivor.

Leen delivered bread in a delivery truck, while Jetty worked part-time in a factory printing brochures and gave piano lessons. Their garden was planted with cactus and palm trees, and a basketball hoop and stand were set up next to the garage; each morning, the postman would throw the *Los Angeles Times* onto the lawn. Leen had a subscription to the boxing magazine *The Ring* and would spend time in the garden reading articles about Sugar Ray Robinson, Joe Louis and Rocky Marciano. He wore slippers and Hawaiian shirts, and would hose down the plants stripped to the waist. He had little contact with his brothers.

In 1958 Leen became a leather dyer, after having worked for a time at an aircraft factory. By then, he'd developed a love of hamburgers and milkshakes. He had made his debut as a featherweight boxer and now, by his own admission, he belonged 'in all honesty, among the heavyweights'. *De Telegraaf* printed a story that, financially speaking, things were not going so swimmingly for him in the United States; Auschwitz survivors sent cheques as a donation together with their concentration-camp number.

On 12 August 1959, Leen drove to Los Angeles City Hall. He had become the janitor at a high school in Culver City, keeping the building clean, and had to adopt American citizenship because it was a public-sector job. A clerk asked him questions relating to a 'Petition for Naturalization (of a married person)': Leen was fifty-one, his race was 'white', his blood pressure was 'high', and he had entered the country legally. The US government 'Alien Registration' form had as its final question: Visible distinctive features? The clerk wrote 'cauliflower left ear'.

The cauliflower-eared janitor drove to the Generalkonsulat der Bundesrepublik Deutschland on Wilshire Boulevard in Downtown Los Angeles. The Frankfurt Auschwitz trials were scheduled to begin in 1963, and survivors were being asked to provide information about Nazi defendants. Leen went to the duty room of the German vice-consul in California and explained about his arrival at Auschwitz, the blocks he had lived in and the sort of work he had done at the camp. The camp authorities had given orders to *Rapportführer* Kaduk to be brutal, but Leen had seen him kicking people of his own free will and smirking when he sent people to the gas chambers. His statement began: 'I am 53 years old and a janitor at a high school in Culver City. My number was 86764, which I still bear on my left forearm.'

Leen quit his job as a janitor in the mid-1960s to start up a small cleaning business. He, Jetty and Joe would drive their van to companies and the residences of Hollywood stars, where Leen would lift the cleaning machine out of the vehicle, Jetty would tidy the rooms and Joe would watch television on the couch or help out. It was hard work, but Leen's humble business venture proved so successful that, for the first time since their emigration, they were no longer in financial hardship.

His income once again took a downturn a few years later, because he'd had to cut down his working hours. He dreamed of the Germans and kept picturing Selli, Jopie and David turning left; he suffered with his joints, his hands and legs were often swollen, and ever since Auschwitz his feet always seemed to feel cold. Dr Perloff from Culver City prescribed him medicines and therapy and Leen sought support from the Dutch Holocaust Survivors of Los Angeles. Together, they would celebrate Sinterklaas, drink advocaat, Heineken or Bols and eat *speculaas*, *boterkoek* and marzipan. They went to evenings out where Dutch traditional costume was worn, tables would be decorated with vases of tulips, waiters would serve Dutch dishes, such as *hutspot*, *boerenkool* or endives, and music would be played by Snip & Snap, Louis Davids, and the Rhythm Five jazz band of Jack de Vries, Maurice van Kleef, Lex van Weren and Louis Bannet. They tried not to talk too much about Auschwitz, Bergen-Belsen, Mauthausen or Birkenau, but it was often unavoidable. Survivors had to complete forms to qualify for compensation as victims of war.

What were the surnames and forenames of the persecuted
    parties?
SANDERS, JOSUA LEENDERT; SANDERS, DAVID JOSUA

Where did the persecuted parties die?
AUSCHWITZ

What reason was given for depriving them of their liberty?
JEWISH DESCENT

What was the cause of death?
PROBABLE ASPHYXIATION BY GAS

19a. Are you still a Dutch citizen?
NO

19b. What is your nationality now?
AMERICAN

The final question on the Dutch government's application form B, as addressed to Leendert Josua Sanders, 10860 Whitburn Street, Culver City, USA:

What was the family relationship between you and the persecuted parties?
[Leen wrote in pencil]: FATHER

For a long time, Joe was told nothing about the boys after whom he had been named. One day he came home from a friend's party, passed by his father's room and heard him sobbing. The next morning Joe asked about it and Leen told him about Selli, Jopie and David, other relatives, and friends and acquaintances. Joe did try asking more at a later date, but by then his father no longer wanted to answer any more questions. 'He is forever searching for the sons he lost,' said his cousin Beppie.

Joe preferred tinkering with his Chevrolet to watching

Muhammad Ali v Joe Frazier, and he also tried imitating Jimi Hendrix on his guitar. He talked to his parents only in English, emphasizing: 'I'm American.' He surfed at Malibu or at other beaches and his knees bore thick calluses as a result, which led to Leen hiding the surfboard. Joe reminded him that Leen's own parents had once forbidden him from boxing; Leen relented and gave the surfboard back.

The war had to be repressed, but contact with fellow survivors remained close-knit. In 1970, Leen received a card from Lex van Weren. The front of it showed a photograph of the cornet that Leen had stolen for Lex in 1944. The trumpet player wrote on the back:

> In commemoration of my old friend LEEN SANDERS without whose help many others from the Netherlands would never have survived the Auschwitz concentration camp. We shall never forget his efforts and altruism.
>
> With all best wishes,
> Lex van Weren
> No. 163848.

In the summer of 1973, Leen travelled back to Rotterdam for the first time in twenty-one years. He was now walking with a stoop, thanks to his rheumatism, and would soon be determined unfit for work. In his own view, the cause of his arthritis was the abuse and hardship he endured at the camps; his other complaints were a result of the anxiety and stress that he'd had to withstand 'so as not to be caught stealing by the SS'. Medical costs were high in the United States, and social provision was poor. He feared that in the event of rejection he would be reduced to living in poverty again and, therefore, made efforts to qualify for an Extraordinary War Pension in the Netherlands.

His application was rejected. Civil servants doubted whether he had really been involved in resistance; was such a thing possible at Auschwitz? Moreover, was there really a direct connection between the war and his medical complaints? Perhaps, in actual fact, these had been caused by his past activity as a boxer.

In Rotterdam, Leen stayed with his cousin Beppie on Schieweg. On the bedside table there was a box containing painkillers and Mogadon sleeping pills. He told a journalist from *Het Vrije Volk* that he'd never wanted to speak about the assistance he'd given people in Auschwitz; it was like singing his own praises. He had simply done his duty, no more than that. Now, however, he did have to 'beat his own breast' about this. He'd resisted the Germans in 1940, 1941 and 1942 and performed life-threatening work in Auschwitz, which had now left him a wreck as a result, and he would prove it, because he needed that war pension 'for when I can no longer work'.

To support his case, Leen fetched out letters and newspaper cuttings that he had brought with him from the United States for that purpose. Bill Minco had written:

That I survived Auschwitz and the period afterwards is a fact for which I have the Rotterdam boxer Leen Sanders to thank: a man who, because of a boxing enthusiast SS man, took on a somewhat privileged position and who acted as an unremitting shield for me, a fellow Rotterdammer. He mothered me, kicked me into touch if he had to, but saw me through it all. His left hook never missed its target, although this was not something he bragged about and only a very few became acquainted with it. However, fewer still wanted to.

In the opinion of Lex van Weren it was beyond doubt that Leen had risked his life at Auschwitz, and he had always tried to give solace to his fellow prisoners 'so that you could hold it together in that deep pool of misery'. Lex called him a godlike figure for the Dutch at Auschwitz, and an extraordinarily exceptional human being: 'exceptional in relation to the selfless help and support he gave to his fellow prisoners'. During the evacuation 'in cattle wagons, he was once again our guardian angel, defending us both literally and figuratively'. Another Auschwitz inmate described him as a resistance fighter at the concentration camp, 'where death lies in wait every second of the day and all human dignity has been annihilated'.

His Rotterdam friend and former De Geuzen resistance fighter Jo Hoek thanked him:

Thirty-five of us came floundering in, exhausted, starving, eyes glazed over, seeing a place that was alien and bleak. As if a gift from God, you came up to us, asking how many of us there were. When we said 'thirty-five', you said very calmly: 'I'll see what I can do for you all; I'll be right back.' Leen, the resulting support you gave us on that day was truly so great, I don't believe you can imagine. I think it's sad that you're now having to make this cry from the heart for your livelihood. You who never wanted to hear a word of thanks, seeing it instead as a duty. You who helped people as human beings, people at the camp who were weak and sick, without making a distinction between whether they were Jewish or not. You, my short, stocky fellow, risked your life to save us. Later, when we'd been at Auschwitz a little longer, we discovered that this approach was typical of you. Wherever there was a Dutchman in need, you were there to fill the breach.

Leen visited government agencies to fight his corner and wrote letters in which he stated: 'I upheld my duties as a Dutchman, as a soldier, in sport and in the concentration camp.' He'd had to pay the price for that with his health; at 'Gross-Rosen I was given the beating of my life from which I still suffer greatly to this very day'. One SS man in Auschwitz had landed him punches that were harder than 'all the others received in my whole boxing career put together'.

He flew back to Los Angeles, where Dr Perloff wrote to a Dutch civil servant: 'It is felt that this man is completely and totally disabled to do any type of work.'

Government experts examined Leen for post-concentration camp syndrome and 'resistance invalidity'. They demanded further medical information from Dr Perloff, requested bank statements to prove that his income had suffered as a result of his problems, and sought additional testimonies about his war years. A committee required nineteen months to reach its verdict: REJECTED.

'Mr Chairman, I should first of all like to thank you for having afforded me the opportunity to speak as the authorized representative of Mr Sanders of Rotterdam, consequent on the rejection of the application to award an Extraordinary Pension for 1940–45.'

It was 22 August 1986 and Eva Mendel-Sanders was appearing

before the court in Utrecht. Her husband, Lou Sanders, was Leen's second cousin, whom Leen had saved at Auschwitz. She was engaged in a final attempt to provide Leen with an Extraordinary Pension. The civil service had continued to stonewall, and in July 1986 the application had been rejected yet again. Eva appealed the decision at once, requesting that the case be given priority owing to 'the poor health and advanced age' of her client. The officials could not give that undertaking, and additional investigation was required for the umpteenth time.

Eva had brought a stack of squared paper with her containing entries such as 'stealing from the SS food supply was in fact resistance and sabotage'. She tried to find the words to describe Auschwitz and concluded this part of her case with the words: 'Mr Chairman, the report about the camp that I have just submitted does not come from third parties. Unfortunately, my husband and I speak from experience, because both of us went through the hell of Auschwitz personally.'

Included among the submitted appendices were testimonies made by boxing champions and fellow survivors, as well as financial details and Leen and Jetty's medical files. A former training partner made a statement about the theft of identity papers in 1942: 'What is relevant here is that Leen Sanders took these risks as a Jew in order to resist the Nazis.' Lex recounted how 'for us, Leen Sanders was a true pillar of strength and a refuge for countless people owing to his commitment and courage. All superlatives actually fall too short for what he did and for what he meant to the Dutch. If there was one man who committed sabotage in every area and wherever he could at Auschwitz, then he was that man.'

Eva looked the chairman squarely in the eye:

Ten days after his arrival, Mr Sanders heard that his wife and children had been murdered and it will not be difficult to envision the intensity of this man's sorrow and despair. At the same time, there arose in him enormous rage against the Nazis and a will to survive. Yet, over the passage of time, past events have come to the surface, resulting in Mr Sanders suffering not only from physical complaints but also psychological problems: phobias, fits of crying, pains throughout his body, anxiety and distress through visions of persecution as a result of his time spent at Auschwitz and on the death march, a feeling of being under great strain, and insomnia. At present, he is in a state of such confusion that there is a risk of his withdrawal from the world. His doctor in California expressly advised him to go back to Rotterdam, which he proceeded to do recently. His sorrow will never abate, but in his native city he will be able to re-establish many contacts. Before the war, Mr Sanders had been a celebrated boxer both at home and abroad, and in Rotterdam many old sports friends can take him with them to all kinds of boxing matches.

She concluded under the heading 'indescribable circumstances' as follows: 'He succeeded in increasing his fellow prisoners' chances of survival at great risk to his own life. This assistance was in conflict with the SS objective of exterminating everyone and, therefore, was a manifest act of resistance.'

Once again, a committee required months before reaching its decision: there were 'no terms whereby L.J. Sanders can be awarded a special allowance'. The rejection 'is sustained in consequence'.

It was 1989. The veteran pro boxer was now sitting in a wheelchair. Leen had Alzheimer's disease and was living in the Laurens Antonius Binnenweg nursing home on Nieuwe Binnenweg. He was able to look out onto a patio and a courtyard garden filled with plants and flowers. Once a week, there was a 'disco afternoon'. Leen could receive visitors in the Grand Café, and Jetty would come by tram or taxi almost every day. The rage and aggression within him ever since the end of the war was no longer present, and for the first time in a long time he seemed happy. According to Joe, his father imagined himself living once more in pre-war Rotterdam.

Eva Mendel-Sanders would sometimes stop by with her husband, Lou. Government specialists had carried out a further examination of Leen's case, and the outcome was announced in December 1989. Leen received apologies. The report stated: 'The emotional and psychological strain to which you exposed yourself during the occupation and which has reduced you to a total invalid has been underestimated by us.' On closer inspection, he was found to have 'participated intensively in resistance, such that it can be assumed on that ground that you were exposed to exceptionally severe and prolonged stress'. At long last, Leen was awarded his Extraordinary War Pension. Eva told him the good news; Leen no longer understood what she was talking about.

Bep van Klaveren died on 12 February 1992. Leen died on 8 April 1992 at the age of eighty-three. Two days later his bank account was credited with more than 100,000 guilders, the amount still owing to him in arrears as his war pension.

Years before, when making his will, Leen had told a notary: 'I want to be cremated. After all, they burned my whole *mishpocha* [family network].' He had his wish, and the reception after his cremation was attended by boxers, former boxers, Rotterdammers and Amsterdammers, and by Jews and goys alike. Lex said: 'The extent to which that man helped prisoners is unimaginable.' Bill Minco wrote an article about his saviour and sent it to Jetty: 'My first introduction to Leen was his loaf of bread. To some people it is an injustice that no statue has been erected.'

SOURCES

Bibliography

Beckman, J.F., *Odyssee 1940–1945*, self-published, Leiderdorp, 1993.

Bell, Leslie, *Bella of Blackfriars*, London: Oldhams, 1961.

Benda-Beckman, Bas von, *Het Oranjehotel. Een Duitse gevangenis in Scheveningen*, Amsterdam: Querido, 2019.

Boas, Jacob, *Boulevard des Misères. Het verhaal van doorgangskamp Westerbork*, Amsterdam: Nijgh & Van Ditmar, 1988.

Boasson, Herman, *Uit het nabije verleden. Kamp-episoden en Kamp-begrippen*, Amsterdam: Jimmink, 1981.

Bogacka, Marta, *Bokser z Auschwitz. Losy Tadeusz Pietrzykowski*, Warsaw: Demart, 2021.

Bordewijk, Ferdinand, *Karakter*, Rotterdam: Nijgh & Van Ditmar, 1938.

Borowski, Tadeusz, *Stenen wereld. Verhalen uit het kamp*, Amsterdam: Contact, 2005.

Braber, Ben den, *Zelfs als wij zullen verliezen. Joden in verzet en illegaliteit*, Amsterdam: Balans, 1990.

Brecht, Bertolt, *Der Kinnhaken und andere Boxgeschichten*, Frankfurt am Main: Suhrkamp, 1995.

Brusse, M.J., *Het rosse leven en sterven van de Zandstraat*, Rotterdam: W. L. Brusse, 1912.

Cadsand, Kees van, *Ontsnapping uit de dodenmars. Herinneringen van Louis de Wijze aan de concentratiekampen en de transporten*, Amsterdam: De Bataafsche Leeuw, 2015.

Cohen, Elie, *De afgrond. Een ego-document*, Brussels: Paris-Manteau, 1982.

Cohen, Elie, *Beelden uit de nacht. Kampherinneringen*, Baarn: De Prom, 1992.

Creveld, I.B. van, *Verdwenen Buurt, Drie eeuwen centrum van joods Den Haag*, Zutphen: De Walburg Pers, 1989.

Czech, Danuta, *Auschwitz Chronicle*, New York: Henry Holt, 1997.

Dassen, Patrick, *De Weimarrepubliek 1918–1933*, Amsterdam: Van Oorschot, 2021.

Deelder, Jules, *Bep van Klaveren. The Dutch Windmill*, Utrecht: L. J. Veen, 1992.

Deyong, Moss, *Everybody Boo*, London: Stanley Paul & Co., 1951.

Döblin, Alfred, *Berlin Alexanderplatz*, Frankfurt: Fischer, 2014.

Egger, Willem, *Surinaamse rug Joodse buik. Emoties over de slavernij en de Sjoa*, Libertador, Voorburg, 2009.

Fairweather, Jack, *The Volunteer. The true story of the resistance hero who infiltrated Auschwitz*, London: W. H. Allen, 2019.

Fedorowicz, Andrzej, *Gladiatorzy z obozów śmierci*, Warsaw: Bellona, 2020.

Feringa, M.M.S., *De stadsdriehoek van Rotterdam. De westelijke waterstad tussen Boompjes, Blaak en Schiedamsesingel*, Rotterdam: H. Gemeentelijke Archiefdienst, 1993.

Fransecky, Tanja von, *Escapees: The History of Jews Who Fled Nazi Deportation Trains in France, Belgium, and the Netherlands*, New York: Berghahn Books, 2019.

Fraunberg, Bero von, *Damals im April. Chronologie zum Seeshaupter Mahnmal*, Seeshaupt: LesArt Verlag, 2010.

Garcia, Max, *Auschwitz, Auschwitz, I Cannot Forget You . . . As Long As I Remain Alive*, Santa Clara, CA: Think Social Publishing, 2009.

Greenman, Leon, *An Englishman in Auschwitz*, Elstree: Valentine Mitchell and Co, 2001.

Groeneveld, Gerard, *Rotterdam Frontstad*, Nijmegen: Van Tilt, 2016.

Grunberg, Arnon (compiler), *Bij ons in Auschwitz. Getuigenissen*, Amsterdam: Querido, 2020.

Haenen, Marcel, *De bokser. Het leven van Max Moszkowicz*, Amsterdam: Querido, 2018.

Harding, John, *The Whitechapel Whirlwind: The Jack 'Kid' Berg Story*, Chichester, W. Sussex: Pitch Publishing, 2019.

Hees, Karel van, *Cor Eversteijn, Bokser, herenkapper*, Rotterdam: Post Editions, 2011.

Heinz, W.C. (compiler), *The Book of Boxing*, New York: Total Sports Publishing, 1999.

Hen, Jozef, *De bokser en de dood*, Amsterdam: Moussault's uitgeverij, 1967.

Hess, Sales, *KZ Dachau. Eine Welt ohne Gott*, Münsterschwarzach: Vier-Türme-Verlag, 1985.

Hogervorst, Sandra, *Rotterdam en het bombardement*, Veldhoven: Erimon, 2015.

Huizenaar, Theo, *De waarheid over de bokssport*, Rijswijk: Sijthoff, 1980.

Italië, G., *Oorlogsdagboek van dr. G Italië*, Amsterdam: Atlas Contact, 2009.

Jong, Wilfried de, et al., *Boks! Een beeld van een roemruchte Rotterdamse bokshistorie 1947–1960*, Rotterdam: Koppel, 1999.

Kessel, Sim, *Hanged at Auschwitz*, New York: Cooper Square Press, 2001.

Keune, Martin, *Knock-Out*, Berlin: Bebra Verlag, 2015.

Kiecol, Daniel, *Wir in den wilden Zwanzigern: Charleston & Co. an Rhein und Ruhr*, Düsseldorf: Droste, 2016.

Kielar, Wieslaw, *Anus Mundi. Five Years in Auschwitz*, London: Viking, 1981.

Langbein, Hermann, *Menschen in Auschwitz*, Vienna: Europa Verlag, 1995.

Levi, Primo, *Is dit een mens*, Amsterdam: Meulenhoff, 1987.

Lewis, Morton, *Kid Lewis. His Life and Times*, London: Robson Books, 1992.

Liber, Jan, *Helpers weg! Laatste ronde, roman uit de bokswereld*, Amsterdam: Uitgeverij Nieuwe Wieken, 1947.

Liempt, Ad van, *Gemmeker. Commandant van Westerbork*, Amsterdam: Balans, 2019.

Margolick, David, *Beyond Glory. Joe Louis vs Max Schmeling, and a World on the Brink*, New York: Vintage Books, 2005.

Mechanicus, Philip, *In Depot. Dagboek uit Westerbork*, Hilversum: Verbum, 2008.

Mechanicus, Philip, *Ik woon, zoals je weet, drie hoog: brieven uit Westerbork*, Amsterdam: Balans, 1987.

Meijer, Bertus, *Vooroorlogse herinneringen van een Rotterdamse arbeider*, Rotterdam: Rotterdamse Kunststichting, 1971.

Minco, Bill, et al., *Kerst 1944. Herinneringen van mensen uit het voormalig verzet en overlevenden uit concentratiekampen*, Linschoten: Uitgeverij Mingus, 1982.

Minco, Bill, *Koude voeten. Het relaas van een Joodse scholier uit het Geuzenverzet*, Nijmegen: SUN, 1997.

Mohr, Joachim, et al., *Deutschland in den Goldenen Zwanzigern*, Munich: Penguin, 2021.

Naarden, W. van, *Herinneringen vanaf 1924 en de oorlog 1940–1945*, self-published, La Nucia, 1983.

Opzeeland, Ed van, *Davidster als ereteken*, Kats: De Buitenspelers, 2006.

Ossendrijver, Josua, *Verdoezeld verleden. Kind van de oorlog*, Hilversum: Verbum, 2014.

Pérez, José Ignacio, *KO in Auschwitz*, Madrid: Corner, 2022.

Prähofer, Hans, *Wie es war. Kriegsende und Neubeginn in Mühldorf am Inn und seinem Hinterland*, Mühldorf: Heimatbund Mühldorf, 1985.

Romer, Herman, *Rotterdam in de jaren dertig*, Baarn: Europese Bibliotheek, 1981.

Rost, Nico, *Goethe in Dachau*, De Bilt: Uitgeverij Schokland, 2015.

Schaik, Paul van, et al., *'Allemaal jongens die lekker uit de voeten konden': 17 portretten van Rotterdamse oudboksers*, Rotterdam: Trichis Publishing, 2002.

Schippers, Hans, *De Rotterdamse Zandstraatbuurt en zijn inwoners*, Amsterdam: Amphora Books, 2022.

Schuldman, Ken, *Jazz Survivor. The Story of Louis Bannet, Horn Player of Auschwitz*, Edgware: Valentine Mitchell, 2005.

Shawver, Katrina, *Henry. A Polish Swimmer's True Story of Friendship from Auschwitz to America*, Phoenix, AZ: Ribbon Falls Press, 2017.

Sobolewicz, Tadeusz, *Aus der Hölle zurück*, Frankfurt am Main: Fisher, 2011.

Springmann, Veronika, *Gunst und Gewalt. Sport in Nationalsozialistischen Konzentrationslagern*, Berlin: Metropol, 2019.

Steinberg, Paul, *Speak You Also. A Survivor's Reckoning*, New York: Picador, 1996.

Stroman, Ben, *Stad*, Rotterdam: Brusse, 1932.

Szafran, Eleonora: *Mistrz. Tadeusz 'Teddy' Pietrzykowski*, Warsaw: Ringier Axel Springer, 2021.

Thyn, Nico van, *Survivors: 62511, 70726. Two Holocaust Stories, From Amsterdam to Auschwitz to America*, self-published, Fort Worth, 2016.

Toepoel, P.M.C., *Boksen als sport en als zelfverdediging*, Rotterdam: Nijgh & Van Ditmar, 1922.

Troost, Peter, *De meisies van de Schiedamsedijk*, self-published, Rotterdam, 2014.

Tyminski, Kazimierz, *To Calm My Dreams. Surviving Auschwitz*, Auckland: New Holland, 2011.

Ulreich, Carry, *'s Nachts droom ik van vrede. Oorlogsdagboek*, Utrecht: Mozaïek, 2016.

Voet, H.A., *Tussen Hofplein, Oppert, Grotekerkplein, St. Laurensstraat en Coolsingel*, Rotterdam: Gemeentelijke Archiefdienst, 1993.

Vortmann, Jürgen, *Hans Breitensträter, Boxer und Sportstar der 1920'er Jahre*, Norderstedt: Books on Demand, 2021.

Vuijsje, Marja, *Ons kamp. Een min of meer Joodse geschiedenis*, Amsterdam: Atlas, 2012.

Wiarda, Dick, *Trompettist van Auschwitz. Herinneringen van Lex van Weren*, Amsterdam: Balans, 2020.

Wiesel, Eli, *Nacht*, Amsterdam: Meulenhoff, 2006.

Wind, Eddy, *Eindstation Auschwitz. Mijn verhaal vanuit het kamp 1943–1945*, Amsterdam: Meulenhof, 2020.

Wittman, Rebecca, *Beyond Justice. The Auschwitz Trial*, Cambridge, MA: Harvard University Press, 2012.

Würger, Takis, *Noah. Von einem, der überlebte*, Berlin: Penguin, 2021.

Zirkzee, Hans, *Jazz in Rotterdam. De geschiedenis van een grote stadscultuur*, Rotterdam: Lecturis, 2015.

Testimonies of Auschwitz survivors in the Netherlands Institute for War Documentation (NIOD)

Bannet, Levie
Beckman, J.F.
Blitterswijk, Leendert
Cats, J.S.
Cohen, Abraham
Cohen, Elie
Franschman, Louis
Furth, Jacques
Janssen, Josephus
Kluger, Hermann
Minco, Sebil
Naarden, Wolf van
Nab, Jan
Pach, Arie
Poons, Bep
Prins, Hartog
Pront, Jonas
Schimmer, Coenraad
Schnog, Leo
Spetter, Ies
Turksma, Ary Berti
Vries, Jacob de
Wolf, Jacob de
Zilverberg, Simon

Testimonies of Auschwitz survivors in the National Archives of the Netherlands (Nationaal Archief)

Berclouw, Hannah
Egger-Jas, Engelina
Kleef, Maurice van
Knap, Izak Simon
Pront, Jonas
Sanders, Jakob Josua
Sanders, Leendert
Weren, Samson van

Articles

Algemeen Dagblad, 'Voor hen is het nog oorlog', 1 June 1974.

Bataviaasch Nieuwsblad, 'Het Hollandsche pendant: Leen Sanders', 26 February 1940.

De Telegraaf, 'Merkwaardige figuur in de ring. Sanders vol vertrouwen tegen Locatelli', 2 March 1940.

De Telegraaf, 'Nederlanders in Amerika, bokser en bollenkweker in de ring des levens', 6 August 1959.

De Telegraaf, 'Smartegeld uit Holland voor Leen en Charlotte?', 9 August 1974.

Groot Rotterdam, 'Leen Sanders getrouwd', Rotterdam chronicle, 8 July 1932.

Het Parool, 'R'eddende trompet. Hoe Lex van Weren het concentratiekamp doorkwam', 12 May 1980.

Het Vrije Volk, 'De sport redde Sanders het leven', 22 June 1945.

Het Vrije Volk, 'Leen Sanders in de ring', 18 March 1946.

Het Vrije Volk, 'Leen Sanders terug om zijn recht te halen', 30 August 1974.

Kontakt, 'Het brood waardoor de hemel open ging'. Bill Minco in August 1992.

Limburgsch Dagblad, 'De verbijstering van ex-Auschwitzer Lex van Weren', 3 May 1980.

Rotterdamsch Nieuwsblad, 'Leen Sanders werd schipper van z'n huwelijksbootje', 1 July 1932.

Rotterdamsch Nieuwsblad, 'LATE HAVER KOMT OP! Locatelli eveneens aan Sanders' zegekar', 5 March 1940.

Rotterdamsch Nieuwsblad, 'Bokser Leen Sanders na 40 buitenlandse jaren: "Ik ben blij dat ik terug ben"', 2 November 1985.

Rotterdamsche Parool, 'Leen Sanders. Eens bekend bokser. Thans zakenman op Aruba', 28 May 1952.

Trouw, 'Elie Cohen overleefde als arts het vernietigingskamp', 2 September 1992.

Veritas, 'Duitsche concentratiekampen', 13 June 1945.

Volksdagblad, 'Leen Sanders een groot Rotterdamsch Bokser', 23 April 1937.

Weekblad voor Israëlitische huisgezinnen, 'Een van de beste boksers ter wereld', 6 July 1934.

Newspaper archives

Algemeen Handelsblad
Berlin Morgenpost
Berliner Abendblatt
Berliner Herold
Chronique à Oran
Daily Telegraph
De Telegraaf
Düsseldorfer Stadt-Anzeiger
Düsseldorfer Nachrichten
East London Observer
Echo d'Algers
Haagsche Courant
Het Laatste Nieuws
Het Vaderland
Het Volk
Het Vrije Volk
Le Miroir des Sports
Le Parisien
Maasbode
Nieuwe Rotterdamsche Courant
Oran-Matin
Paris-Soir
Rotterdamsch Nieuwsblad
Rotterdamsche Parool
Volksdagblad
Voorwaarts
Vorwärts
Vossische Zeitung

Magazines

Auschwitz Bulletin
Boxing
Box–Sport : Deutschlands größtes Box–Magazin
Groot–Rotterdam
L'Auto
Nieuw Israëlietisch Weekblad
Sport Echo
Sportrevue 't stadion
Sportwereld

Miscellaneous source material

Wartime dossier of Leen Sanders via Leonard Sanders and the Sociale Verzekeringsbank.

Manuscript and life story of Lou and Eva Sanders, 1989, as transcribed by Frans Keijsper.

Leen's testimony in the Frankfurt Auschwitz trials via the Fritz Bauer Institute in Frankfurt.

Oral history of Maurits Wolder and Max Garcia via the USC Shoah Foundation in Los Angeles.

Information about and testimonies of Kazik and Karl Egersdörfer, *Zapysiterroru* (Terror Chronicles), Witold Pilecki Institute in Warsaw.

Transport lists via the Netherlands Institute for War Documentation (NIOD) and the National Archives of the Netherlands (Nationale Archief).

Registration cards Dachau, Auschwitz, Mühldorf and other concentration camp information via the Arolsen Archives, Internationales Zentrum über NS-Opfer, Bad Arolsen.

Information about Leen's blocks and work in Auschwitz via the Auschwitz Museum in Oświęcim.

Cigarette box, Sander Turksma: via the Jewish Museum (Joods Historisch Museum) in Amsterdam.

Letters/postcards to Leen from: Jo Hoek, Leon Greenman, Lex van Weren, Dr Slagter, Jack de Vries, Dr Cohen, Bill Minco, Ada Minco, former Geuzen Blitterswijk, Pietersen, Man in 't Veld, Hoek, Moock, Nibius, Blom.

With thanks to

Ben den Braber
Bram Oosterwijk
Josua Ossendrijver
Leonard Sanders
Joe Sanders
Ger Taubman
Melchior de Wind
Ms B.W. van Oostrum, Sociale Verzekeringsbank